Paul
Thanks for
doing the
Spotlight
Good Luc

Napkin Logic

48 Great Business Ideas, Lessons, and Rules

Insights to make you a better business person and entrepreneur

by

Philip Edholm

Philip Edholm

ISBN: 1494904659

ISBN-13: 978-1494904654

DEDICATION

This book is dedicated to my wife Suzanne who has stood by my through the good times and the bad times. Life is better with you at my side. It is also dedicated to all of the mentors that have been there for me in my career. Without your guidance, knowledge, insights, constructive criticism and occasional humor, I would not be the businessperson I am today.

CONTENTS

Table of Figures

Philip Edholm

ACKNOWLEDGMENTS

A book like this comes not from an individual alone, but from the environment around him or her. Therefore, acknowledging that environment is only appropriate.

First I would like to thank my wife Suzanne, for not only putting up with me while I was writing, but for being there for so many years. She is anchor and also was an editor/commenter on the book. My thanks to my children Karl and Christina for putting up with me through the years, I hope this gives you some insight into your Dad.

For Tony Rybczynski, Bill Selmeier, John Yoakum, and Bill Morgan, who all took the time to edit and comment, this book would not be nearly as good without your insights and thoughts. Together you cleaned up my wandering prose, told me to take out the bad jokes, and helped me be clear and concise, as much as can be expected. I especially want to thank Tony for all of his efforts in cleaning up my prose and typos and for assembling all of the acronyms, you are the best friend an inferior writer could ever have.

Finally, to the thousands of people who I have worked with through my business career, you provided the insight and inspiration for this book. You showed me how to soar and sometimes how to stumble. Together we created magic and changed the world and occasionally failed miserably. You gave me your insight and you let me develop the principles in this book with you. You let me help you succeed through listening to my insights. For all of you, this book reflects how we all are interconnected and impact we have on each other. As you will find out, that impact is the most important thing, and I really hope you have fun and make some money as well.

Chapter 1 Introduction

Welcome and thank you for buying this book, or at least picking it up somewhere. I set out to make this book intentionally different than most business books. I wanted to cover a wide range of topics and leave you to do some of the thought process as well. The intent was to cover each as if they were being described to you by a mentor using a napkin or some paper. By contrast, it seems to me that generally, business books fall into four categories:

Textbooks that take a single topic and delve deeply into it, often without any linkage to the rest of business or other topics. Textbooks range from the typical college book to the newer "*Subject* for Dummies" form that assumes you know nothing. These books are great for learning a topic, but often go too deep for someone who does not want to become focused in that area.

The one great idea book. Great idea books start with one or maybe two premises or concepts. They then spend at least 250 pages, often using increasingly arcane examples, to clearly demonstrate that the premise is correct. Occasionally there is a clear implementation strategy and you come away with a plan to use the one big point. This is the reason that typical business books often can be very clearly synopsized in 5 pages, the key point only takes 5 pages to clearly enumerate. Great examples of this are "Crossing the Chasm" (Moore, 1991)and "The Innovators Dilemma" (Christensen, 2003). The concepts are great concepts and I have used them continuously since I read enough of each book to get the concept (or a synopsis). The problem is that you are paying for/reading a whole book when you really only wanted the 5 page synopsis.

The Executive Memoir or Vanity Book. This is a book written by a renowned business leader that describes their experiences and management style. Jack by Jack Welch (past CEO of GE) is an example of this type of book. While I thought that overall it was an entertaining read, most of us are not CEOs of Fortune 20 multi-national companies that are organized as multiple P&L business units. While Jack's stories are entertaining, most of us are hard pressed to use much of the business insight that comes from that exalted role (that one point about 20% market share notwithstanding). In the end these books are less about changing us and more about learning

Philip Edholm

about them. And sometimes the great author looks slightly less excellent with time. I still have a copy of Odyssey by John Scully, detailing his path from Pepsi to Apple, not much detail about almost bringing Apple to its knees. The executive vanity book of today can become the anchor of tomorrow. Similarly, the biography of Steve Jobs is just that, a great biography, there is little that any of us can use as real business insight.

The "group" topic/how to book. This is more of a lesson book such as "10 Habits of Highly Effective People" that can be applied to an individual or an organization and are more of a how-to manual. It is a set of things in a specific area. It generally has a longer structure as each topic is detailed. Often the outcome of this type of book is that one or two of the topics are interesting, many do not apply, or are already implemented or being used. While this type of book is great for organizing, it generally does not provide the insights to grow your intellectual capacity.

I have tried to do something different with this book. As I am not enough of a renowned business person to write a vanity book. and rather than take one or two concepts and drive them into the ground, my goal was to take 40-50 key lessons learned in 40 years of business and set them forth in a way that they are easy to understand, thus the napkin metaphor. Providing only enough edification to make it reasonably clear that they are true and of value. This book is a combination of a bunch of "great idea books" and "group topic/how to book" rolled into one. Depending on your skill and knowledge, some of the topics may not be new to you. In fact, in some cases you may know more about the topic than is described. However, you can be reasonably sure that the next topic will be in an area that you do not have the same level of skill or knowledge in and it will be of value. My goal is to have at least 10-20 of the topics in the book be of value to you, either today or at some later point in your career. And I believe for most readers there will be a number of real epiphanies as well.

Most of the topics in this book started as exercises in mentoring my employees and associates in real life business situations, often on a napkin or a white board, sketching out the very same diagrams you will find in this book.. Typically someone with less experience in an area would ask a question or present something that required them to understand a basic business principle or how to analyze or think about a topic or challenge.

Through the years I have found myself regularly repeating these same "lessons" or "rules", often having people come back later and say they understood something clearly for the first time. This book is sets these forth as topics that can be consumed, but the tone I have tried to achieve is essentially a written mentor with examples where appropriate.

The topics range from short to not so short. For example, the Chapter on Cash is King is only a couple of pages. However, some are over 10 pages to completely cover a topic. If the topic is interesting, there is additional reading or study, both in book and Internet form listed in Appendix 1. This enables the reader to take the knowledge points conveyed in this book and both expand and check where appropriate. Finally, in the web link at the back is a link to the book web site where the spreadsheets used to generate many of the figures are located, along with all of the diagrams in PowerPoint. This is intended to enable you to rapidly use this information in your actual role.

Finally, I have been asked why 48 topics, why not more or less? The reason is very simple, I wrote topics based on a list of what I thought would be interesting until I got to a point where I thought the book was deep enough.

Approaching this Book

There are at least three ways to approach this book, based on your experience and time tolerance: the business beginner, the seasoned professional with a specific business area focus, or the business generalist.

If you are a beginner in the business world, it may be good to read this as a complete book, in a single pass. Hopefully the structure in a continuous reading will help you understand the journey you are taking and build knowledge to succeed. After reading it in this way, my hope is that you will remember key topics and revisit them as the challenges in your career change and require that new knowledge or skill. I find that many of the business books on my bookshelf are never revisited, I hope this one will be different for you.

If you are a seasoned professional in one aspect of business, this book can be an excellent way to expand you knowledge to the areas you are not well versed in. You can use your knowledge in your field of specialty to analyze those sections and understand how the information in this book relates to your primary area of focus relative to depth and clarity. This should help you understand better how this book can help you in the new areas, and hopefully engender trust in the other topics when you see that your skill topics are well covered.

Finally, if you are a business generalist, this book can serve two purposes, potentially to open up some new areas of thought, and also to help you clarify and explain things to those you are mentoring as you build your organizations going forward.

A couple of final suggestions, for some the best way to approach this book may be to have it in a place where it is consumed in little pieces. While there is some level of continuity between the chapters, generally each chapter or topic can stand on its own, so making this a continuous read is not in any way necessary. It is great book to have for a quick read, in the bathroom, on an airplane between the meal and the movie, on the train to work, or other short times. You may find some chapters you will read in depth, reviewing and re-reading sections, while other you may skim and then come back to sometime in the future. Finally, keep this book where you can find it if a topic or area comes up that you skimmed or read, it may be helpful when you get to that crucial point in your career to review the key topic.

Light versus Heavy Chapters

While the length of a chapter generally is an indicator of whether the topic in that Chapter is a heavy analysis or a light conceptual one, the following are the chapter numbers by relative intensity.

If you wish to start off on a lighter foot, I would encourage you to start with the "Light" list, as the first couple of chapters have some of the heaviest analysis. Chapters not listed below are generally in the medium level.

The Light List

If you want to start with light reading, I would suggest this order of Chapters. These may also be best when you have a little time available.

Chapters: 4, 6, 7, 9, 10, 18, 22, 23, 24, 30, 31, 32, 33, 34, 41, 42, 43, 45, 47, 48

The Heavy List

These are the Chapters with the most analysis and detail and are the most challenging to read, both in time and focus:

Chapters: 2, 3, 15, 16, 27, 38, 39

How the Book is Structured

The book has 48 topics/Chapters in seven major sections. Each section is in an area of business, so the chapters are not arranged in an order that requires sequential reading. Where a Chapter uses some information or concept from an earlier chapter in the book it will be noted with a reference to that chapter, though this not prevalent. The sections are:

Business Models and Business Analysis

This section is devoted to how a business operates and how different factors can impact the operation of the business. It is intended to be a primer on business finance for the non-finance person pared down to a set of reasonable essentials. It starts with the basics of Profit and Loss and then moves to more complex business issues from a financial perspective. It is first as it has a few key concepts that are used in other areas of the book.

Business and Management Concepts
This section is devoted to a few high level concepts of business and management that are not tied to any single typical business function. It is intended to open your thoughts to some new ways of looking at business and the world that business resides in. It includes some key management concepts as well as some views of organizations and structure.

Strategy and Vision
The strategy and vision section has essential points on strategy that can be added to the strategic discussion and help in understanding the strategic process. While I considered adding more in this section, I decided to keep it short and succinct.

Selling
I once worked for a salesman who had become president of the company and he often said "nothing happens until you get an order". While I would suggest that all other areas of business are equally important, the selling area has a number of critical points that lead into marketing as well.

Marketing
Before you can sell, you have to have your marketing bases covered. The focus of this section is to overview a few key areas: how marketing and sales relate, what are the elements in a marketing plan based on transactional volume, and a few key concepts that have continually been used by winning teams.

Technology
The technology section is relatively brief, reflecting the complexity of the area and the fact that many technology areas are so very market/industry specific. However, as a technologist, there are a few topics that I feel are good for the non-technologist to understand, and even may help the technologist as well.

The Business of You
The last section in the book relates to you and how you relate to your work life. It is based on observation of the workplace and individuals through the years. It has both some points that are important to think through early

in your career as well as some points that may help you clarify and decide on career paths later.

Glossary of Acronyms and Definitions

At the end of the book there is a Glossary of the acronyms used in the book and their meaning. In many cases, acronyms are the barrier to entry into a profession or industry. As this book is based on a career of learning int he technology industry, the terms used are from that industry. The Glossary should help those from other fields and industries to understand some of the terms.

Who Am I

When I started to write this book, I realized that many of the readers would logically ask why they should put any stock in the concepts and topics I planned to cover. In the interest of having you understand the background in business that I come from, I put together a brief bio.

I was born in Germany, but moved to Northern California when I was less than 2 years old. I grew up in Redding, then a small town. After High School I went to UC Berkeley to study Physics. While there I decided to change to engineering and received an offer to attend General Motors Institute (now Kettering University), the premier co-op institution in the US. I pursued three engineering degrees: mechanical, electrical, and industrial and ended up completing my degree in the ME/EE category. To complete this degree, I wrote a thesis that defined a mechanism to save GM over $100M by optimizing assembly factory operation and was awarded a distinguished degree.

After graduation I spent 4 years working for GM in both supervision and engineering roles in the assembly facility in Fremont, CA. During this time I played an active role in developing the next generation of data networks running on broadband cable technology and in exploring how to implement and use this technology in the manufacturing environment. In 1982, GM closed this facility, and with my wife pregnant with our first child I decided to stay in California rather than pursuing a role with GM in the Midwest.

I joined a start-up networking company named Sytek and started as a Systems Engineer and Consultant. I quickly broadened my role and became the manager of the SE group and then of Technical functions in

Philip Edholm

Sales and Marketing. During this time I was on the IEEE standards group
that defined Ethernet and created the concept of a multi-protocol interface,
a technology that was critical in early network evolution.   I eventually
moved into a role as a salesperson because it became clear that to lead a
sales and marketing function I needed the experience of actually being a
salesperson and having a quota. In my sales job, less than half my income
was from a base salary, so I was highly leveraged and learned the skills to
win. In my first year as a salesperson I was at 105% of my quota, when I
left in my second year I was the top salesperson.   I moved into the role of
VP of Marketing and was a key part of selling Sytek to Hughes in 1988. It
was one of the first big M&A deals in the data networking industry. After
Sytek became Hughes LAN Systems, I continued in Marketing and then
was asked to run the North American sales organization and do strategic
planning.

In the early 90s I spent 5 years in early stage start-ups and new technologies.
These companies, Protocol Engines, Blyth, and XNET were opportunities
to create and grow technologies from scratch, to develop and sell business
plans for funding, and to create marketing and sales organization and plans.

In 1995 I joined Nortel to drive convergence. While Nortel wanted me to
define the path for them to data networks, I saw the opportunity to
converge data networking with the real-time communications of the PBX
(Private Branch Exchange for corporate voice communications) through
VoIP (Voice over IP). Over the next few years I drove the creation of the
VoIP technologies at Nortel as well as the acquisition of Bay Networks.
This led to Nortel being a major player n the enterprise market. From
2001-2009 I was in the role of CTO (Chief Technology Officer) for this
business unit as well as CSO (Corporate Strategy Officer) in the later years.
In this role I drove the technologies and strategies that defined Nortel in
the enterprise market. A number of these are detailed in this book. In
2009 Nortel declared bankruptcy due to poor management decisions at the
corporate level. Even though the enterprise business was strong and
growing, this had a major impact. The enterprise business was sold to
Avaya at the end of 2009 and I drove the integration of the two product
lines and the R&D teams and resources. In addition I drove the
Technology Strategy and Innovation for Avaya. In 2012 I decided it was
time to strike out on my own and created PKE Consulting to use my range

20

of knowledge and skills in helping companies in creating transformation through Strategy, Technology and Innovation. And I wrote this book.

In my career there are a few things I am particularly proud of:.

Received Frost and Sullivan Lifetime Achievement Award for Growth and Innovation in Telecommunications in 2007. This is a prestigious award given by one of the largest industry analyst companies in recognition for contributions to creating the new VoIP market.

Have been recognized by Internet Telephony magazine as one of the "Top 100 Voices of IP Communications" and as one of the "50 Most Influential People in VoIP" by VoIP News.

Did 3 "Great Debates" in the early 2000s at the VoiceCon (now Enterprise Connect) conference. These presidential style debates on the emergence of the VoIP revolution were seen as seminal events in the development of the new technology.

Have 13 patents issued with an additional 11 patents pending across a range of technologies. I am proud of the range of these patents from systems, hardware, core software and operating systems, VoIP, collaboration and next generation social media.

Recognized by the IEEE (the Institute of Electrical and Electronic Engineers) as the originator of "Edholm's Law of Bandwidth". This is described in Chapter 40, not just the Law, but how the analysis of data can lead to clear perception of major trends. Being one of a handful of recognized technology law originators is a source of real fulfillment

Co-founder of Frame Relay Forum (the first industry technology forum), IEEE 802.3 contributor, developed first multi-packet APIs (later became NDIS and ODI).

Drove strategy that led to Microsoft/Nortel Integrated Communications Alliance resulting in 20% revenue increase and 1,200 new customers (increase of 6x). This is discussed in some detail in Chapter 16.

Defined and delivered Nortel integration into Avaya for product portfolio and the R&D organization resulting in $1.2B in 2011 revenue.

Philip Edholm

I sincerely hope you enjoy this book and find in it the topics and knowledge that will help you in your career.

Phil Edholm, Pleasanton, California, 2014

Business Models and Business Analysis

This first section is about some business basics, particularly around operating financial models and discounting and margin. Each chapter is designed to clarify some key points in understanding how a business is operating and to see how some of the key analysis points apply. If you are an advanced business person, it may be more of a review, though I have found that some senior people have said they had a better view on something they have dealt with for years after reading this section.

If you come from the technical or sales or even the more process functions of marketing or sales, or from manufacturing or supply chain or human resources, this section should give you a basic understanding of the terms so when you are in a business model or analysis discussion you can better relate to what is being discussed.

Finally, the terms and models in this section are applied in different ways in other parts of the book, so the language is important.

Chapter 1 The Basic Business Model

I decided to start this book with a simple business P&L (Profit and Loss)Business model and the terms that go with it. The reason for this is that many of the later chapters use some of these terms and constructs to illuminate the specific points Even though many people have spent years in business, it is easy to lose track of the underlying basics that drive a business. The intent of this section is not to be a complete business finance book, but to just clarify some basics to enable the reader to understand other concepts in the book. If you are a finance professional or have a clear understanding of business finance, this section can be skipped, but before you do, read and answer the question in the next paragraph. This book is only focused at the P&L side of business finance and does not include any significant review of balance sheets or other financial issues.

An interesting test to see if someone understands the concepts of business is to ask the following question, "If you have a business that has 50% Gross Margin and 10% Gross Profit and *has no change in these ratios with volume*, and if you discount your product/service by 10%, how much volume increase do you need to break even on the discount?" Before reading further think about what your answer would be.

Often the first answer someone will give is that you need to double the volume, or sometimes the person answering will start doing complex analysis of the margin and the impact. However, the answer is very simple...if your profit is 10% and you discount by 10%, you have given ALL of your profit away. If there is no change in the business model with volume then you can NEVER break even.   The key point in the question is the one in bold italics - *has no change in these ratios with volume*. This means that the question is not sensitive to volume. If you did not understand this subtle point, take the time to read the section, it will clarify a few concepts.

From a business perspective, the fundamental goal is to make a profit on revenue. While a profit can be defined as some paper construct, in reality, the primary goal is to generate unencumbered cash. In all cases, analyzing a business based on cash is the clearest way to understand the relative performance of the business. In the later sections of this chapter a brief discussion of non-cash items is included, but for clarity, this chapter will primarily deal with a cash type analysis.

Revenue and Cost

Business is very simple, the business delivers a product or a service and the customer pays for that product or service, which becomes revenue for the business. To deliver the product or service, the business has costs which must be paid for. After subtracting the costs from the revenue, the result is the income or gross earnings on the business. If the costs are relatively low compared to the revenue, the business is very profitable, if the costs are equal or higher than the revenue, the business is going out of business.

If revenue is obvious, costs can be easily defined into a few buckets:

CoS - The Cost of Sales - this is the cost of the goods or the cost to deliver the services that were sold for the revenue. The critical point there is that these costs are only incurred after the order is received, though in the case of services they may be the allocated cost for equipment plant or labor that would vary dependent on revenue. It is important to realize that not all CoS are in fact variable. For example, if I buy a factory to build a product, that cost of the factory will be allocated into the products built in each quarter. As volume increases, the allocation per product decreases and the CoS would decrease. If volume decreases, the CoS would go up due to these fixed costs. Fixed CoS may also include the Supply Chain staff and other items. Note that in some industries CoS is referred to as Cost of Goods (CoGs). This is typically in a product business. In this book I have used the more generic Cost of Sales to include services businesses

R&D - Research and Development - this is the cost of developing future products or services. The key is that these costs generally do not contribute inn period to current revenue, but are generating value for future revenue.

SG&A - Sales, General and Accounting - in this category are two costs. Generally I believe these should be separated for clear understanding as in the next two items.

S&M - Sales and Marketing - this is the cost that is spent in period associated with generating the revenue before the order is received.

G&A - General and Accounting - these are the costs associated with operating the business, including insurance, accounting, core services, executive management (and in a public business costs of compliance such as with the Sarbanes/Oxley Act in the US

Simple Profit and Loss Model

Using revenue and these four costs (CoS, R&D, S&M, G&A), we can define a very simple P&L model as shown in Figure 1-1. In this simple P&L model, revenue is $100 (it can be thousands, millions, or billions, depending on how grandiose you want to be in your planning). For the $100 in revenue, the Cost of Sales is $40. The result is a Gross Margin of $60 or 60%. Gross Margin is the money left over after deducting the CoS. Gross Margin can be expressed as a dollar amount or as a percentage of revenue. With R&D at $14, Sales and Marketing at $25 and General and Accounting at $7, this leaves $14 or 14% of Gross Profit (this is before taxes or other costs such as financing interest). Similarly to Gross Margin, each of these costs can be expressed a a percentage by dividing the cost by the total revenue. This is a helpful way of comparing businesses or business models that have different values as the percentage is a relative comparison. Obviously, if we increase the costs or decrease the revenue, this can move from showing a profit to a loss, never a good thing in a business.

Revenue ($)	$	100
Cost of Sales ($)	$	40
Gross Margin ($)	$	60
Gross Margin (%)		*60%*
R&D Cost ($)	$	14
R&D (%)		*14%*
SG&A Cost ($)	$	32
SG&A (%)		*32%*
Sales and Marketing ($)	$	25
Sales and Marketing (%)		*25%*
General and Accounting ($)	$	7
General and Accounting (%)		*7%*
Gross Profit (pre-tax $)	$	14
Gross Profit (pre-tax %)		*14%*

Figure 1-1 Simple Profit and Loss Model

This simple model will be used at different points in the book to illustrate specific impacts of product, channel and sales decisions. Examination of the business model reveals some very specific things. A dollar spent in any of the four areas of cost is a dollar lost from the bottom line or Gross

Profit, Similarly, a dollar of discount is a dollar lost from Gross Profit. The point is to clearly understand that we can think about the model as having a set of knobs: the list price, the discount from list price that is given to the customer, the Cost of Sales, the costs of R&D and SG&A. If we think about each of these as a knob, it becomes easy to understand that there are options in 'tuning' the P&L for maximum profitability.

Impact of Volume and Discounting

A phrase often heard in business is, "You cannot make it up in Volume." While this is often true, in fact volume does have different and understandable impacts on the business model. Figure 1-2 shows a traditional volume business model with revenue, fixed costs and variable costs shown versus volume. This is a chart that you would see in your first year business class. The critical point is that the costs from the P&L Model above have both fixed and variable elements.

Generally, certain costs are totally independent of volume, for example, R&D and G&A have very little variable relationship to volume. However, both CoS and S&M have fixed and variable component. In the case of CoS, certain attributes such as a building lease costs

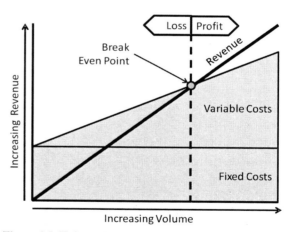

Figure 1-2 Volume Business Model with Break Even

may be fixed relative to volume, while other costs, components for example, will change with volume. Similarly, S&M has both elements. A salesperson base salary will be fixed, but the amount of compensation paid as incentive pay can vary with volume. The point is that having a clear understanding of these costs is critical to managing your business. In this model, the flat horizontal line of fixed cost is the cost that the business will have to spend even if it does not receive a single order or sale. The variable cost line to the upper right is the added cost for each unit of sales volume.

It starts from the base of fixed costs. This can be the cost of the product or the cost of a service. The revenue line starts at zero as each unit of revenue adds from that point. At the breakeven point, the revenues equal the costs and from there forward as volume increases, the business will generate a profit. Prior to that point the business is not generating a profit.

		No Discount	10% Discount				
			No Volume increase	10% Volume Increase	25% Volume Increase	50% Volume Increase	Break Even 16.67% Increase
Revenue ($)		$ 100	$ 90	$ 99.0	$ 112.5	$ 135.0	$ 105.0
Total Cost of Sales ($)		$ 40	$ 40	$ 42.0	$ 45.0	$ 50.0	$ 43.3
	Fixed Cost	$ 20	$ 20	$ 20	$ 20	$ 20	$ 20
	Variable Cost	$ 20	$ 20	$ 22.0	$ 25.0	$ 30.0	$ 23.3
Gross Margin ($)		$ 60	$ 50	$ 57.0	$ 67.5	$ 85.0	$ 61.7
	Gross Margin (%)	60%	55.6%	57.6%	60.0%	63.0%	58.7%
R&D Cost ($)		$ 14	$ 14	$ 14	$ 14	$ 14	$ 14
	R&D (%)	14%	16%	14%	12%	10%	13%
SG&A Cost ($)		$ 32	$ 32	$ 33.0	$ 34.5	$ 37.0	$ 33.7
	SG&A (%)	32%	36%	33.3%	30.7%	27.4%	32.1%
Total S&M ($)		$ 25	$ 25	$ 26.0	$ 27.5	$ 30.0	$ 26.7
	Total S&M (%)	25%	28%	26.3%	24.4%	22.2%	25.4%
	Fixed S&M	$ 15	$ 15	$ 15	$ 15	$ 15	$ 15
	Variable S&M	$ 10	$ 10	$ 11.0	$ 12.5	$ 15.0	$ 11.7
General and Accounting ($)		$ 7	$ 7	$ 7	$ 7	$ 7	$ 7
	General and Accounting (%)	7%	8%	7.1%	6.2%	5.2%	7%
Gross Profit (pre-tax $)		$ 14	$ 4	$ 10.0	$ 19.0	$ 34.0	$ 14.0
	Gross Profit (pre-tax %)	14%	4%	10%	17%	25%	13.3%
Percentage Change in Gross Profit $			-71.4%	-28.6%	35.7%	142.9%	0.0%

Figure 1-3 Impact of Volume and Discount on the Business Model

To analyze the impact of discounting, we return to the P&L Model in the previous section. Assuming that the CoS, (which was $40/40% of the revenue) has both a fixed and variable component, the impact of increases in volume can be analyzed. Let's assume that half of the cost is fixed ($20) is fixed and half ($20) is variable. Of the other costs, we assume that R&D and G&A are fixed, regardless of volume and that 40% of the $25 of S&M is variable and will change with volume and the remainder is fixed. If we assume that the company extends a 10% discount, if there is no volume increase we know it will result in a 10% loss in Gross Profit. However, what if volume increases as a result of the discount and the variable costs lead to increased profitability? Figure 1-3 shows some comparative P&Ls for different volume levels based on a 10% discount.

The first column shows the P&L at the non-discounted price and a defined volume ($100 in revenue). The other five columns are all calculated at an average discount of 10%. The first column shows what happens if the volume does not change. In this case, the revenue is reduced by 10% and the Gross Profit drops by the same. To make it easy to understand what is happening as the volume changes, the fixed and variable costs for both CoS and S&M are shown. If we look at the 25% volume increase column as an example, the revenue is now $112.5 (Discounted Price x 1.25 Volume - $90 X 1.25 = $112.5). Both the COS and S&M Variable costs are multiplied by 1.25 (COS - $20 X1.25 = $25 - S&M - $10 x1.2 = $12). With a 25% increase in volume in this model, the Gross Profit $ increases from $14 to $19, an increase of 35.7%. The last column is calculated at the breakeven point, which requires an increase in sales volume of 16.67%. The last line in the figure shows the relative decrease and increase in the Gross Profit Dollars for each volume analysis.

For many people, seeing data in tables like Figure 1-3 is hard to understand. Therefore, the following two figures show the same information, but displayed as charts to easily see the changes that the different examples represent. Figure 1-4 shows a graphic comparison of the percentages in the examples above. This graphic makes it simple to see the impact in the changes in percentages of revenue that go to each area. Starting from the top are the percentage of the total revenue used in each area (CoS, R&D and G&A respectively) and concluding with the Gross Profit % at the bottom.

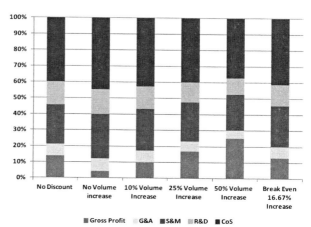

Figure 1--4 Percentage Graph of Volume/Discount Impact

Philip Edholm

Figure 1-5 shows the same data but in $ blocks. This makes some very important points clear,. For example, we can see that, while a 10% increase in volume gets almost to the same volume ($99), it has significantly reduced Gross

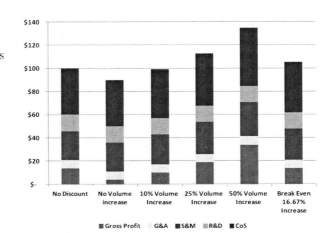

Figure 1-5Dollar Graph of Volume/Discount Impact

Profit. These figures should help you visualize the impact of changing the knobs, without doing all of the analysis.

Figure 1-6 shows a comparison of the base revenue and the discounted revenue against the fixed and variable costs shown in Figure 1-2. This is a clear view of how and why the breakeven point moves to the right to an increased volume level with a reduction of revenue per unit volume of a discount. The slope of the line is reduced by the discount..

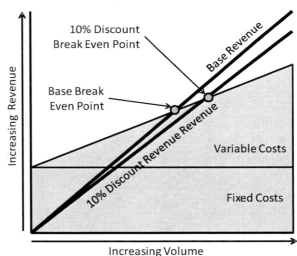

Figure 1-6 Impact of Discount on Breakeven Point

The lesson in this section is often related to a term in marketing called "elasticity of demand". The point is that pricing can have a variable impact on demand and volume. The challenge is to understand the requirements of the P&L model for a given discount and then test the market elasticity to see if the demand and volume increase required to maintain the model or increase Gross Profit are there. In the example above, a test to assure that a 10% discount would generate a minimum of a 17% increase in volume would be required. Once a point is reached where decreases or increases in price have non-linear changes in demand, the edges of the elastic zone have been reached.

Testing in a target market or in a limited way is often a good way of assuring that your discounting will deliver the required volume increases. Without a clear understanding of these dynamics and the business model, pricing and discounting becomes a series of shots in the dark without clear outcomes and goals.

Conclusions

I hope this brief introduction has given the neophyte sufficient knowledge of basic P&L and business models to understand the other concepts in the book and has given the more seasoned business professional a couple of points to ponder.

Philip Edholm

Chapter 2 Business Impact of Go To Market

The term "Go To Market" (GTM) is generally used to define the path that
a product or service takes from the End Producer to the End Customer.
End Producer refers to the company that creates the recognizable thing that
the customer is purchasing, while the End Consumer is the person or entity
that actually uses that item, versus in some way selling it to someone else.
Sony is the End Producer of a television, even though many of the
components are made for them by others. Similarly, Ford is the End
Producer of the car, even if the tires are bought from Goodyear. Someone
who integrates multiple products together and sells them as a system and
positions their value as integration, not as a complete product is not an End
Producer, such a party is actually a Channel, either a reseller or a
Distributor. The End Customer is the company or entity that actually uses
the product or service. I use the term End Customer here to clearly
delineate that, while the Channel is also a customer of the End Producer, it
is not the End Consumer. The Channel is one or more tiers of companies
that sit between the End Producer and the End Consumer. While the
generic form of Channel can refer to one or more of these companies, the
terms Reseller and Distributor have more detailed meaning. Generally the
Reseller takes ownership of the product, making them the "customer" of
the End Producer, consequently the sale to the actual End Consumer is
between the Reseller and the End Consumer.

Figure 2-1 shows three GTM paths: first is direct where the End Producer
has a direct sales relationship with the End Customer and then a single and
two-tiered channel/distribution. In the single tier case, the End Producer
sells to a Reseller that then resells to the End Customer. In some cases, the
channel may have two tiers, a Reseller who sells to the End Consumer, and
a Distributor who sells to a number of Resellers. The two tier model has an
additional distribution tier that provides a mechanism to reduce the points
of interaction of the End Producer when there are many Resellers. In the
case of electrical power, the End Producer may be the operator of an
electrical generating station. The End Producer sells the power to a grid
distribution company, who may sell it again to a local electric company,
who in turn sells it to the consumer. Even though the "power" changed
hands through this process, it was not altered from the end producer to the
end consumer. There are limited cases of three or even more tiers, but the

issue is that the margin must be distributed across the tiers and the result will be less profit for each layer.

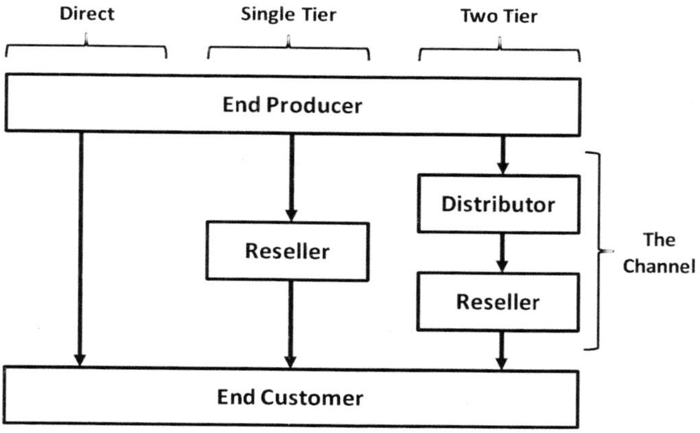

Figure 2-1 Go To Market Models

There are four primary reasons for having Channels for the distribution of an End Producers products or services:

Ability to reach new markets either geographically or size.

Adding Channel produced value to the product or service.

Integrating the product or service with other products or services into a more complete and competitive solution for the End Customer.

Transforming the products into a service offer to the End Customer.

It is critical to understand each of these to evaluate the value of the channel and how it will impact the overall business model.

Channel Reach

The capability of a channel to reach customers that are not easily reached through a direct sales relationship is a predominant reason for Channels between the End Producer and the End Customer. There are at least two major areas this comes in: for geographic considerations or for costs of addressing the customer. Often, for markets outside of the home company of the End Producer, a channel is the only way to address the market. The channel provides local sales and support and has both local presence and language support.

Another is to increase the reach of the End Producer to customers that cannot be addressed directly. As this section is just looking at reach, the assumption is that there is no" value add" to the transferred item, that is covered in the next two areas. Figure 2-2 shows how the reach of an End Producer is increased by using Channels.

As we move down the pyramid of customers, the volume (size) of the sale decreases and the number of End Customers increases. In the large volume case, the End Producer can have a direct relationship with the End Customer. A good example of this is IBM selling computer systems to the Fortune 1000 company. The annual sales are large and the number of

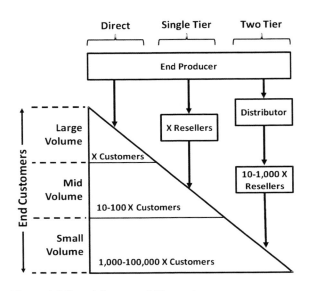

Figure 2-2 Reach Impact of Channels

customers is low. As the number of customers increases and the size of the sale drops, Resellers that cover portions of the market increase the reach. A good example of this is the new car dealer selling a specific car make in a specific geography. Finally, when the number of Resellers that sell to the End Customer reaches a large number, an intermediate distribution layer is often required. A good example of this is in the distribution of beverages. The End Producer (Coke or Pepsi) sells to the regional Distributor, who then sells to the retail store (Reseller), who sells to the End Customer. Though this is a typical two-tier model, the Distributor is adding value as they typically transform the soda syrup into bottled beverages.

As the intent of this book is not to belabor the intricacies of channel distribution, but rather to define it for other topics, those intricacies will not be explored here. The impact of the internet and direct marketing will not be considered, though they have a dramatic impact on the models. However, it is interesting to note that often End Producers may employ all of these at the same time. It is important to note that the role of the Reseller versus the Distributor in two tier distribution is different. The Reseller has the relationship with the End Customer and the distributor aggregates a group of channels to present a single interface to the End Producer. It is sometimes called a "Value Added Reseller" (VAR). The role of the channel is similar in both the single and two-tier model, but the Distributor essentially takes some of the work from the End Producer in the form of warehousing, order management, and billing/account receivable management. Often this is associated with lower volume to the Reseller where the Distributor, by aggregating together products from multiple End Producers creates an economic value.

Later in the book, Chapter 21, "How Small is Too Small" there is a detailed discussion of how to allocate sales between direct and channels. This analysis demonstrates how channels, through their aggregation of multiple End Producers products, can address market segments that are not available directly.

Channel Value Add and Systems Integration

Two other reasons for having a channel are related to the channel adding value beyond simple reach. First, the Reseller may add specific value to the product or service that is not within the capability of the End Producer. For example, a software VAR may buy computers from a computer manufacturer and add a software package that they have developed that does office management for doctors and deliver the combination to the end customer (the Doctor). This Value Added Reseller is now a channel for the computer manufacturer and is adding value. A company that buys a basic truck chassis and installs a tow truck package is similarly a VAR. The key point is that the VAR is adding something that it has developed and/or manufacture and then sells the combination. In the software industry this is referred to as an Integrated Software Vendor (ISV) who builds a software product on a framework like Microsoft Windows™. If the Reseller sells the result under its own brand name, the relationship is referred to as an Original Equipment Manufacturer (OEM), where the End Producer is the OEM.

Another value channels can add is the integration of products or services from multiple End Producers into an integrated solution. Large resellers called "Systems Integrators" (SI) in the technology sector(e.g., IBM and HP), often deliver volumes of products in an integration deal that would not be possible for the End Producer of that product to sell directly, but the End Customer sees value in acquiring those along with others from an integrated source. Smaller Systems Integrators may deliver similar solutions for smaller End Customers or may focus in a specific niche. A good example of a system integrator is the general contractor that builds a custom house. The general contractor generally has a road map of requirements (the architectural design), but it is left to him/her to put everything together into a complete solutions (your new house).

Often VARs and Systems Integration go hand in hand as the value a Reseller/Channel brings to the End Customer. The capability of channels to integrate multiple products or services and provide specific value adds creates great value in the market. For an End Producer, having a relationship with this level of channel is not only about economics, but also about reaching customers that would not buy any in other way.

Service Transformation Channels

Finally, there is a type of channel that takes a product from the End Producer and turns it into a service. When a taxi cab company buys a car from the car manufacturer and then uses it to deliver the taxi service, they are doing a service transformation of the product. Similarly, when the power company buys a generator and sells power, it is a service transformation. Or the wireless carrier when it combines technologies and smartphones to create great new services. The key difference in this model is that the End Producer often does not participate in the ongoing revenue stream, though revenue sharing has become an interesting new model in many industries.

Understanding the Impact of Channels on the Business Model

A key point in defining GTM is a clear understanding of the way channels (i.e. Resellers, Distributors, SI's) impact the business model. While you will need to clearly understand the specifics of your industry and market, there are some basics that allow you to define how channels can be used and valued.

First, it is important to understand how a channel impacts the flow of revenue and cost. This is often not obvious, even to a seasoned business person. I was once in a meeting with a senior executive with over 35 years of business experience in which he insisted that there was no difference between the gross margin with or without a channel. Very simply, when you sell your product through a channel, you are giving some of the end customer revenue to the channel in exchange for the value they bring. Figure 2-3 shows a very simple comparison from the perspective for the End Producer of direct versus channel and the allocation of the components of the business in a simple one tier Reseller Model. You could do a similar analysis for the channel's business.

	Direct	Example 1 No Change in EP Costs	Example 2 S&M Cost Decrease	Example 3 S&M and CoS Decrease
End Customer Spending ($)	$ 100	$ 100	$ 100	$ 100
Channel Revenue	N/A	$ 100	$ 100	$ 100
Channel "Discount" ($)	N/A	$20	$20	$20
Channel Discount off of list %	N/A	20%	20%	20%
Channel Mark-up %	N/A	25%	25%	25%
Total Channel Absorbed Costs	N/A	$ -	$ 16.0	$ 20.0
Absorbed CoS	N/A	$ -	$ -	$ 4.0
Absorbed S&M	N/A	$ -	$ 16.0	$ 16.0
Reveunue to End Producer	$ 100	$ 80	$ 80	$ 80
Total Cost of Sales ($)	$ 40	$ 40	$ 40	$ 36
Fixed Cost	$ 20	$ 20	$ 20	$ 18
Variable Cost	$ 20	$ 20	$ 20	$ 18
Percentage Decrease in CoS versus Base			0%	10%
Gross Margin ($)	$ 60	$ 40	$ 40	$ 44
Gross Margin (%)	60%	50%	50%	55%
R&D Cost ($)	$ 14	$ 14	$ 14	$ 14
R&D (%)	14%	14%	14%	14%
SG&A Cost ($)	$ 32	$ 32	$ 16.0	$ 16.0
SG&A (%)	32%	32%	16.0%	16.0%
Total S&M ($)	$ 25	$ 25	$ 9	$ 9
Total S&M (%)	25%	25%	9.0%	9.0%
Fixed S&M	$ 15	$ 15	$ 5	$ 5
Variable S&M	$ 10	$ 10	$ 4.0	$ 4.0
Percentage Decrease in S&M versus Base			64%	64%
General and Accounting ($)	$ 7	$ 7	$ 7	$ 7
General and Accounting (%)	7%	7%	7.0%	7.0%
Gross Profit (pre-tax $)	$ 14	$ (6)	$ 10.0	$ 14.0
Gross Profit (pre-tax %)	14%	-6%	10%	14%
Percentage Change in Gross Profit $		-142.9%	-28.6%	0.0%

Figure 2-3 Impact of Channel Cost Absorption

In this simple example, the customer spends $100 for the product or service. This is often referred to as the "street price" as it may be a discount from the list price. Many products have a "normal" discount from the list price, which means that using the street price for analysis is the only reasonable path. The "street price" is independent of the channel or path to the customer. In the direct case on the left, the entire $100 of revenue goes to the End Producer. If the CoS is $40 then the Gross Margin is $60 or 60% of the $100 of revenue. On the right, a channel is added. The End Customer pays the same $100 for the product or service, but the channel only pays the End Producer $80. The $20 that goes to the Channel is the discount the End Producer allows the purchase below the *street price*. Note that if the street price and the list price are different, the

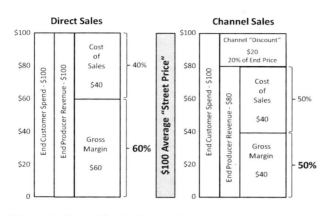

Figure 2-4 Gross Margin Comparison

actual discount from the list price may be much higher than this 20%. For example, if the list price is $120 and the street price is $100, then the channel discount would be expressed as a $40 or 33% discount from list, though the real impact is the 20% discount form the street price or revenue that the channel received. Now the End Producer revenue is not $100, but $80. Assuming the CoS has not changed, then the $40 of COS is now 50% of the revenue and the Gross Margin is reduced to $40 or 50%. While a reduction in Gross Margin is not necessarily bad, assuming that the costs for the End Producer have not changed, the loss of margin will flow through to a loss of Gross Profit.

Obviously, having a channel instead of direct selling does not make sense unless the channel is changing the business model in one of two ways: absorbing costs or increasing volume. The third option, that the channel can charge more for the product than the End Producer is so rare that we will not consider it here. To show how cost absorption and volume increases can change the business with channels, we are going to use the same P&L models from Chapter 1 "The Basic Business Model". The first analysis assumes that the sales volume remains the same, and we will change some of the other variables of cost to see the impact. Figure 2-4 shows how costs need to be changed when a channel is in place.

The direct column is the same as before and all of the channel values are N/A (Not Applicable). The result is that there is no change in the End Producer (EP) costs. This model generates a $14 Gross Profit or 14%. All three channel examples make the assumption that the channel buys the product from the e End Producer at $80 or a 20% discount and then sells the product for $100. While this is a 20% discount from list, it can also be thought of as a 25% mark-up.

Example 1 assumes that the End Producer continues to incur all of the costs that were incurred selling direct. As can be seen, the P&L now goes from a profit to a loss. This is obvious as the discount to the channel comes directly off of profits as was discussed earlier. The 20% discount is greater than the 14% profit. If the channel is not extending reach or reducing cost, then it is not going to be positive to the a comparison with direct..

Example 2 shows that the End Producer has reduced the cost of S&M by 64% (from $25 to $9), assuming that the channel is going to absorb those costs as shown in the $16 in S&M Absorbed Costs. By reducing cost based on the channel, the End Producer is now profitable again, but has had $4 or 28.6% reduction in Gross Profit.

Example 3 shows that by the channel taking on 10% of the CoS by having warehousing and some other work, the End Producer has now returned to the same level of profit as in the direct case.

The problem with this simplistic case is that the $20 of cost ($4 of CoS and $16 of S&M) absorbed by the channel has actually just moved to the channel. If the cost to do these activities is the same for the channel as the End Producer, then there is no way for the channel to make a profit. It is always interesting to listen to people who do not understand the requirement of profitability of the channel and their assumption that the channel will just absorb costs so the End Producer can have a profit. The point is that if the model is static in terms of costs and volume, then in the end, the available Gross Profit HAS to be split between the End Producer and the Channel. SO, why the interests in channels? Because they change other factors in the business model.

The first challenge is to understand if costs change between direct and channel. As is discussed later in Chapter 21 "how Small is Too Small", for low volume products the channel costs may be reduced by aggregating the cost of sales with other products. Also, the channel may have reduced costs due to proximity to the customer and therefore can reduce the S&M costs. So we need to analyze the more complex case in which some of the cost is absorbed by the channel, and also in which the volume increases and variable costs do not increase as fast as volume.

Channel Volume and Cost Impact

Another way of analyzing the cost of the channel is by assuming that in addition to transitioning costs to the channel, going to a channel model

	Direct	Example 1 No Volume Change	Example 2 50% Volume Increase - no reduction in variable costs	Example 3 50% Volume Increase - reduction in variable costs
End Customer Spending ($)	$ 100	$ 100	$ 150	$ 150
Channel Revenue	N/A	$ 100	$ 150	$ 150
Channel "Discount" ($)	N/A	$20	$30	$30
Channel Discount off of list %	N/A	20%	20%	20%
Channel Mark-up %	N/A	25%	25%	25%
Total Channel Absorbed Costs	N/A	$ 10.0	$ 15.0	$ 15.0
Absorbed CoS	N/A	$ 2.0	$ 4.0	$ 4.0
Absorbed S&M	N/A	$ 8.0	$ 11.0	$ 11.0
Reveunue to End Producer	$ 100	$ 80	$ 120	$ 120
Total Cost of Sales ($)	$ 40	$ 38.0	$ 56.0	$ 53.0
Fixed Cost	$ 20	$ 19.0	$ 28.0	$ 28.0
Variable Cost	$ 20	$ 19.0	$ 28.0	$ 25.0
Percentage Decrease in CoS versus Base		5%	7%	12%
Gross Margin ($)	$ 60	$ 42.0	$ 64.0	$ 67.0
Gross Margin (%)	60%	53%	53%	56%
R&D Cost ($)	$ 14	$ 14	$ 14	$ 14
R&D (%)	14%	18%	12%	12%
SG&A Cost ($)	$ 32	$ 24.0	$ 33.5	$ 32.0
SG&A (%)	32%	30%	28%	27%
Total S&M ($)	$ 25	$ 17.0	$ 26.5	$ 25.0
Total S&M (%)	25%	21%	22%	21%
Fixed S&M	$ 15	$ 11.0	$ 17.5	$ 17.5
Variable S&M	$ 10	$ 6.0	$ 9.0	$ 7.5
Percentage Decrease in S&M versus Base		15%	29%	33%
General and Accounting ($)	$ 7	$ 7	$ 7	$ 7
General and Accounting (%)	7%	9%	6%	6%
Gross Profit (pre-tax $)	$ 14	$ 4	$ 16.5	$ 21.0
Gross Profit (pre-tax %)	14%	5%	14%	18%
Percentage Change in Gross Profit $		-71.4%	17.9%	50.0%

Figure 2-5 Impact of Volume Increase of Channel

will increase volume. To make this a more reasonable analysis, certain elements of the model are fixed. The R&D and G&A are fixed $ amounts. It is assumed that the sum of CoS and S&M costs must total the amounts in the earlier model at that volume point. In order to assure that the channel partner has profit, it is assumed that its costs can never be more than 50% of its mark-up. This gives the channel partner 10% of revenue as its margin, with its Gross profit being that less its G&A (as S&M and CoS are in the other 10%). Figure 2-5 shows how an increase in volume by going through the channel can impact the Gross Profit.

In this example, the fist column shows the base case for reference. Figure 2-6 shows the same examples as a chart.

The first column in both Figures 2-5 and 2-6 are the baseline of a direct business with 60% Gross Margin and 14% Gross Profit. Only Sales and Marketing (S&M) and Cost of Sales (CoS) vary in the models,: the costs associated with R&D and G&A are fixed for all four models.

Example 1 is going to a channel with no volume change. The channel.

Example 1 is going to a channel with no volume change. The channel "discount" is 20%, resulting in a revenue to the End Producer of $80 instead of $100.

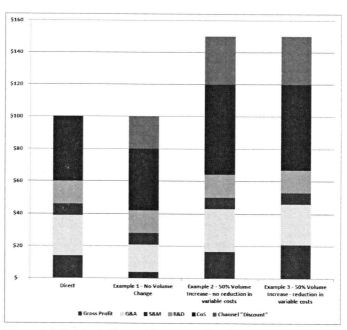

Figure 2-6 Graph of Channel Impact on Profit

However, it is assumed that there is some reduction in CoS due to the channel managing final shipment and delivery, and the End Producer spend on S&M is reduced by $8. As a result, the End Producer has a net reduction in spending of $10. When combined with the net reduction in revenue of $20, the result is a reduction of the Gross Profit of the End

Producer of $10 or from 14% to 4%. While the business is still profitable, the profit has been reduced by over 70%.

Example 2 shows the model if moving to the channel results in a 50% increase in volume due to the extended sales reach of the channel. In this example, there is no decrease in the percentages of total revenue (End Customer spend) spent on CoS and S&M. These costs are assumed to be linear, with the channel absorbing 10% of revenue or $15 of these costs. Those costs have been arbitrarily allocate as $4 of CoS and $11 of S&M. The End Producer's costs in both categories have been reduced by that amount. For example, in the S&M category, a linear rate would have had the End Producer spending $37.5M on S&M with End Customer spending of $150, but as can be seen, this has been reduced by the $11M that was absorbed by the channel. The result is that the End Producer Gross Profit is now increased to $16.5, but as a percentage, it is the same 14% as in the direct model (this is not by design, but a coincidence of this set of numbers).

Example 3 shows the impact of a reduction in certain variable costs because of the 50% volume increase by using the channel. While the absorption of costs by the channel is unchanged, the CoS has been reduced by $3 from Example 2. This is based on a 32% increase in variable CoS cost versus the 50% increase in volume. Similarly, the S&M has been increased only by 25% for the 50% volume, as it is assumed that much of the variable S&M costs are now in the channel. The combined impact of channel absorption and volume increase demonstrates the value of the channel in growing the business. In this example, the Gross Profit has increased 50% to $21 and has increased to 18% of the End Producer revenue.

Adding Distribution to the Mix

The two-tier model of adding a distribution layer has many of the same factors as in the previous analysis. The distribution layer can impact the business model in two positive ways: by decreasing absorbed costs and increasing volume.

Let's take an example of a distribution organization which has established business relationships with a large number of End Customers. While they may not sell heavily a particular product from a single End Producer, this organization may have a broad range of products from a number of End Producers, thus realizing significant improvements in processes. While a typical distribution organization may only mark up the product by 2-5%, they may absorb 50% more in cost than would have been incurred. Efficient ordering and inventory management, combined with efficient warehousing and movement can reduce these costs significantly compared to the direct sales by the End Producer. In addition, the aggregation role it plays to the next tier results in added efficiency. For example, products from multiple End Producers can be combined in shipment and accounts receivables are more easily collected. If the volume through the distributor is 10 times the volume of the End Producer if it was done direct, there is no question that the costs are going to be reduced through the volume processing. The smaller the End Producer is as a percentage the better this reduction. The key to this part of the value of the channel is to clearly understand the cost alternatives to using the distributor versus doing the function as the End Producer.

The second value of the Distributor is increasing volume. Just as in the previous models for channels, if the distributor opens up a very small increase in volume, then it will easily justify the distributor discount.

Conclusions

While the use of channels is a complex part of the business process, it is relatively simple to understand the levers and outcomes that using channels generates. A clear plan around cost absorption, volume change, and efficiency will enable an organization to take advantage of the channel. If you are a channel or distributor, having a clear understanding of the challenges and opportunities you deliver to your End Producer partners is critical to structuring your business.

An analysis of channels specific to a particular market/industry is left to the reader. Using the same analysis techniques used in this chapter would produce a clear understanding of the variables.

Chapter 3 The Knobs Behind Gross Margin

As was discussed earlier, Gross Margin is a critical business concept. An added dollar of margin is a dollar of profit (or less loss if the business is unprofitable). Below the gross margin line, the primary variable based on sales volume is variable sales compensation. However, margin has a set of components that need to be understood. The following equation is a good way to think about Margin:

$$
\begin{aligned}
&\text{List Price} \\
&\quad - \text{Street/Customer Discount} \\
&\quad - \text{Channel Discount} \\
&\quad - \text{Standard Cost of Sales} \\
&\quad - \text{Other Costs (volume variable)} \\
&= \text{Gross Margin \$}
\end{aligned}
$$

The calculation essentially subtracts these four elements from List Price to arrive at the Gross Margin. So, for Gross Margin we have 5 factors (or knobs): Price, Street/Customer Discount, Channel Discount, Standard Costs, and Other Costs.

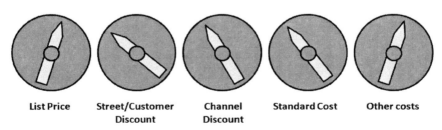

| List Price | Street/Customer Discount | Channel Discount | Standard Cost | Other costs |

Figure 3-1 Knobs of Gross Margin

One easy way to think of these factors is as a set of knobs and to use that analogy to understand the resistance to changing a knob and the value delivered. At the same time it is valuable to understand as a pictogram the steps from Revenue to Gross Margin and the impact of each of these elements. To simplify the visualization, we will use the same $100 Street Price that we used in Chapter 1: The Basic Business Model. Figure 3-2 shows the "waterfall" of the impact of the knobs on the Gross Margin that the company receives.

In this simple model, the list or published price is 25% higher than the average selling price (the Customer or "Street" price). The result is that a 20% discount from List Price gives us the $100 Street Price that matches the other models. As this model assumes the product is being sold through a channel, the channel discount of an additional 36% (corresponding to a 25% channel mark up) reduces the actual company

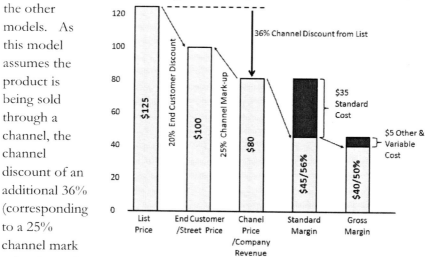

Figure 3-2 Basic Waterfall of Gross Margin with a Channel

revenue to $80. Next we remove the "standard" cost of the product (this is the expected average cost to build the products and deliver to the customer), and finally there is an adjustment for other costs and variables from the standard. In this model "Other and Variable" is shown as an additional cost, reducing Gross Margin. This can also be a positive to Gross Margin if actual costs are lower than projected standard costs. Though warranty is generally accrued into SG&A, sometimes to separate it from the S&M activities it is shown as another cost. If it is not shown there, it is important to think about warranty costs as an additional cost impacting the Gross margin. The result in this case is $40 in Gross Margin or 50% of the $80 sales price to the channel that is the End Producer's revenue.

Remember, the way to think about increasing margin is to think of how difficult each factor is to move versus the value it will accrue to Gross Margin. To better clarify this process, let's look at each factor in more detail.

End Customer Discounts

End Customer Discounts are both the easiest and most complex item on this list. Depending on your specific market, a discount from list may be expected and may be relatively volume independent. As we covered a significant detail on discounting and controlling the impact in the previous chapter, the key concept here is to clearly understand how you manage the discount. For example, in a grocery store, the discount may have two very different elements, a "normal" list price for an item that is based on the general mark-up in the industry over the channel price, or a "special" price that is generated by a temporary reduction in the channel price. This concept of dual pricing works well for products for which buying preference can be changed through significant price reductions (Coke versus Pepsi for example). In many cases of this type, there will be three types of buyers: those with a price-independent preference for Product A, those with a price-independent preference for Product B, and those with a price dependent buying behavior. A critical factor in this type of discounting is clearly understanding the demographics of the target customers in these three groups.

In more complex purchases, there is an expectation of discount based on the industry/product and the customer volume/importance. The auto industry is a good example of how discounting becomes less controllable by an individual vendor and becomes part of the process. Dependent on the economic conditions and the type of vehicle, customers come to expect a discount. In this environment, it may be better to set a list price that enables "continual" discounting to meet the expectation.

In very complex sales such as technology sales into enterprises, discounts of a specific level are seen as an entitlement. If Wal-Mart goes to buy computer systems for their internal use, they expect to get a relatively large discount from the list price. Depending on the industry, these discounts can range up to 50% or even higher. In this environment, the list price is set to accommodate these discounts, so the list price becomes a "reference". Managing the trade-off between volume and customer "importance" in the mechanisms for discounting is critical. The challenge is managing these through a channel that may not provide clear data about the End Customers and volume becomes a significant problem to manage. In many cases this leads to complex individual added discounts on a deal by deal basis. This is often exacerbated as a large customer may expect a significant discount, even at low volume (we are Wal-Mart after all).

In the end, the ideal way to manage End Customer discounting is to assume a standard discount and then use the resulting price as a standard and minimize the variance. This is especially true when the End Customer is hidden by the channel. In the grocery store example, the ability to shift discounts based on an individual is very challenging, though targeted coupons are a way for driving this. Generally, this discount is best understood and managed, but may not be an area for substantial change to the Gross Margin. The one exception to this is when End Customer discounts are driven by individual negotiations, for some discussion of this, See Chapter 22: The Customer Always Lies.

Channel Discounts

When looking at Channel Discounts (or conversely, Channel Mark-ups), both the End Producer and channel sides need to be understood. From a End Producer perspective, minimizing the channel discount is optimal from a financial perspective. From a channel perspective, maximizing the mark-up is optimal. In the end then, the channel and the End Producer are in conflict based on the financial value of the outcome. If we think about a very simple change in the model as shown in

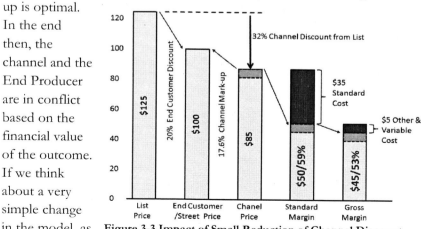

Figure 3-3 Impact of Small Reduction of Channel Discount

Figure 3-3, a reduction of the channel discount from 36 to 32% has a carry

49

through increase in the Gross Margin of $5. This reduction in discount results in a reduction in the mark-up of the channel from $20 to $25 or from 25% to 17.6%.

As can be seen the Gross Margin is now $45 and 53% with no other changes. While the actual Gross Margin Dollars changed by $5, the Gross Margin percentage only went up by a little over 3% as the denominator in the gross Margin percentage is now $85 instead of $80. The medium grey areas shows how the discount reduction flows through to the Gross Margin. Assuming the R&D and SG&A costs do not change, this 3% increase will flow to Gross Profit.

So managing channel discounts is a critical value. How can this be effectively managed? Generally there are three ways to think about the discount the channel receives as related to the value it delivers in the overall acquisition process.

Channel Generating Buying Preference

If the channel is driving End Customer buying preferences instead of the End Producer, generally the channel will expect and receive a higher discount. In this case, , the decision about which product to sell will be made on which delivers the greatest value to the channel. This is combination of two factors: how much discount the channel gets, and how much it costs the channel to deliver that End Producer's products versus others. Assuming that the street price and the delivery (ordering receiving, installing, etc.) for two products are the same, the channel will generally move to the one that has a higher discount. This then exposes a strategy around using process simplification for the channel as a way to justify lower discounts and higher margins. For example, an investment of $1M in developing a sophisticated order management system would be justified if discounts could be lowered by more than 1% on a $100M business based on this being a competitive advantage. The only forewarning here is that often this type of trade-off is relatively short lived as the channel's competition will react and copy the move. In this mode the End Producer must clearly understand all of the factors that will drive the channel preference. From a channel perspective, clearly understanding all costs associated with a specific choice is critical.

End Producer Generated Buying Preference

A very different model is where the End Producer is actually driving the buying preference. While this is partially true in the grocery model (all those TV ads for sodas and beer), and in the car business, in many ways it is a shared responsibility with the channel. In Chapter 20: Value Add Selling Model, the value of the channel as a service capability is discussed, so having the channel create buying preference through service can be associated with a End Producer product/vision based buying preference.

The key difference in the End Producer generated buying preference is that the channel is now fulfilling the customers decision, so the discount should not reflect the work that the vendor is doing in S&M to generate that preference. Again using the same model, we now reflect a much lower channel discount to reflect the channel not driving buying preference.

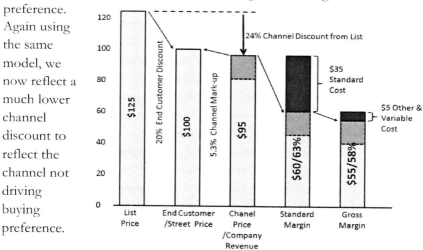

It is important to remember

Figure 3-4 Impact of Significant Channel Discount Reduction on Gross Margin

that this model may generate higher Gross Margins, but not increase Gross Profit as the End Producer S&M is now much higher as discussed in Chapter 21: How Small is Too Small?.

It is generally simple to understand when discounts fall into this category versus in the channel driven buyer preferences. If the customer can buy the product easily in multiple outlets, then the buying preference will generally be End Producer driven. While this is true of groceries generally, it is much more complex for other items like autos. In major urban areas, a purchase of a specific brand auto may have little channel influence as there are multiple dealerships in close proximity. Alternatively, in a rural area where the distance between dealers is much higher, the dealer may have a much larger impact in preference. This is often a significant reason in reducing the channel versus reducing discounts. BY decreasing the competitive footprint, the channel discount can be maintained. When GM reduced the number of dealers in its channel, a significant reason was to concentrate volume to reduce the discount level to maintain viable dealer business models.

Mixed Buying Preferences

Often, the channel and the End Producer share responsibilities in the GTM process. There are a number of excellent ways to think about this, but for purposes of this section, it is best to reduce it to how to manage when this is variable across the served End Customers. In Chapter 20 How Small is Too Small, the topic of how to distribute customer deals and relationships to the channel is discussed. However, in many industries, a specific channel partner may have a mixed role: in some End Customer relationships the channel is the lead and in some the End Producer is the lead. Having a clear plan as to how discounting is managed in this case is critical. If the revenue is split 50/50 between these two, a bad choice will either open the End Producer up to displacement in the small deals if the discount is too small to cover the channel costs or leaving significant Gross Margin if the discount is too large, resulting in not enough S&M to cover the costs of the End Producer sales activities in a large deal. In this case a base discount with targeted end customer discounts works well. This requires a simple process to define how the larger deals are tracked and managed. One critical challenge in this area is managing the demands for discount from the channel because the End Customer "needs" a price. This makes the End Producer dependent on the channel to both validate pricing as a factor and to not have the channel use an artificial price point of effectively increase the discount.

Avoiding Cyclical Discounting

One critical area to be aware of is allowing your business to get into a cyclical discounting modality. In the auto industry, this was often referred to as the end of the month deals to make the numbers. When a vendor sells through a channel, this can become a significant issue. If the channel begins to understand that the End Producer will significantly alter pricing on a cyclical basis and the channel has enough volume predictability and sufficient predictability in its sales funnel to buy using that cycle, the vendor will rapidly find that the discounts are being significantly impacted. This generally is caused by having a low backlog, in which case the End Producer is heavily seeking revenue at the end of a financial period and is willing to extend "special" discounts to get the volume. The challenge is that after only a few periods of this process, the buying pattern will become ingrained in the channel, and the discounts will essentially become institutionalized. The only way to avoid this is to have sufficient backlog/run-rate, where there is no driver to dramatically change end of cycle volume by intense discounting. One significant way of analyzing discounts is to plot discounts over the period. If there is a statistically significant increase in discount at the end of the period, this is an issue and needs to be addressed.

Standard Cost

Standard Cost is the expected cost of the product at the planned volume. Generally it includes all costs for manufacturing the product and delivering it to the customer (or channel). Included are raw materials, components, and labor, as well as the costs of the factory facilities and operations.

The impact of a reduction of Standard Costs from $35 to $25 is shown in figure 3-5 based on the original model in Figure 3-2.

As can be clearly seen, the $10

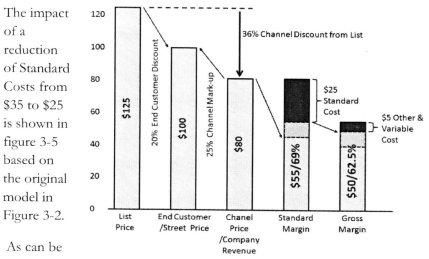

Figure 3-5 Impact of CoS Reductions based on Channel Volume on Gross Margin

53

reduction in cost flows all the way through to Gross Margin. However, this actually represents a 28.6% reduction in standard cost. Achieving this would be a challenge in any businesses and would require significant investment in one of three areas, dependent on the business and how optimized each area is.

Product Design

One critical way to reduce Standard Cost is to reduce the cost through a modified design. The Japanese concept of Kaizen is often applied to the product itself. For example, in one iteration of the Toyota Camry had a 50% reduction in the parts in the bumper assembly. Similarly, continual examination of parts and other items can reduce cost. Of course, product design for cost reduction must be considered based on volume versus cost. This is a simple analysis that will quickly determine the value of an investment. Another way is to have a specific budget for continuous cost reduction based on the assumption that you can continually reduce your costs.

However, when looking at product design, it is important to understand if you are in an industry segment where cost reduction is expected. Certain segments either have expectations about cost decreases (the PC industry of the 90s), or an expectation of value increase (the PC industry today) where a continual investment in replacement and cost reduction is required, but is actually reflected in the price reducing or being the same for higher value (the next larger processor in a PC and added memory at a specific price point).

Having a clear view of investments that are required to maintain or increase the price points versus cost reduction that can be done without impacting price is critical. These can all be analyzed against the business model to optimize the investment strategy.

The Supply Chain

Whether you manufacture your own products, buy from someone else, or have your product made for you, managing the cost of manufacturing is critical. Similar to the product design, having a clear understanding of how to reduce the manufacturing costs for a defined product design is very important.

The processes of Kaizen, or continuous improvement and leané Six Sigma to reduce steps are well defined for managing a process that you control. Similarly, being aggressive with suppliers and vendors you use can often reduce the standard cost.

In any case, having a clear understanding of how the manufacturing components compare is critical. Often, product design issues appear as manufacturing cost, or conversely, high manufacturing costs may lead to product design choices that are non-optimal.

Service Labor Costs

While the two areas above refer to a product oriented business, when there is significant non-manufacturing labor in the offer, optimizing the cost of that labor is critical. Because the actual hourly/monthly/yearly costs of labor are very industry, regional, and other factors specific, it is very hard to define mechanisms to effectively manage those in the short space allowed for this topic. However, the universal factors of rate mark-up, utilization rate and efficiency can be clearly seen in any non-manufacturing labor business.

Mark-up and Utilization Rate

Assume that your business is selling hourly services. If you sell an hour of labor for $100 and the salary/benefits you pay to the employee is $40, then it is relatively easy to calculate the Standard Cost. As your headcount costs are static (assuming this is a full-time employee), that part of the equation is fixed.

Gross Margin = Annual Revenue – Annual Costs
Gross Margin = ($Billed/Hour * Billed Hours) – (Employee Cost + Infrastructure Costs + Management Costs)
Gross Margin = ($Billed/Hour * Billed Hours) – ((Hourly Cost * 2080) + Infrastructure Costs + Management Costs)

Key Factors:
Ratio of $Billed/Hour to Hourly Cost
Ratio of Billed Hours to 2080

As can be seen, other than the infrastructure and management costs associated with the employees, the critical factors are the ratio of the billable hour rate to the actual cost per hour and the ratios of billable hours to 2080 (52*40). Note that available billable hours are always less than 2080 because of vacations, training and other activities (this is not true if your employees work overtime and you bill or they are salaried yet bill more than 40 hours per week, as is common in both the legal and consulting businesses). If we assume 4 weeks of vacations and holidays and one week of training, then the maximum (100%) billable hours is 1880 (47*40) The ratio of actual hourly costs to billed hourly costs is easy to analyze and understand. The following examples show a fixed $40 actual employee rate and vary the charged rate from $100 to $120. The infrastructure and management costs have been set at 25% of employee costs for simplicity of analysis (the employee costs are multiplied by 1.2 times the annual cost). This is a comparison of the impact of slight rate changes on Gross Profit..

$100 Billable Rate
Gross Margin = ($100*(1880 * 70%)) – (($40 * 2080) + (20% * ($40 * 2080)))
Gross Margin = ($100 * 1316) - (($40 * 2080)*1.2)
Gross Margin = $131,600 - $99,840
Gross Margin = $31,760

$110 Billable Rate
Gross Margin = ($110*(1880 * 70%)) – (($40 * 2080)*1.2)
Gross Margin = $44,920
Increase versus $100 = 41% higher

$120 Billable Rate
Gross Margin = ($120*(1880 * 70%)) – (($40 * 2080)*1.2)
Gross Margin = $58,080
Increase versus $100 = 83% higher

As can be seen, an increase in hourly billing of 20% results in an increase of Gross Margin of 83%. Obviously, if the billing rate and actual costs are closer then this will become even more important.

The utilization ratio is also easy to analyze. For example, in the legal profession, the drive to maximize billable hours is paramount. If the billable hours exceeds the compensated hours, the business is now in a great position. Having a clear view of these factors is critical and should be analyzed to optimize at all times. For example, a plan to increase billed hours in the above example by 10%(from 70% to 77% for example) would mean that the Gross Margin would increase by the same 41% as a 10% increase in Billable Rate as shown previously.

70% Utilization
Gross Margin = ($100*(1880 * 70%)) – (($50 * 2080) + (20% * ($50 * 2080)))
Gross Margin = ($100 * 1316) - (($50 * 2080)*1.2)
Gross Margin = $131,600 - $99,840
Gross Margin = $31,760

77% Utilization
Gross Margin = ($100*(1880 * 77%)) – (($50 * 2080)*1.2)
Gross Margin = $44,920
Increase versus 70% = 41% higher

84% Utilization
Gross Margin = ($100*(1880 * 84%)) – (($50 * 2080)*1.2)
Gross Margin = $58,080
Increase versus 70% = 83% higher

The result of both of these examples is that a clear plan to optimize billable hours and increase rates is critical for margins in service businesses.

Increasing Efficiency

Obviously the other factor in a services-oriented business is efficiency. If the time to do a task that is billed and paid as a task can be reduced, and there are sufficient billable tasks to keep the employees busy then the result will similarly impact Gross Margin. This can be of value in bid-based businesses and where there are fixed rates (auto repair often has fixed hours for a task for example). Understanding what is standard and having a plan to improve it is a great way to increase Gross Margin in this type of business. Using the techniques of Kaizen and Lean/Six Sigma to examine the labor content and working to reduce it is important. Even in a small business, a slight reduction in task cycle time can result in increased efficiency. If a waitress spends 25% of his or her time getting condiments, drinks, etc. and that can be reduced by 50% by effective restaurant layout, then that can result in a 12.5% reduction in work per table or a 10% increase in covered tables. This can reduce the number of required waiter staff by 10%. The resulting reduction in labor cost and increase in average tips for the remaining servers will be good both for the restaurant owner and the staff.

Other and Variable Costs

Assuming you are using a Standard (or estimated) Cost for your business management, this is the area where costs are accrued up at the end of a period. While there are some costs (warranty for example) that can be included here (this is not the normal accounting practice), generally these costs are the variables. If you planned your Standard Costs at a specific volume and you exceeded that volume by 20% and some of the Standard Cost was fixed factory cost, then that cost per unit is actually less. The result is that there will be an increase in gross margin because of a reduction in Standard Cost versus the volume. Similarly, if you planned to buy parts at a specific price and due to volume or market fluctuation the price increased, the increase would reduce the standard margin to the gross margin.

Modeling Gross Margin Change

Often a plus/minus model is used to plan changes in Gross Margin. Figure

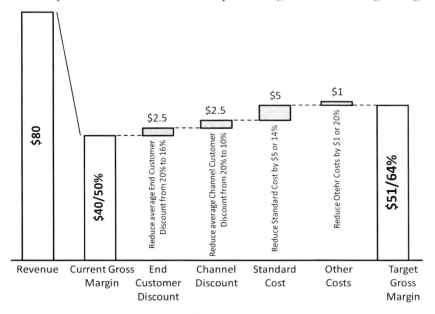

Figure 3-6 Modeling Gross Margin Changes and Impact

3-6 shows such a model using the data from the earlier models and some of the changes that could be accomplished.

In this example, all of the changes are increasing Gross Margin: other examples may have negative changes as well. In this case, the discounts are reduced, the Standard Cost is reduced, as are the other costs. The result of a plan to initiate all of these changes would result in a change from a Gross Margin of $40 to a new Gross Margin of $51. From a percentage perspective, the Gross Margin Percentage increased by 14 percentage points. Assuming that the company was generating 10% Gross Profit with the 50% Gross Margin, now the Gross Profit would be 24%, an increase of 140%. Assuming there is a linear relationship between Gross Profit and company value (company value is generally defined as the value of a company based on its stock price or market value if sold), this would result in a 140% increase in company value..

Gross Margin and the factors that enable a business to control and manage it are critical to the success of any venture. Continual examination and questioning of all the factors that go into it should become a regular part of any business process.

Philip Edholm

Chapter 4 Cash is King

This is a simple concept, but one that is so critical to thinking about a business that, is worth a Chapter. The goal of a business is to generate cash, period. After that cash has been generated, whether it is used to pay dividends, enrich the owners, make acquisitions, fund growth, or revenue to buy back stock to increase shareholder value is irrelevant. It all starts with cash. It is important to remember that the P&L we did earlier is not necessarily cash. You can have a great P&L without actually generating cash. For example, a rapidly growing business will use cash to increase inventories and accounts receivable for increased shipments today and in the future. If the company is growing rapidly, the result may be a P&L that is positive, but with cash being used for inventory and receivables. This will show up as assets on the balance sheet, but the result is not a generation of cash. This is not bad, but looking beyond the P&L, cash is still important, especially to understand if the increase in inventory is in saleable products or in things that will become obsolete.

A great example of P&Ls without cash generation happened in many of the telecommunications service providers in the early 2000s. The Internet was exploding and new Internet companies were cropping up all over the place. In the Internet access and transport business the growth of new companies was explosive. A new Internet Carrier company would get funded with a few hundred million dollars and then go to the equipment suppliers and buy equipment with an initial payment and financing from the equipment supplier. The result was that the equipment supplier was often taking on 80% of the revenue as a debt liability from the Internet Carrier. Using this debt asset, the End Producer would then get additional debt funding, increasing the general liability of the company. The result was a great in-period P&L, while simultaneously increasing both assets and liabilities from the debt. In 2002/3, when the Internet bubble burst, many of these new companies failed or were sold for asset value and much of the debt assets had to be written off. The result was a debt liability without a corresponding asset. The key was for example Nortel (which later went bankrupt at least partially from debt built up during this period), generated over a billion dollars of profit in 2001, but actually had to borrow capital to fund cash. This was due to the End Producer funding discussed above and also building inventory, much of which would later be written off at a 90%

loss.

Cash is the major measure of the flexibility of a company to survive changes and disruptions in the market. While innovation and adaptive management is critical, without cash, even the most innovative companies will fail. It also is the best measure of a company that owns a strong market position. When a company is in a leadership position, it is always generating cash. In late 2011, Apple generated over $13 billion of cash in a single quarter, a direct reflection of the dominant market position in tablets and iPhones.

When I was part of Sytek, General Instrument (a cable equipment provider) owned 57% of the company. As the General Instrument's executive team had come out of the cable television industry, they started every conversation about performance with cash. This was directly tied to how the cable business was built, often bootstrapped and built on generating cash to fund the business. As part of their business philosophy there was a clear recognition that each element of the business either increased or decreased cash. If average pricing could be increased by 5% without impacting volume, the result is cash. A decrease in discounts, product costs, or operating costs becomes cash.

While actual quarter to quarter increase or decrease in cash is a significant measure of the health of a business, there are a couple of other cash analysis points that should be understood: cash on hand and current ratio.

An interesting and not often used measure of a business is cash on hand and what is called the current balance. Cash on hand is a simple measure of how many days of cash there is based on the cost of the business. So if a business has total expenses of $100K per day and has $2M cash, it would have 20 days cash on hand. In small businesses, less than 10 days cash on hand is considered very dangerous, while in large corporations, typical cash on hand is over 100 days and often over 200.

The current ratio is a measure of a company's liquidity. It is expressed as shown. A Current Ratio of under 1 is an indicator

$$\text{Current Ratio} = \frac{\text{Current Assets}}{\text{Current Liabilities}}$$

that the company would not be able to pay back its short-term liabilities (debt and payables) with available short-term assets (cash, inventory, receivables). Together these two indicators are a good measure of the cash situation of a business.

So remember as you analyze your business, or even your investments: **Cash is King** and there is no substitute. When cash and P&L are not aligned, look closely at both the business model and the sustainability of the business with a clear eye to both the Current Ratio and the Cash on Hand.

Business and Management Concepts

This section is devoted to a few high level concepts of business that are not tied to any single typical business function. It is intended to open your thoughts to some new ways of looking at business and the world that business resides in. The topics are designed to make you more effective both as a manager and as a leader. It includes some key management concepts as well as some views of organizations and structure

Chapter 5 The Value Add Economy

How services or products are valued is highly dependent on their relative complexity and scarcity in the market. However, there is generally not a defined way to think of the elements in an economic system and their relationship to value and "commoditization ". In this chapter the concept that in any macro or micro economic area a defined layered system of values can be identified is explored. The concept of "value add" refers to how value is added in a system above the commodity value. If we start with commodity value being work that virtually anyone can do (shoveling dirt for example), we next add value above it: what dirt to shovel, where to put the dirt, building a better shovel, etc, finally completing the value with the design of what is requiring the dirt to be shoveled. The concept is that in any economic ecosystem, whether small or large, the layers of value can be defined as they add up from the lowest base value levels. This is a key concept that other sections in this book will refer to and that is key to understanding many areas of business.

The Basic Concept of Value Layering

To begin, we can start with the concept of a system with layered value. For simplicity sake, it is easy to divide value into three layers. Here I have described the layering in terms of services, but the concepts can also apply to products, as you will see later. These layers are shown on Figure 5-1.

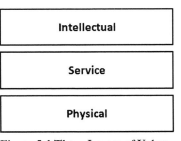

Figure 5-1 Three Layers of Value

Physical Value - this is value that is simple to deliver and can be delivered by a broad range of individuals or entities. It requires relatively low levels of training and or skills and is readily available in the market. Generally in work, physical value is associated with a relatively short term event and not with a sustained activity. Traditional labor is physical, but so is driving a Taxicab or a UPS delivery van.

Service Value - this is value that is defined and delivered not in a specific activity, but in the sustained capability over time. It generally includes both the organization of risk as well as structuring and managing the delivery of components during the time in a variable way. Service value is available through a smaller set of providers than physical value.

Intellectual Value - this is value that defines new capabilities or structures that are not well understood. It is limited in available capability and generally requires advanced training, experience, or knowledge not generally available in the market.

While it is interesting to think of these layers in terms of work, what becomes more interesting is to begin to contrast value with the number of available providers. In Figure 5-2 there are two different ways of looking at the layers. In the left is the relative value accrued to the provider of that layer of value, while on the right are the relative number of providers. As can be seen, the two are inverted pyramids of value/scale. On the left, the number of participants/providers increases from the top to the bottom (from intellectual to service

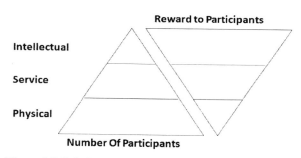

Figure 5-2 Relative impact of Value Layers on Participants

to physical), while on the right the reward, set by the market value decreases. So the intellectual has a small number of participants with high reward, while the physical has many participants with low reward, and the Service layer is in between

Examples of Layered Models

Some simple examples of economic systems where layering can be well understood are next illustrated with three examples.

Building a custom home

In building an on-spec (not pre-sold) custom home the three functions can be well understood. At the Intellectual Value level are the architect and the developer. The architect receives 5-10% of the home value for a deliverable that is essentially a few sheets of paper. However, contained in those sheets is the intellectual value of how the house will function, look, and accommodate the residents. The developer may in fact do no labor per se, but his intellectual value is organizing the financing, managing contractors, and scheduling all of the activities to get the work done. In some ways the developer may have a dual role at both the intellectual and the top of service layers. At the Service Value level are the contractors and sub-contractors. Each of these takes responsibility for a piece of the work and delivering within the framework defined by the developer and built to the designs of the architect. Finally, at the Physical Value layer we have the actual tradesmen that do the labor (the carpenters, plumbers, electricians, painters, etc).

In this system it is easy to see how the value accrual is tied to both the complexity/knowledge of the work as well as the number of providers. The developer and architect do well in financial compensation, while the laborers do much less "well".

Fashion/Clothing Industry Segment

Another example is the fashion or clothing industry. At the intellectual level are the designers that create the designs that the industry wants. For many of these designers, their role is to create new trends and designs. These are then conveyed to the market through two service segments, the manufacturers of clothing and the retail companies. While these organizations may not create the intellectual value, they manage the processes that translate small volume designs into high volume deliverables to consumers. Finally, the physical value in the eco-system are the employees in the retail stores and the employees in the manufacturing plants generating the actual clothing.

As in the home example, it is easy to see how the highest individual value accrues to the designers, while there is high value to the service organizations (and their management) that manufactures and distributes the clothing. Finally, the physical value of retail sales and clothing manufacturing are relatively low paid and less valued roles.

Health Care/Hospital

In the Healthcare industry, there are doctors, typically at the top as the

Intellectual providers. Below these are the nurses, X-Ray technicians and physical therapists that are in the Service category, while at the Physical layer are the janitors, the untrained orderlies, receptionists, etc.

In this example, value accrues to the doctors and to a lesser extent to the service layer, very little to the physical providers like the orderlies and the kitchen cooks.

Value Decay

In the world of nuclear physics there is the concept of the decay of an isotope. What this means is that a radioactive isotope actually changes to emit radiation, and in doing so often changes to a state that is no longer radioactive. In physics the concept of a half life is when 50% of the material has decayed to the new state. In the value ecosystem, decay is also always happening. What this means is that things that start as intellectual value and have a limited provider set often move down to being a service value and then may eventually decline to be a physical value. As the capability or value is able to be delivered by a wider and wider audience, it is decaying. While these trends are easiest to recognize in fast moving areas such as technology, they generally apply across the board. This is a concept that has long been understood and is often referred to as "commoditization".

A simple example from the last 15 years is the support and maintenance of personal computers (PCs) in the workplace. In the late 90s, most companies had on-staff employees who were tasked with managing and supporting the PCs used in the organization. This role was part of the Information Technology (IT) group and was generally considered to be a "good" job. In the early 00's, organizations began to contract outside companies who provided this work as a service, so that by 2005, PC support had transitioned from an in-house role to something that was purchased on a service contract (as with many things this was not universal, but was the predominant trend). The result was that individuals who had built their job around doing PC support found they were now employed by a services company that contracted to their previous employer, often with both reduced income and benefits as well as reduced career options. Between 2005 and 2011, the next change in PC support occurred: as the number of people capable of providing basic PC support increased as the complexity reduced, the services organizations began to outsource their use of people and increasingly the actual provider was no longer an employee, but rather an individual contractor. In fact, in many ways PC support has moved now to the same level as bank tellers. A friend of mine who works for a major bank in the US told me that in the typical bank branch in that company, there are only 2 or 3 full-time employees: the branch manager and the operations manager and maybe a high-wealth agent in key branches. All the other employees are part time and the predominant role of the operations manager is to hire and arrange the schedules of these tellers. While the change in banking has taken many more years, the same change as occurred in PC support occurred in bank branches where 20-30 years ago all of the employees were full-time. In the bank branch this was due to automation and simplicity in the role, reducing both training and knowledge.

Both of these examples are illustrations of how value decays and the delivery point of value moves down in the Value Model. In the hospital, the movement of certain functions from a physician to a physician's assistant is a similar path. These illustrate key factors that drive value decay. The mechanisms to deliver the value in these spaces become better understood, automated and easier to use. The result of this is that the training, practice, and knowledge required to deliver the value decrease significantly. Often this transition comes because the area matures, the rate of change decreases. Also when things mature the mechanisms can become standardized. This combination reduces the intellectual (or service) value in the area and drives value decay. In the consumer electronics business the value decay is continually demonstrated. When a new technology such as Blu-ray enters the market, the price of the players is high. As the technology becomes integrated into standard chips and optical devices, the number of manufacturers increases and prices rapidly drop.

While many more examples could be illustrated here, once this concept is understood, then the impact can be analyzed. If we assume that value of a specific knowledge or skill will decay, what does that mean to individuals, organizations, and even societies?

Managing Value Decay

If we know that value is going to decay, then we can identify how it is going to decay and even when (remember that half-life concept). The concept of managing decay can be applied to an eco-system, but more importantly it can be applied to individuals, organizations, or even social entities like countries. In all cases, managing the decay process has two key elements: identifying the decay drivers and

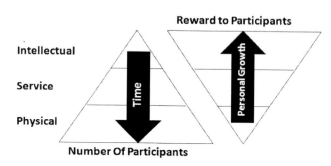

Figure 5-3 Personal Value Layer Transitions

understanding the timing and direction of the decay and deciding whether to jump up to the next level of value or to take advantage of the decay process in providing the value as it decays. If I am in the process of delivering an intellectual value and I can clearly see that that value is moving down to being a service value, I must choose to either transition to new intellectual values or to manage my value in the service arena. The key here is that continuing to only do the value that is decaying will assure a negative outcome.

Managing Individual Value

For the individual, there is nothing more important than managing your own personal value. If you had become a PC support person in the early 90s, it would have seemed as though you were on top of the world. It was a good job, you were seen as an expert and the pay and opportunities were commensurate. the number of PCs in business was exploding, so the demand for the skill was high. As the 90's progressed into the 00's, the change in this area caused by value decay began to happen The PC environment became more standardized, plug and play reduced complexity, training programs increased the pool of available talent, and organizations standardized their PC software. The result was what was described above, the job prospects for a PC support person were now much reduced. As an individual, the PC support person of the late 90's was faced with a decision.

If he/she stayed in that area they would follow the decay curve. The alternative is to either move up or change within the decay.

An obvious step would have been to actively move up from the PC support function to other IT functions. For example moving to application operation, in an area such as databases or data centers would have been a good choice. If that is not an option, realizing that moving into training and process management for PC support would have enabled a higher value role within the PC support arena (versus the now physical value of actual support). This would have retained a role in the services layer akin to the Operations Manager in the bank branch.

The key to understanding the value system as it applies to you is to always examine the skills and values that you bring to the market and identify the areas where those skills and knowledge areas are decaying (and the rate of decay). Then look at what the new areas are that are coming into your level. If you are in a service level today, look at what things are considered "expert", but are becoming standardized, trained, etc. Keep an active lookout for the new capabilities you can add to your service portfolio to keep your value up. If you are in an intellectual space today, identify how it will move to service and how to either optimize your value in that transition or begin to identify the next areas of intellectual value you can provide. If you are already in a physical value role, begin to think about how to move up to a service value role to accelerate your capabilities and career.

Managing Company Value

Companies often face the same value decay impact as individuals, though the mechanisms by which transitions happen may be less clear and many times the decay appears to be a growth opportunity as it is expanding the market. The key is to actively understand that operating a business at each level of the value pyramid is different and requires different thought processes and planning. Transitions from one level to another are very traumatic for an organization as they generally require both significant structural as well as employee changes.

Obviously the first point is to understand where your company is today. While many companies have all three elements (this is discussed in the next section), it is easiest to define the company by the highest level of value it provides. For a company that has a broad divisional structure this will vary by division. General Electric has groups that provide physical value (light bulbs) to intellectual value (nuclear design). As you examine your company in this way, you will see how it delivers that value to your customers. Then examine whether that value is changing. This change can come in many ways. For example, the capability you provide as an intellectual differentiation may become part of a "service" offering. This has often been a trend in technology where a new capability is purchased separately for a time and then acquired as part of a larger purchase. The field of technology is littered with companies whose capability became part of the Windows™ Operating System. If you find that key element of your market value is in areas that are in potential transition, then you have to plan as to how you will change. Either you must begin to structure your business for the new value level of delivering that capability, or you must actively identify new areas at your current value level to bring into your portfolio. Again, technology, being a relatively fast moving area, enables clear views of how this is accomplished. Companies like Cisco have consistently invested and acquired technologies and products that expand their value. What is interesting is that where those technologies are consistent with the company value (intellectual high value systems), they have been successful, acquisitions like the Flip video camera that was a physical value product failed.

Another critical decision is how vertically integrated the company is. Does the company directly participate at multiple levels of the value ecosystem or does it focus on one area? This is a complex decision, but not being clear about this opens the company up to significant challenges and danger. An excellent example of how a vertically integrated company can succumb to changes is Wang Computers. In the mid-80's, Wang had a very successful business building an integrated ecosystem that delivered word processing. They integrated together the software, hardware, support and customer engagement in this space and created a very successful company. However, the vertical structure was being challenged, not by a single competitor, but by an alternative ecosystem that had defined layers and significant strength. The new PC systems, with applications running on a standard OS on hardware from many manufacturers and printers from other manufacturers became a huge challenge. The Wang products and architecture, limited to word processing became marginalized, not because the Wang solution was not good, it was no longer viable as a vertically integrated company. If

Wang had chosen to focus on their intellectual value of the word processing software and forego the vertical revenue of hardware, they may have succeeded in creating a sustained company. Would Wang have created an integrated suite of productivity software that could have eclipsed Microsoft Office is unclear, but not changing guarantees failure.

A successful example of such a transition is Unisys, a company that started life as a products company and moved to services as it became obvious that it could not sustain an intellectual product position over time.

Figure 5-4 shows the differences between horizontal and vertically integrated companies. One of the big challenges is to understand where the value comes from in the organization. When I joined Nortel in 1995, we held a strategic planning session. One of the key "strengths" of the company that was identified by the senior management was the advanced manufacturing capability. Even in 1995, it was becoming clear to some that the actual manufacturing of electronic devices was moving away from being a key component of delivering the intellectual value in the device. A number of companies devoted to the service value or delivering low-cost, high-quality

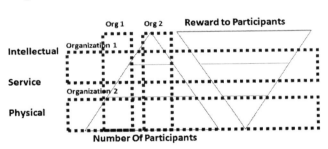

Figure 5-4 Managing Corporate Value

manufacturing on a turn-key basis had emerged. By 2005, Nortel had almost completely exited direct manufacturing. Not clearly understanding that manufacturing was not a clear advantage and that vertical integration was actually a disadvantage resulted in a slower exit from manufacturing operations and loss of competitiveness. Understanding the limitation in managing a vertically integrated company often requires challenging core assumptions of what a company's value is. If a core strength is something that many others are providing, then you must either focus to compete in that area alone or realize that delivering a higher value through those lower level elements is the right plan. However, in all cases, you must remember that value will continue to decay.

There is no cookbook recipe for managing these transitions, but ignoring these forces will hamper organizations in managing the change. It is critical to understand where your value derives from, how it is decaying and have a clear plan as to the transitions and changes. This will drive business and organizational restructuring to assure that the company is poised for success.

Managing Societal Value

This topic is included for completeness, however space does not allow a more detailed analysis: so I'll be brief. The same concepts of value add can be applied to societal structures within a society. If we examine the relationship between countries in the modern global economy, we can readily see how values have decayed over time and moved between countries. For the US and key Western European countries, lifestyle has been largely based on high societal intellectual value. Whether this is realized through technology, entertainment, or organizations, the society as a whole has defined its value level based on being "predominantly" intellectual versus other societies/countries. To sustain this level requires two key attributes: a recognition that this is in fact critical to the well-being of the society/country, and active investment to assure that new intellectual values continue to come into the system as current values decay. If a country/society allows itself to be displaced from the intellectual value level, the transition to the service value level and the impact on GDP and personal well-being will be profound and cause massive societal disruptions.

In the US our investments in creating the next level of intellectual value has been a critical component of assuring a societal value level. The space program, the defense investments of the 80's and 90's, the investments in healthcare and medicine have all delivered an ongoing stream of new intellectual value to build on. As a society we have to assure that we continue to make those investments. Similarly, Western European and other societies need to examine their values is a similar light. The transition of many services to Asia are an indication of the challenges in the global eco-system that both global telecommunications and English as a universal language have enabled.

Conclusion

Continually evaluating and re-defining value add in an economic system is critical to your personal value, your company or organizational value, and societal value. Hopefully this framework will enable you to analyze the value eco-systems you inhabit and define the best paths to assure success.

Chapter 6 Skin in the Game

This is actually a very simple concept: whenever possible, *it is incredibly valuable to have people personally linked in some financial way to the outcome that you want to happen.* The fact that I have a chip in the game causes me to move from being a spectator to a participant, as being a spectator now has a cost associated with it and no control.

In poker, the ante is a simple way of assuring that all of the players have a minimum interest in actually participating in each hand. Without the ante, a player would simply fold any but the best hands while waiting without consequence for a "killer" hand. In Texas Hold-Em, this is even further driven by having two of the players on a "blind" that requires an even larger commitment. Both of these are mechanisms to assure that the game does not include spectators who have no "skin in the game".

In business, there are some obvious "skin in the game" positions. A salesperson who has a significant part of their income based on actual customer sales has a lot of skin in making sure that happens. Stock Options are a great way of getting skin into the game.

There are some things that, while appearing on the surface to be skin in the game, in fact may have less impact than expected. The broad annual bonus based on total corporate performance may be great in a small company, but as the company gets larger, the linkage of personal contribution to actually generate this decreases. In Nortel in 2001, the company exploded through its financial targets. However, the growth and increase in revenue and profitability was predominately due to one division, the optical group. In the enterprise division, the performance, while exceeding the goal was nowhere near the level of success as the optical team. However the annual bonus plan was based on achieving the corporate goals and did not include any accelerators for individual divisions. In another example, some companies set bonus targets so high that there is little chance of achieving them, reducing their value even more.

Similarly, in a company that is kicking off a new business venture, while the new group may be having spectacular success in delivering the new technology, the greater company may be missing its goals. When I was recruiting Sales Engineers for new roles outside of sales, they would tell me proudly that they had achieved over 90% of their goal in each of the last 8-10 quarters. My response was that this was relatively uninteresting as a measure of success. This role typically would support a large group of 30-50 salespeople and 15-30 individual Systems Engineers in the region. When you average out all of the sales revenue for a group of that size, it is almost always going to be in the 85-95% of goal range. This is the way some compensating plans are structured.

The key message is that skin in the game needs to be tied to something that the individual can both impact and understand. It also needs to be tied to a meaningful impact measurement. Annual bonuses need to be tied to smaller team goals as well as individual goals, for example, including an accelerator on the corporate bonus number based on the team achieving a tightly defined set of goals. Another area is to define a goal range for the anticipated impact. If the average region varies from 80% of goal to 110% of goal, then use that as a basis for the bonus. If the region is at 80% of goal there is no bonus, at 95% there is a 100% bonus and at 110% there is a 200% bonus.

But skin in the game extends beyond employee compensation. One critical factor is to get customers to have skin in the game as well. For example, if you are hosting a seminar, there is often a suggestion that it should be free. However, if you can charge a small pre-registration fee, there now is an invested incentive for people to attend. It is much easier to skip something that has no cost versus something you have paid for in advance. The technique of having specific training and certifications attached to your products or services and creating value for customers who have that training is a great way to get skin in. The technicians in the customer will select your products as it validates their training and knowledge.

In one company I created a discount program that was designed to get the customers skin into the game. The program, called a Volume Procurement Agreement (VPA) worked like this.

A customer choose the level of volume that they forecast they would do with the company over a calendar year. This defined a specific discount amount, with higher volumes resulting in greater discounts. There was no monetary penalty for not achieving the goal, however, there was a quarterly volume goal. This goal, 16% for Q1, 33% for Q2 and 70% for Q3 were required achievement levels to maintain the discount for the NEXT quarter. So a customer might sign up for a $500K VPA with a discount of 20%. If the customer dropped below the achievement goals, they would drop to the $250K VPA at a 16% discount level. So, at the end of Q2, when the customer had only booked $155K of purchases against a $166.66K goal, the salesperson could come in and say, "If you buy the $12K of products you know you need but have not processed orders for, you will protect your discount for the rest of the year. Based on you buying at least $400K worth of product, that is a 5% discount on $245K, or a discount of $12,25K. So if you buy the $12K before the end of the quarter it is essentially free." By having the commitment from the customer to reach volume levels to retain something of value to them, they had skin in the game. In virtually all cases this technique got the end of the quarter order. It is much better than asking your customer to give back something, which almost never happens.

Another great example of this is an employee event. A company I was in had tradition of hosting an annual family picnic at a facility that included food, beer and wine, and events and games. For the first couple of years we just allowed everyone to get as many tickets as they "needed", without any commitment to attend. The result of this was obvious (in hindsight of course), employees got extra tickets for their friends they thought might come and many ended up not coming. They had no skin in the game. The result was that 30-40% of the tickets we bought were not used at the event. As the tickets were subsidized, this resulted in lost spending by the company. As the company that did the event required us to actually buy the tickets in advance, we tried a system to have the employees pick up the tickets at the event so we could estimate the shrinkage. This proved to be very difficult. In the third year we instituted a new system. The company continued to pay for the picnic ticket, but we required every employee to buy a raffle ticket for each attendee. The raffle tickets cost about $5 (versus the $25 for the picnic) and all of the proceeds went to buying prizes to be raffled during the event. The result of this was that the attendance drop-out rate went to less than 5% and the employees were happy as they got to win something. The employees had skin in the game. One final interesting observation was that instead of giving one raffle ticket for the $5, every attendee was given 10 raffle tickets. While those of us that understand statistics realize that the chance of winning is no greater if everyone has 10 tickets versus if everyone has one ticket, the perception generally was that the was a much greater chance to win with 10 tickets...so the skin in the game perception was actually doubled in value, merely through an exercise of distributing more tickets.

Finally, when there is no skin in the game, it is easy to have everything go wrong. Early in my career I was a Systems Engineer for one of the best salespersons I have ever known. He meticulously built up an invitee list for a local event in Silicon Valley, inviting over 75 people from the likes of HP and Stanford to see early data networking products. The event was held in a local hotel and we had some snacks and I had set up a demo system. As the time for the event to start came and went, not a single attendee came. I know this was not due to lack of effort or real contact, it was because no one had skin in the game and occasionally, everybody will do something else.

Always analyze the motivations, outcomes, and rewards of the people involved in any activity and understand clearly who has skin in the game and how does their skin get rewarded. If you concede that the skin is not right, make sure you get it right. If you get this right, your chances of success are much higher.

Chapter 7 Decisions, Decisions, Decisions

In the mid-2000s, at the annual Nortel Executive Leadership Team retreat, the President extolled his philosophy of good decision making. He said that he believed that every decision required two people to make it and the tension between these two decision makers is what caused good decisions. The audience was aghast, and many of us realized that this concept would have serious negative ramifications. That individual was later indicted by the US Dept of Justice for financial fraud, so the question is how the tension led to that set of bad decisions.

Having a senior leader espouse such a concept has caused me to watch decision making and how it impacts organizations. That view and being a decision maker for almost 40 years, I believe, has given me a clear view of decisions and how they are optimized. Here are some key thoughts about decision making.

Own the Decision

One person must own the decision. Group decisions are prone to being compromised (that camel as a horse thing). How that individual is identified can be either by delegation from above in the organization or by agreement in the group, but in the end one person must own the decision.

Once the decision maker is in place, identifying the questions that must be answered and the data that must be gathered to answer the questions, becomes the process of the decision making. As there are entire books on the process of decision making, the focus here is on the participation of the stakeholders in that process. In any decision process there are two types of stakeholders to the decision maker: the stakeholders who are limited to providing input to the process and those who are (or feel they are) entitled to veto the decision. While both groups may be impacted by the decision, the former sees their role as merely providing input, while the latter believes they have the right to reject the decision made. If we have a single decision maker, then the veto class of individual feels they can essentially disagree with the decision based on their personal interpretation of the answers and the data. Managing this group after the decision is made is crucial.

Clear Decision Criteria and Data-Based Decisions

The key to decision making is to have a clear understanding of when the decision is required and when there is enough gathering and analyzing data to make a clear decision. It is important as it is not just for the decision maker, but for the stakeholders to agree in advance in what the level of data is going to be. If this is not clear, data "creep" can replace making a decision. This is either due to uncertainty, or the desire to not make the decision (and be held accountable). I have seen senior executives use a request for more data as a way of not making a decision that would require other actions they did not want to take. The result is that the executive is able to say they "could not" make a decision, when in fact they "did not" want to make a decision. In the 80/20 Principle, Richard Koch suggests that you can get 80% of the data from the first 20% of analysis. In fact, this has been proven to be the key to success, understanding when you have enough data. Make your decision too soon, and you will make bad decisions: wait too long and you have missed the window for decision impact. The result is that the decision window needs to be based on two factors: how long until the decision will lose value, and how long to get to that 80%.

After the Decision is Made

For most organizations, this is the single biggest issue: we are often really good at making decisions, but really bad at living with the outcomes. This generally comes in two forms: 1. people questioning the decision and attempting to get it changed without any change in underlying criteria or data, or 2. sticking with a decision even when it is clear that the criteria or data have significantly changed.

In the first case, some of the stakeholders do not agree with the outcome of the decision, even thought the data and analysis clearly defined the decision outcome. Rather than accepting the decision and moving forward, they choose to question the decision without new data or bring up new criteria or data in an attempt to get the decision changed. Often this can be recognized by someone starting a discussion with "I know we decided, but the team did not consider....." As a manager, this level of activity cannot be accepted unless there is a major change as discussed later. It is critical that everyone understand that minor factors that were not considered are not sufficient to re-evaluate every decision. If it was decided during the decision process that that factor was not critical, then let it lay. This becomes a critical part of the decision process: acceptance. The point is to have all of the stakeholders have ample opportunity to bring up the decision criteria they think are important and then the data that enables a clear decision to be made. If that has been done, there should not be any surprises after the decision is made. A good example of this occurred in the early 2000s in Nortel. There were three separate groups pursuing a similar path to a new product. A team was formed to decide which path or combination of paths was the right answer. After defining the criteria for the decision and the data, a decision was made. However, one of the groups felt that the decision, which was not to use their technology as the primary future vehicle, was the wrong decision. That group repeatedly brought up a succession of less and less relevant points to try to defray the decision. Senior management listened to this discussion but was not clear that the decision had been made. The result was that this team did not focus on the actions resulting from the decision, but continued in an orthogonal direction, resulting in a 6 month slip in the final product and tens of millions in lost sales. Senior management must make it clear that decisions made are not to be questioned or revisited. If a stakeholder tries to bring up a new criteria, they need to be censured for not bringing it up earlier...unless.....

On the other hand, relevant new criteria or new data emerging since the decision was made clearly impacts the decision process. For example, a decision made on an assumption that there will be a specific event at a point in the future may need to be revisited if that event does not occur or is seriously delayed. Similarly, if new events occur that were not anticipated in the decision process, then he decisions may need to be revisited taking those events or data into account. A good example of this happened in Avaya in 2009-2011. In 2009, as part of the Avaya strategy, Avaya decided to build a new desktop device that could replace the telephone. It was decided that the device would be a small tablet sized (10.5" screen) device and would use the Android operating system with a new user interface. This device was seen as defining Avaya going forward. In the original planning, end user pricing of much less than $1,000 was anticipated. At the time the development started, there were few tablets in the market (the iPad was not announced until the middle of 2010), and the product seemed unique. In addition to the tablet, the product would include video so it

could be used as a desktop video system. As the product neared
completion in mid-2010, the market had changed significantly: Apple had
introduced the iPad, and there were a number of Android tablets coming
out. The price point for a basic tablet of the type being built was around
$400-500, but the tablets in the market did not include video. In fact, at
that point it became clear that most, if not all, of the decision data was now
invalid (competition, price point, etc.). In addition, it was obvious with the
introduction of the iPhone4 in August 2010 that Apple would include video
in their products soon. This was followed by general announcements of
video in many tablets. So by the time the Avaya product was introduced in
the fall of 2010, it was too large (5 times the thickness of the iPad, too
expensive - list price of $2,0000 versus $500, and too limited - no app store
or other programs). Rather than having a clear examination of the
decisions, Avaya proceeded to introduce the product, and build thousands
of units. The result was a significant failure. By the middle of 2011, Avaya
was focused on moving the user experience to the iPad and was finally able
to introduce that to the market in early 2012. If the decision to build a
hardware device had been revisited in the middle of 2010, it would have
been obvious that the development path at that point would fail. The
company could have positioned the hardware platform as a demonstration
(and provided it to customers as was done, but without the expectation of a
completed product). This would have allowed the company to focus on the
iPad and Android platforms at least 6-9 months earlier and with
significantly increased resources. The lack of examining the decision cost
many millions of dollars and market position.

What is clear is that when a decision is made, part of the decision process is
defining when that decision would be validated. For decisions that have
investment over an extended period, there should be a clear intermediate
check-point where the criteria and data can be examined to see if the
decision is still on the right path. This also becomes a way of defraying the
questioners- "We will look at that in 6 months, in the interim we are
proceeding". As part of this process, clearly defining the criteria and data
that could change will enable easy future evaluations. If the decision was
based on assumptions, clearly describing those assumptions in the decision
process enables them to be reviewed in the future. Doing this will reduce
the probability of a bad decision continuing to a bad outcome. Of course,
even the best decisions can become failures with bad execution. A critical

part of any decision is assuring that it can be executed.

Philip Edholm

Chapter 8 Understanding Self Interest

For many of you, this chapter may be the least fulfilling. I did not set out here to cover motivation ala Maslow, nor to have an in-depth discussion of psychology, but rather to make the point that most employees operate from their own self-interest and understanding this will enable you to more effectively manage.. and understand yourself. While this may appear to be obvious, the impact when building an organization can be significant.

Three Types of Employees

When I was in University (though it was called General Motors institute when I was there, it is now Kettering University, so I will use that designation), I had a number of multi-class series such as heat transfer, thermodynamics and fluid engineering. In many of the multi-class series, in the first class the professor would introduce a theme of the series. In the first class of a management series of three or four, the professor said something like this:

> *"There are three kinds of people in the workplace:*
>
> *"People who need to work to provide them income to do other things in their lives. This is the vast majority of people, representing almost 90% to 95% of the workers,*
>
> *"People who are upwardly mobile and are in pursuit of money and power and the luxury/lifestyle that comes with it. This is around 5% to 10% of the workforce.*
>
> *" And finally, there are people who work because they love what they are doing and are there for the work itself. This last group is around 1% to 2% of the workforce, but is the most important as you can always find the other 98%"*

As I left that class, I was unconvinced. How could it be that only 1% or 2% of the workforce was truly motivated by what they were doing? As a child of the 60s and 70s and still a bit of a hippy in my heart, I felt this was not true.

After almost 40 years of being in the workplace, I can clearly say that, while the actual percentage may be slightly higher for the last category, I really do believe this view is correct. A few personal glimpses into this.

The Educated Booth Cleaner

While I was at University, I was in a co-op program, so I worked about half the time in industry. While this is an excellent way to learn and get exposure to jobs and work skills, it also exposes you early in life to a broad range of individuals and thoughts. In one of my work terms, I was assigned to the maintenance department and drew the role of supervising the second shift booth cleaners. The booth cleaners were the workers that cleaned the paint build-up in the spray paint booths in the auto assembly plant. As their job was not tied to the assembly line and the repetition thereof, the job was highly desirable.

Bob (not his real name), one of the booth cleaners that was working for me was about 35 years old (I was probably 20 or 21 at the time). On the weekends we would come into the plant that was shut down to clean the booths when the line was not running. As it was only myself and a small team (about 20), and the cafeteria was closed, I typically would eat lunch (called that, even though it was at 8PM on second shift) with the hourly team. During these lunches I talked with Bob and found him to be very articulate and intelligent. As we talked, I found out that he had a Masters Degree in Psychology from the University of California at Berkeley. When I asked him why he was working in a blue collar job at General Motors, he replied that is fit his lifestyle. He then went on to say that he loved second shift because it left him clear in the day for other activities. And then he said something that has stayed with me my entire life: "Do you know the difference between you and me?" he asked, "Your job is to get me to produce as much output as possible, while my job is to sleep as much at work as I can so I can do other things while I am off....and I average 4 hours a night."

Sleeping at work in an auto plant was almost an epidemic. We continually found beds that employees had built in the material racks, so this claim was not that farfetched. What it demonstrated to me was that a clearly intelligent and well-educated person had made a clear and thoughtful decision that work was totally secondary to the other things in their life.

This was a clear example of the first category, he worked to do other things in his life.

Toyota and GM

In the late 70s, with the competitive threat of Japan and recent oil embargos fresh in everyone's mind, one of the television networks did a documentary comparison of GM and Toyota. As I remember (I have not been able to locate an archive), it contrasted GM and their operation in Kansas City, MO with the Toyoda City (that is right, the parent name is Toyoda) in Japan. They spent time on the differences, the dormitories and apartments for the employees in Toyoda City versus the typical US factory. However, as they examined the factories, one key point came forward: absenteeism in the US factory was between 10 and 100 times higher than the Japanese rate. In fact, analysis of that time put US auto plant absenteeism as high as 18%. (O'Reilly, 1989)This meant that of six workers, on any given day one did not come to work. Beyond the burden of carrying 10-15% additional workers on the payroll, high absenteeism has a huge impact on quality in an auto plant. If the person trained to do a job is not there, people must move around to cover that specific job. In a typical group of 30 employees, there may only be one or two spare employees. If three people are out, one or two will be sent from a central pool. However, these employees will have had no training on the jobs they are going to have to do. This analysis found the majority of the in-factory defect quality difference between GM and Toyota was due to absenteeism (this does not include design-in quality). In order to better understand this, the TV team secured an interview with an employee who was classified as a habitual absentee. He typically missed one day each week, and due to the protection of the union, was not terminated for missing work. The sincere interviewer, after first detailing why absenteeism was so bad and making GM non-competitive, asked why the employee missed one day a week. After a few seconds of thought, the answer was "Well, I tried living on three days' pay and I just can't do it." His work was defined not by responsibility or maximizing income, but rather on the minimal amount of work that allowed him to do other things in his life. This second confirmation convinced me that there was validity to the concept, crushing my idealistic views of human behavior forever.

Life on the Delta

The concept of there being a large group of people who fundamentally worked only because they had to support their lifestyle seemed to be obvious. However, in my daily life, working in Silicon Valley in start-ups where we thought we were changing the world, the evidence of this large group seemed to be limited. In the mid 1990s, I bought a vacation home on an island in the California delta. This island, with 75 lots primarily with house trailers was a great escape from the pressures of the work world. Reachable only by boat, it was isolated. The thousand miles of inland waterways in the center of California offered the best water skiing around and a great family opportunity to explore and play. After buying a lot with a double-wide trailer, we became familiar with our neighbors.

On one side we had a married couple. He was a service person for a welding equipment company and his wife worked at Costco. On the other side was an auto mechanic. As we met the people around us, it became clear that this was not the same group as in our hometown and at work. As we began to sit at night around a fire drinking beer, I began to understand their view of work. Work was not something they saw as critical to their lives, but something they did so they could spend their weekends at the delta. No one talked about their work in a societal construct, about creating technology or changing the world. Work was something they did from Monday to Friday so that they could ignore it on the weekends.

The Big Question

All of this leads up to the big question: if you were to walk up to 10 people totally at random on the street and ask them this question:

"if I offered to pay you your current salary and benefits for the rest of your life, including the raises and increases you would expect to get, and would not require you to go to your job any more, but with the one stipulation that you cannot do any meaningful work for the rest of your life, would you accept?"

In other words, I will pay you exactly what you would make for working if you guarantee not to do any work.... My best guess is that at least 7 and probably 8 or even 9 of the people you ask will say yes to this proposition. This is the challenge we face, not just self-interest, but self interest where work is only a means to an end and therefore is treated as an inconvenience.

Philip Edholm

Short Answers

I wanted to close this section with a set of great recommendations about how to manage this, but I do not think it is that easy. Obviously when you hire, looking for that 1% - 2% that are focused on the role, the technology, the vision and not just on money is critical. Identifying the upwardly mobile 5% - 10% is critical and assuring that their skin in the game is commensurate with the output you require. But we still have to have that 90% - 95% that sees what they do as nothing more than a prerequisite for the rest of their lives. I believe the key is to show them a clear tie between your company/organizations success and their ability to continue with their lives. It needs to be as clear as:

Absenteeism generates quality issues

If we have quality issues we lose sales

Lost sales means reducing production

Reducing production means losing jobs

Absenteeism will eventually cost you your job.

As this message sinks in, peer pressure and group dynamics will emphasize it to all of the employees in the organization. Similarly, a lack of interest and enthusiasm will spread.

The Fremont CA GM Assembly Plant, that GM shut down in 1982, re-opened in 1984 as a joint venture with Toyota. Even though 75% of the employees were the same, there came a change in culture and the clear realization that their actions could lose jobs and impact their lifestyle. The result was a drop in absenteeism from as high as 18% in the GM days to under 2% as part of Toyota, even though it was still a union shop (this facility was actually closed in 2010 and is now the home of Tesla). The actual closing of the GM plant made it clear that just showing up occasionally is not enough, you have to produce for that job. I always wondered if that booth cleaner Bob still worked there.

In the end, you have to make this a case of self interest for your employees. Define a clear path of how each employee impacts the company and how that enables the company to provide a salary and benefits to the employee. When I talk with salespeople, they often tell me that I am more accommodating and more sympathetic than other executives. I respond very simply, "Unless **you** make a sale, we don't sell any products. If we don't sell products, the company can't pay my salary. If I don't get a salary, my kids don't get food on their plate. It is really important to me that my kids eat, so me helping you to sell something is very important to me." And it really is important to clearly understand and communicate a similar message.

Chapter 9 Management by Walking Around

At some point I heard about this as a business concept, but it was after I had "found" the concept on my own. While it appears to have come from HP and was popularized by Tom Peters and Robert H. Waterman in their 1982 book: "In Search of Excellence: lessons from America's best-run companies", (Waterman, 1982) the concept is one that I believe is critical. In fact, as we will discuss, it can be dramatically extended to "Management By Virtually Walking Around". I actually started walking around when I was a foreman working for GM. I found that getting out of the office and walking around and talking to the employees was great way to get a sense of how things were going. I remember once when we had a problem with a conveyor and I had a couple of the employees helping me push the car bodies across an unpowered gap. My manager, the General Foreman asked how I got them to do that. He asked because he had worked with them for years and assumed they would never do something like that, helping out on their break. I told him that I just asked. Later I asked a couple of them why they did it and they said it was simple, I was the first foreman in years that actually seemed to care about them as people. The longer term foremen saw this as a job of managing numbers and did not try to connect with their employees. While this was great for the company and the employees did not mind, in the end I got a union grievance for the audacity of asking workers to pitch in on their break.

The key point is to change the relationship from one of reporting to interacting. rather than having all interaction with a manager be through a formal process such as status reports or formal meetings, the interaction occurs randomly and out of the manager's office or the formal structure of the meeting room. In fact it is sometimes referred to as Management by Wandering Around.

By changing the paradigm, two things happen. The conversations become significantly more direct and uncensored. An impromptu conversation allows discussions that are not framed in a context of meeting a plan or report. For example, a simple question like "What is giving you a headache today?" may open the door to a critical issue that is limiting success. Or a question like "What was the best thing that happened last week?" can find a success or capability.

Another outcome is a perception by employees that the manager and management team is both interested in what that individual is doing and what the team is doing. In structured status reports and briefings, the contributions of individual teams often do not come through, nor is it clear the manager appreciates the level of effort and contribution, even if the manager does understand. This is because the timing and interaction in formal meetings makes it difficult to clearly identify and comment on success and effort.

MBVWA

The big change that is see in business today is that the distributed nature of teams has dramatically limited the Management By Walking Around (MBWA capability). Unless the entire team is physically co-located, there is no way to walk around. However, in addition to the airplane there are clear tools to forge a similar management style without physically flying to the space. The point is to do the same thing in a virtual way, hence Management by *Virtually* Walking Around or MBVWA.

While there are virtual reality applications like Second Life and web.alive that use avatars and virtual environments to create a virtual world, these are often perceived as cumbersome, and both the employee and manager have to be in the virtual environment at the same time. Therefore, after the initial meetings, either in person or by video, the simple phone call can often suffice. Driving time is ideal for these calls, as they are less about details and more about interaction. The first few times it will be awkward, but with repetition comes familiarity and expectation.

For my direct employees that are physically located away from me, my goal is to have a conversation at least once a week on an unscheduled basis. The first time I call, I make it clear that it is not related to a specific issue or activity, but is just a quick check-in. I generally do this in addition to a weekly or semi-weekly one-on-one call that is more formal. For the one-on-one calls, I have defined formal review of activities and deliverables. Those calls have structure and do not lend themselves to discovery. A MBVWA call would go something like this:

Phil: "Hi John, it's Phil"

John: "Hi"

Phil "How is it going?"

John: "Going well."

Phil: "Is the family well (if you are aware of some specific activity, this is where to put it)?"

John: "Well, my wife and son have colds. (you now have some data that you may need to consider about a deliverable john has on his plate and whether it can be done.

Phil: "Wow, sounds bad, I guess you are pretty tied down, do you need some help?"

John: "No, I think I can handle it." (This has now become a perception of concern, and translated in a re-commitment to getting the project done)

John: "Though it would really help if Steve could get the documentation done, so I would spend less time there." (And a potential road-block has been uncovered.)

...and so on.....

This may be a short call, less than 10 minutes, often less than 5. But it establishes that dialog is accepted and even expected.

Informal for Them, Formal for You

You should actively seek out all of your direct reports. While it is up to you to decide, in most environments, this needs to be weekly. For reports to those reporting to you, a monthly or at a minimum quarterly calls seems most appropriate. If you have 10 direct reports and direct managers with an average of 7 employees per manager, then you have 10 direct reports and 70 second tier reports. If your manager MBVWA interaction takes 5 minutes each per week, then you have a total of 100 minutes for mangers. If the second tier takes an average of 5 minutes every 4 weeks (assuming that employee have their weekly meeting with their direct manager), then you are committing to about 70 minutes per week.

The result is that this activity will take about 2 hours of your week or about 5% of your time (assuming you work a 40 hour week). While this may seem like a lot, it is a relatively small investment of time for the value you will accrue. As you begin to use this technique you will get better at managing the interaction and you will see change in how you and your employees relate. I find the cell phone driving to and from work an ideal way to conduct these calls. I would use the morning commute for European/Middle East and Eastern US and the evening for the west coast and Asia. As these conversations were informal, being in the car does not degrade them. It also becomes a way of reinforcing and preparing for annual reviews. If the review is a surprise, you did not do your job in keeping in touch with your employees.

Philip Edholm

Chapter 10 Good News and Winning

In the 80s I was part of Sytek, one of the early data networking start-ups. Over time I became part of the executive team of the company and the president was George Klaus. George introduced me to a concept of good news, which I have used in every role since.

The concept of good news is to actively seek out the good news in the organization on a regular basis. The reasons for this are simple, in most organizations, staff meetings and status meetings are focused on issues and problems. These are the times when we discuss what is not going well, what needs to be resolved and conflicts. Rarely, other than a report saying that objectives are being met, do these sessions focus on our successes.

The point of actively seeking out the good news is that is always there. I have used this technique in every role I have had since, in multiple ways. In my staff meetings or team meetings, I make it a mandatory for each attendee to come to the meeting with a piece of good news. While it is encouraged that these be business related, I am not pedantic and state clearly that personal good news is acceptable (if you have been on vacation it is generally the norm). At the start of each meeting, I do a roll call of the attendees and they relate their good news item. When someone new joins the meeting or team, they hear the good news, and are asked to come to the next meeting with their own good news.

Frankly, it is amazing how much good news comes forward in this process. Whether your meetings are weekly or less frequent, there are always a few really great wins or successes that come forward. When I have managed larger organizations with managers who had their own meetings, I encourage them to do the same with their teams and then, as a team, identify the 2 or 3 pieces of good news the team wants to bring forward to the next level. The result is that we now have a sharing of good news and wins across the organization. In some organizations we would actively disseminate a couple of good news items each week to let the entire organization know how we were winning.

With social media and the capability to communicate out to the organization, this now can lead to a culture of looking for success and identifying with the win. In a company, cascading good news up to the executive team on a weekly basis can then lead to selecting some number (3 always seemed about right) of key pieces of good news for every week and then emphasizing those down to the organization.

Whether the good news is a sales win, a product release, or even reducing the cost of a purchase of something, it has great positive impact. This impact is both for the general employee population and also for the team or individual that had the good news. For the general employees, in most companies, the continual drone of issues and challenges today completely masks the success and movement of the company. Having a regular reminder that the company is winning and moving forward is critical. For the employee or team that identified the good news, having it be discussed and identified is validation of their efforts.

This brings forth one of the key elements of good news, everybody had wins! Good news cannot be limited to sales wins, it has to extend across the organization and over time all parts of the organization should have their good news recognized. But in order to recognize good news, you have to able to know when you had a win.

Knowing When You Had a Win

In many organizations, identifying when you have had a win is a challenge and often ignored. In sales it is easy, when you get an order, it is a win. In other groups such as a supply chain, or a support group, identifying a win is much harder. You have to understand what is a win for you and your team. Wins need to occur at reasonably regular intervals. They do not need to be at specific times, but the number of events over a time period should be understood. For example, at a minimum for a team there should be a win 3-12 times per year. Think about events and outcomes that your team does and how you both identify them and measure them. Write down the things that happen that really change the game. If you are a support organization, how often do you solve a critical issue on the first interaction? If this is an outcome that delights the customer, then maybe that is a win. If you are an HR group, a month without a voluntary termination may be a win, or retaining a critical employee who had decided to leave. The goal is to understand the wins when they happen, not going looking for wins on a timetable.

In organizations that have longer term programs like engineering, identifying wins along the way is also important. While it is great to have the celebration of the release of a product, if that takes 18 months, it is too long between wins. A team with a long range program like this needs to identify types of intermediate wins: for example, early release of a feature, reduction in size of a developed piece of software, etc. Often, in a team of this type, you cannot define a win in advance, but you need to have a set of criteria in your mind to recognize a win when it happens.

Celebrate Your Wins

As an individual and as a team leader, you have to celebrate your wins. As an individual, stopping to understand your own wins are important. It will re-energize you and break the tedium of the challenges. When I was writing this book, each chapter completed was a win, and I often celebrated each one with a glass of wine that day. As a team leader, celebrating these are incredibly important for morale and success. However, it is also important not to celebrate a false win. Before celebrating a win or a piece of good news, stop for a moment and ask, "Will everyone on my team see this as a real win?"

As a manger of a team, I had an event that I generally identified as a win. It was well defined and important to the company. In one of my MBVWA discussions with one of my employees that often met that win criteria, he commented that another employee who was also a regular identified "winner" was being added to the winning event regularly with minimal activity. What I realized was that this view of the win was having two impacts: it was reducing the value of the win and causing people to feel as if there was less validation of other events. I changed my win criteria to ones where it was more tightly defined to an individual contribution, maintaining the win, but reducing the number of participants in the win. I also began to focus on slightly different ways of identifying wins adjacent to this area.

Plaques Last, Money Doesn't

If you have identified a win and communicated it up and out as a good news, how do you go to the next level of recognition? I have seen two types of programs, a cash or financial reward and some form of recognition object (a plaque or trophy). While most employees appreciate a financial reward, I believe the recognition value and the motivation for the next win are less than if it is accompanied by some form of physical reminder. Often in a company the reward for a small win for a typical employee is $200 or up to $500. This is not an annual bonus, nor is it of great significance, but it can be done so it is of great motivational value.

In rewards, it has to be clear that the reward is for a win. Putting reward money into a regular paycheck will have little value as often this check will go into a bank account as a direct deposit and will not even be seen. Using a reward card guarantees that the reward will be used in a specific event. This is important for the employee's family. If you give an employee a $200 gift card from one of the major credit card companies, it will likely be used to buy a dinner for the family or a specific purchase. That identified use with the family makes the family aware of the reward. I generally send the financial part of the reward to the employee's home to make sure that their family knows that they had a win as well and can be proud of the employee as a family.

At work, the financial impact is gone instantly. So accompanying every reward should be some physical reminder of success. This can be a plaque, a trophy, a pin or something else that is recognized. This is often a greater motivator than the money, especially to the key employees in that 1% that are motivated by the work and, interestingly enough, to the larger group that work to support their non-work lives (See the chapter "Understanding Self Interest").

In my years at Nortel I saw this repeated over and over. Nortel was particularly good at identifying wins and giving out awards, especially physical. In most employees' offices, there was an area set aside with a few award plaques or trophies. It was clear that both the identification and celebration of wins was important and valued. Nortel had very high employee loyalty and this was contributor.

In my time in Avaya we instituted a program to identify a small group of technical contributors that would be recognized as Distinguished Engineers. While this was not a recognition for a single win, it was a recognition for sustained excellence and repeated success. The recognition came with a financial reward, but also included recognition on the employee's business card, a trophy and on their office name plaque. In discussion with the employees that received the honor, while the money was nice, the fact that they had this identification associated with their business card and their name plaque was generally perceived as the greatest honor.

Similarly, the reward of the employee of the month having a special parking place or other reward as recognition for a win can have great value. If you go to the old Bell Labs or IBM research facilities, there are walls of all of the Fellows these organizations have had. The motivation to be a Fellow extends far beyond the financial to the peer recognition that it demonstrates. Physically keeping this reminder tells future aspirants that it is more than a passing fad.

Balancing the Positive to the Negative

The real message of this chapter is balance. As a manger and a leader, it is up to you to balance your interactions with your team and the rest of the organization. While it is great to be a "decisive, action-oriented leader who takes charge and solves problems" (sounds like a line out of a thousand resumes), if you allow your interactions to be limited to negative and reactive, over time, you will lose your capability to lead. You have to balance the leadership of solving the problems with the leadership of recognizing the good and the wins. Having a clear plan of how you and your team and organization will do this is imperative to maintaining a winning culture.

Chapter 11 The Four Types of Management

There are many reasons that managers and their employees and teams fail. It can be lack of capability, knowledge, clear direction, or chemistry. However, one key issue I have seen is that many managers are not clear about the level of interaction and guidance that each of their employees requires for success. This leads to either an employee wandering aimlessly or the manger being perceived as a micro-managing tyrant. In either case, the organization is negatively impacted.

The four types of management came from the experience of starting at the bottom of the management ladder. I joined General Motors as a co-op intern when I was 18 years old. After 5 weeks of office work I was called into a Friday afternoon and told that I should report on Monday to the night shift where I was to be the foreman of the repair yard drivers.

Employee Type	Interaction Frequency	Capability to Self-direct
Entrepreneur	• As required • Decisions • Major reviews	• Defines goals • Develops total plan • Analyzes changes
Direction	• Monthly status • Dialog on plans	• Develops plan to get to goals • Organizes for goal
Management	• Weekly status • Implementation status	• Implements plans • Manages resources • Identifies issues
Supervision	• Daily or more • Task definition	• Task only • Requires immediate instruction

Figure 11-1 Four Types of Management

The next Monday night I came in to find that I now had 20 people working for me and my job was to get them to drive cars in the back repair lot of the auto plant to the appropriate repair station. This was chaos defined. The employees came out of a pool of workers that were used as loaners to cover absenteeism and were different every night and every night needed to be told exactly what to do.

Over the next four years, my work assignments were often as a foreman, either in a production group, or later as a maintenance foreman. In all cases, the workers needed to be organized at the start of the shift, replacements and coverage for absentees needed to be assigned and often instructions or changes needed to be given. The employees even needed to have assigned break times and relief.

As my career advanced into the high-tech market, the employees that I had reporting to me changed and I realized that they required less time and a different focus from me. Out of this came what I see as the delineation of the four types of management: supervision, management, direction, and entrepreneurship.

The challenge for a manager is two-fold: first to understand the level of management that an individual requires and second to determine the level of management that you are capable, comfortable and tolerant of providing. Repeatedly through my career I have seen a mismatch in management type becoming a significant barrier to the success of an employee, and by extension their manager.

Supervision

When I began as a line foreman at General Motors in the Fremont California Assembly Plant, the role was very much that of supervisor. A typical group had about 30 line workers, 2 to 4 so-called "utility men or relief men" that knew multiple jobs and provided relief so the regular employees could go on their scheduled breaks. In addition to the breaks, generally the relief men also could cover for an absentee employee. Finally, there was a "trainer" who was generally a very seasoned senior hourly worker who knew all of the jobs in the group and trained new employees and helped coverage during the shift.

Generally, the General Motors structure in an assembly plant at that time (in the late 70s), was based on a military structure. The hourly workers were the same as the non-commissioned officers and fell into three categories: the line workers were the privates, the relief men the corporals, and the trainer the staff sergeant. The foreman was the first level of salaried or "commissioned officers". Just as first lieutenant in the military, the foreman's role was making sure everyone was in their place doing their job. Above the foreman was the General Foreman, the Department Manager, the Production Manager, and the Plant Manager (Major, Captain,

Colonel, and General). The entire plant was analogous to an army division, with a General and requisite support and combat troops. The assembly workers were the combat troops and the other groups (maintenance, engineering, tooling, HR, IT, etc.) were logistics support.

So what is supervision? It is where the employee requires someone to tell them what to do on a regular basis. Generally supervision is a task-based activity. It is about telling an individual which task to do, generally for reasonably short periods of time. For example, in the morning, when an employee is absent, the supervisor moves employees around to cover all the tasks.

One key factor of supervision is outcomes, or the lack thereof. It is never acceptable in a supervision relationship to tell someone what the outcome is going to be and assume they can define the path. A supervisor needs to assure that the steps to the outcome are well aligned. The supervisor is assigning work or tasks. In addition, these steps/tasks often need to be broken down with tracking and follow-up at intermediate points to assure success. This can be as simple as assuring that someone returned from their break, or checking to see that the task defined is being completed in a timely manner and correctly.

Generally supervision requires daily, if not hourly interactions. In the assembly line group, while the foreman would have some level of paperwork and office work to do (the office was generally close to the line group), the majority of time was spent walking around the group, dealing with issues of parts availability, assembly issues, or problems from further up the line.

Management

The transition from supervision to management is a significant one, both for the manager and the managed employee. In the management relationship, the employee is no longer given a task or element, but rather given a set of tasks that will lead to an outcome. The responsibility for managing those task steps is now the responsibility of the managed employee. One big change is that the managed employee is now responsible for identifying issues and raising them to the manager versus the manager identifying issues by continually checking each step.

The transition from supervision to management can be recognized by the communication of the outcome. In the management relationship, the manager will generally start by defining the outcome and then what the steps are that need to be accomplished to reach the outcome. In most cases, there will be a discussion between the managed employee and the manager about these steps. A discussion of timing and completion times along with a mutual discussion of checkpoints and goals will occur.

The result of this is that the management relationship makes the managed employee responsible for the completion of multiple steps: this was actually done by the supervisor in the supervisor relationship. The managed employee is now acting in a supervisor type role. In the management relationship, the development of the plan is still the responsibility of the manager, while its execution, tracking and operation is the responsibility of the managed employee.

Direction

The next level of employee and manger relationship is direction. In Direction, the manger does not need to define the steps to accomplish the goal, but rather defines the goal or outcome and the directed employee is responsible for creating the plan to get there. Obviously, the manager may be consulted about his or her view on the steps and there may be a review cycle of the plan and how it will create the outcome, but the key change is that the directed employee must be capable of mapping out a series of independent activities that together can accomplish the goal or desirable outcome. The directed employee is capable of creating the plan to get to the outcome, without significant intervention.

A clear change between managed and directed employees is the lack of clear process steps or stages being communicated by the manager in the kick-off of a project. One good example is that a managed employee might be given a Gant or Pert chart of the program they are expected to manage, while the directed employee would be expected to create this and review it with his or her manager.

Another change is that the directed employee may not have intermediate checkpoints, but may be completely managed to the outcome or goal. While a managed employee will often have built-in reviews and status points, it is common for the directed employee not to have any status checks until completion of the overall program to goal or outcome. This expectation of "set it and forget it" becomes a critical challenge of the transition from managed to directed for many employees. Recognizing when to raise an issue often causes problems for the directed employee.

Entrepreneurship

The final stage is managing employees (or potentially we should now think about associates or collaborators) that are capable of defining the outcomes or goals. While the obvious example of an entrepreneur or CEO comes to mind, generally this is where roles translate high level aspirational goals into a set of defined outcomes that can then be translated into actual work outcomes or goals. For example, "growing the business" or "increasing profitability" are aspirational goals. As was detailed in Chapter 1: The Basic Business Model, profitability depends on many factors. Choosing the right factors to focus on and how to define the outcomes is entrepreneurship. Deciding if a channel engagement that will result in growth in revenue is worth the trade-off in margin and potential profits is an entrepreneurial activity.

The real change in entrepreneurship is that the management of an entrepreneur, while often still there, becomes focused on high level business outcomes not on activity outcomes. The entrepreneurial employee often does not have a traditional manager: instead it may be a board or in a larger company the CEO and an executive council.

Mismatches Create Havoc

Throughout my career, I have seen mismatches of management types creating significant failures to achieve the goals. If what a manager thought they should do and what an employee thought they were receiving are not aligned, problems will ensue. The most obvious of these is when a manager is using a level above that which an employee is capable of being managed to. For example, I once told an employee to put in place a program to assure architectural alignment between three different products. I set out a clear objective and a reasonable time frame. He was a new employee to my team and had come with high recommendations from his previous manager and a significant list of accomplishments and programs he had completed. We agreed that halfway through the time of the program, we would have a review and make sure that everything was on track. I volunteered to provide any additional support, but he indicated he was ready to go. When the time came for the review he presented where he was in the "program". It became clear that he had started to move to the goal without a clear plan and steps as well as not having a time-line or program plan.

My first reaction was to be angry and tear into his lack of planning. As we talked, it became clear that in his previous roles, he had been implementing a plan that had been built by others. It was absolutely clear that he was in the transition from management to direction. What was even more painfully clear was that I was at fault. I had not taken the time to understand his lack of experience with creating the plan and his unwillingness to stand up and ask for help when he was outside his comfort zone. While some would tell an employee that the fault was theirs for not asking, the reality is that it is the manager's responsibility to clearly understand the type of management an employee requires to succeed. The result in this case was that I spent a much larger amount of time with him than normal, building a new plan and steps, but making sure he was part of the thought process. In the next activity he did for me we repeated this process, and by the third iteration he did it on his own. He had made the transition that he was capable of, but needed to be guided through the learning process. The alternative, pulling him off of the project and moving him to a role that was clearly a managed employee role would have shattered his confidence, damaged his career, and probably caused him to leave the company. Recognizing that he needed help through the transition was critical.

Similarly, managing an employee below their capability creates another form of conflict. In this case the employee will feel that they have been micromanaged and will chafe at the lack of freedom to do the set of things that they believe he or she clearly knows how to do without "interference". For example, a peer I worked with had an employee (Steve) who had been in line for a promotion to the position the new peer was in. The new manager had a major program that needed to be implemented and he selected Steve to run the program. As this new manager had come from a direction role, he spent a significant amount of time defining the program he wanted to implement. When he finally engaged with Steve, the overall structure was well established, along with most of the steps and intermediate goals. As he reviewed this with Steve, he made it clear that Steve was not expected to change or modify **his** plan. In effect, he used his management style from his previous role (where he was treated as a directed employee) with an employee who had been in a directed style as well. The result was an immediate conflict and the end result was that Steve left the company. For you as a manager, one of the biggest challenges is to let go of the techniques that made you successful at the previous type of management, because it can cause significant conflict and even failure at the next level.

You Have To Let People Succeed (and Fail)

Another big challenge in your transitions is to let go of what you did well to embrace the new management type and challenges. Often you hear management experts talk about delegation as a critical skill, what this is about is understanding what to delegate and being sensitive to tune that to each of your management relationships.

The concept of letting go is always a challenge. You got to where you are through a set of skills and knowledge that put you at the top of the heap. That is why you succeeded and why you were promoted. Now you are going to have to accept that you may not always be the best at those things, or even worse, you may have to keep your mouth shut!

In many ways, the biggest challenge of moving up the ladder of management types is to be willing to accept the views, decisions, and guidance of those below you, even if you believe you have a better perspective. The reason this is critical is that you need your employees to step up to a type of management that will let you succeed. If you have moved to a level in your organization that requires you to mange using Direction, if you make it clear through your actions that only your ideas are really good, your employees will move to a management type relationship instead of direction type. If you are in a meeting and someone presents a way of doing things, before challenging them and saying to do it a different way, ask yourself if it really will matter if they do it your way instead of the way they have proposed. Even if you want to change, think about how to do it in subtle ways, rather than just saying. "No I know best".

The worst thing you can do is to become the manager who always corrects or attacks your people, no matter how small the difference. The result of this is twofold, first, your people will stop doing the work you need them to do on their own and will let you do the lifting for them. This results in poor productivity, and over time will reduce morale and create significant issues. In addition, it can rapidly lead to the pack or "follow the leader" mentality. If your ideas or concepts are always positioned as right and unchallengeable, your employees will start to look for your indications of direction and preference and then will jump on that path. This is an incredibly dangerous situation as it eliminates dialog and the opportunity to consider alternatives that could be better. The children's story of the Emperor's New Clothes shows that this has been common for a long time, and is just as bad today as then.

I have found that the best way to present an alternative is not to present it as the answer, but as a question. For example, instead of saying, "I think we should do X", you would say "Did you consider X?". If it was considered and rejected, now the discussion can be about the criteria. If it was not considered, the employee can consider it without having it become a directive. The key point is that you are not dictating and correcting, but advising and mentoring.

In the end there may be times when you will exercise your managerial prerogative and demand a path or direction, but that should be left to the end. If you are faced with this conflict, think through not only the outcomes in the event, but the outcomes of how you manage.

Level Check

The key message of this chapter is to understand your management type or types and to make sure you clearly understand the management type your employees need to succeed. If you have a mix of employees, you will be challenged with using different management types simultaneously. While this is possible, it is complex and requires clear thinking.

When a new employee comes to your group or you are interviewing prospects, developing a clear view of that persons management type is crucial. This can be accomplished by simple discussions about how they organize their work and how they completed their last few assignments.

For your existing employees, beyond clearly defining their management types, you should be thinking about which employees are capable of changing their type. This can becomes an active part of your personal development programs for those employees. For example, an employee who has reached a high skill level as a management type might attend a course in Program Management and Plan Definition to develop the skills to move into Direction type. You can use this as an opportunity through mentoring to let the employee have a broader range in defining the steps and the management structure.

I generally am clear about management typing with my employees and where I see them fitting. While in recent roles most of my direct reports have been direction or entrepreneurial types, I still find it is important to consider if an employee fits into those types. Occasionally I find an employee that has been represented to me as one type that really does not have all the skills to succeed with that type of management. I can say without qualification that using these techniques has enabled me to help all of the employees who worked for me through the years.

Chapter 12 Differences in Management Styles

Before anyone reacts to the religious reference, this chapter has it has its roots in a real story and relationship. While I am generally agnostic, I was primarily raised in the Protestant side of Christianity. When I was young, my parents firmly believed that I should have a religious education so they mandated that I should attend church. Mind you, this was not attending with them, but was me attending on my own. My parents would drive me to church and pick me up after the service/Sunday school at the church of my choice. Over time. my choice of churches was somewhat friend driven. I attended a Lutheran church, an Episcopal church, had a short time in the Mormon church, and ended up joining and sticking with the Methodist church through my high school years. I actually choose the Methodist church as they had the best youth program and, at least in my opinion of the day, the best looking young ladies.

In the late 80s, when I was VP of Marketing at Sytek, one of the leaders on my team was Peter Filice. Pete and I worked together in different capacities through the years, both as peers and with Pete on my team. In many ways, he and I were perfect complements: I was always focused on the big picture, the end goal, the transformational change, and Pete was always clear that, while that was nice, not having a plan to get there made it irrelevant. He was the operational Yang to my visionary Ying.

Pete was from an Italian family and Catholic. He attended Santa Clara University (with my wife as it turned out), and maintained a strong focus on the Catholic church.

As we worked together, I realized that we had drastically different management styles. When someone came to work for me, I would give them a set of tasks to do (or directions to go) and would let them run with the ball. As discussed in the last chapter, my preferred management approach was a direction style, with trust in the employee's self-completion. Many times the result would be great, but occasionally I would be surprised when the employee could not complete the task or get to the goal. As I worked with Pete, I realized his strategy was very different. Every employee, no matter how experienced or seasoned would have a regular weekly meeting and Pete would review in detail what the employee had done in the previous week and what they intended to do in the next week. Pete started all of his employees in a Supervision/ Management style and then let them earn their way to greater flexibility.

Over time, I realized that our management styles were much less about how we managed and much more about our basic expectations of new employees that we were unfamiliar with and whether they could be counted upon to deliver that which was expected. I realized that where I fundamentally believed that they would/could do the right thing, Pete assumed they would not. Over time I came to see this as a philosophical difference. Just as some religions assume that man is inherently sinful and others assume man comes to the world without sin, your view of people will drive your management style.

Catholic Style Manager

The Catholic Manager (no offence intended), assumes that a new employee or co-worker is unable to be depended on to complete tasks without oversight and some level of supervision. The assumption leads the Catholic Style Manager to immediately structure the interaction with that individual in a way to assure that he or she is in complete control of the process. This generally takes the form of task lists, regular reviews and detailed reviews of activities and plans. This level of detailed and focused management continues until the Catholic Style Manager concludes that the individual has demonstrated their capability beyond a doubt.

Just as in a religious view that assumes men are inherently flawed, this style of management assumes that a new employee is flawed until they prove themselves worthy. The only way to prove that an individual is worthy is to go through the structured process and, by completing the process, the individual has demonstrated that they can move forward.

The Catholic Style Manger, especially early in their career, can be highly effective. While applying the process of their management structure, he or she generally gets predictable results as well as often identifies those sinners that would have failed without the process. The result is that the Catholic Style Manager has a ready reinforcement of the validity of the approach.

However, as time moves on and the roles change, this style of management can become an issue. As new employees come into the manager's orbit, the process that assured success may become very tedious to those that have moved beyond. Applying this process to a mature employee at the direction type of management (see the previous chapter) often generates a significant kickback and even resentment.

Protestant Style Manager

The Protestant Style Manger (again, no offence intended) comes at the process in exactly the opposite way. The new employee is assumed to capable of doing the job, which is why he or she is here after all. The Protestant Style Manager assigns a task or goal and assumes that the employee will complete it or ask for help. The results of this are potentially much more variable than those of the Catholic Style Manager. While often the outcomes are great and the employees feel "empowered", there will be the occasional (and even regular) failure. If an employee does not complete his or her task or goal, this is much to the surprise of the Protestant Style Manager. He or she does not understand how that individual could fail, after all they were assumed to be capable and without sin.

The result is that the Protestant Style Manager is perceived as not operationally focused, "a great thinker, not a deliverer". Over time, this can lead to one of two things: 1. promotion to a role where it is acceptable due to the seniority of the employees, or 2. failure if the organization is not capable of using the individual.

The challenge for Protestant Style Mangers is generally that they assume a uniform level of capability and manage to that level or type. When they get an individual that does not meet that type or level, their management style stays where it has been effective with others and then the manager fails with that employee.

Protestant Style Managers will get great evaluation marks from their employees, but only from employees who are capable of working with that type of leadership. From an employee who needs more guidance, assistance and control, the manager will be seen as not caring.

Agnostic is Best

Once you understand that each of these management styles has certain hallmarks, it is probably easy to see where your personal proclivities lie. However, I believe fundamentally that great managers and leaders integrate three things together: understanding how to apply both styles, evaluating each employee for the ration of styles based on that employee's type of management required, and focus on employees that fit in the comfort range of the manager

Using these three techniques, a manager can assure that they are operating in their comfort zone and, within the time constraints of their role, assure that their employees are comfortable with the management style and how it is applied.

Having a clear understanding of both management styles and the ability to use both in a situational basis is optimal. If you are a less senior manager and have been a traditional Catholic Style Manager, identify an employee that you have not gone through your process with. Look for someone that through your early discussion and reputation you believe should be trustworthy. Try pulling back your personal management processes for this individual. If the result is positive, you now know how to accommodate a greater management range. If the result is less than positive, you know either the employee was not right or your evaluation was wrong.

If you are a Protestant Style Manager in a less senior position, try establishing a structured task-based status and review process with your least senior direct report. Set weekly meetings and clearly review what was accomplished in the previous week and what is on the horizon for the next week. But do not stop here: be clear that you want to understand how each action leads towards the larger goal or outcome that that employee is driving towards.

For each of your employees, complete the Type of Management evaluations discussed in the previous chapter. While the Catholic and Protestant styles can be applied to all types, I will argue that as employees move from supervision to direction types, the management style should change as well. Imagine for a moment a Protestant Style Manager in a supervision role. In this role, the manager would assign an employee to a job, have someone do the necessary training and assume that the employee will be able to do the job. If the employee, for whatever reason, misunderstands the instructions, they could easily make a simple error in the work. That error might mean that 100 sets of tires were installed on the wrong rims and sent to the final assembly line in error. The result was over 100 cars that needed to have their wheels removed and the tires moved to another rim. As you no doubt surmised, as a 20 year old foreman, this exact event happened to me, though in all good faith I can plead extenuating circumstances. I was asked to take over the tire room on second shift the day before Christmas as a single day job to fill in for the normal foreman who was taking vacation. At the lunch break the employees appeared to have imbibed a bit and somehow the whole process got off track. However, I did not make the checks to assure that things were on track: I assumed that the employees would do things right.

Seriously, as you understand the type of management that is required for each of your employees, evaluate the style of management you will use as well. Clearly plan out for each employee both elements and how you intend to move the employee forward over time or to evaluate whether the employee has reached the limit of their growth.

Finally, as you recruit and hire for your team, keep a continual thought process on how the person you are thinking about bringing into the team fits into your personal management comfort zone. If you know that you are generally a Protestant Style Manager and have trouble building into your day the time to effectively do detailed management, avoid individuals who require regular management at a task and activity level. Discuss a recent program and how they interacted with their manager in completing that goal.

Conversely, if you are inherently comfortable as a Catholic Style Manger, you may want to take care to avoid hiring people who start the interview process by describing themselves as "self starters" or "self motivated and managed". Applying a rigorous structure to such an employee may immediately create conflict. If you decide that this individual is ideal for what you need to do, then it is time to evaluate your ability to change your management style to reflect this.

In the end, neither style is right nor wrong. By having a clear view of how your management style reflects in the interaction with your employees and a clear view of how it fits into the Four Types of Management, you can become significantly more effective. This will enable you to leverage those employees that work well with guidance and direction, while still being able to use the capabilities of employees that need more structure and instruction. The key is to let your style be dictated by the employee, not try to make all of the employees fit into a style that you are comfortable with.

Chapter 13 Kicking Off a Team

There is nothing more exhilarating and terrifying than the first meeting with a new team of employees that have just found out you are going to be their new leader. Whether this is a promotion, a lateral move or you have been hired from the outside, you are going to be immediately evaluated as to whether your new team believes you can lead them to success and whether they will be successful and satisfied working for you.

You start by doing a quick round of introductions, and now it's your turn. In brief, you need to make people clear on your goals, your management styles, why you are there and ultimately why they should trust you.

I want to be clear. This chapter is not intended to tell you what to say. It is even less intended as a how to guide. It is intended to give you an idea of how you can begin to develop your own story/strategy for what might be one of the most important events in your work career. The first thing to remember is that each of the employees in the room is not only evaluating you, they are evaluating themselves in light of you. Each is asking the same question: "can I succeed with this new manager?"

Your Personal Introduction

The first thing I do is introduce myself. I generally like to cover three topics in my introduction: who am I, how do I manage, and how I see the team. I do not try to lay out an intense plan of action at this point as I have not heard from them as to their views. Starting by outlining your 30/60/90 day plan indicates you do not value their input and views. This is not to say that I do not have such a plan. but I do not put it out there without asking them, either individually or as a group, what they think the key issues are.

Who am I

My review of who I am is always limited. I talk for less than two minutes about roles I have held, mention a couple of recognitions. Then I focus a bit on how teams that I have led have succeeded. I am very clear in that this is a reflection of the team. I always use the word "we", never "I" and focus on how the team succeeded. The team is not interested in what you did to glorify yourself, but in how your skills and knowledge will help them succeed. Another critical point is to make sure that they understand why you are there.

While there is often a desire at this point to justify why you are the leader, you must be very careful not to start with something that will de-motivate your employees. In one session of this type the new leader began by saying. "I have been very successful in my career. I am now independently wealthy and I am only here because this seemed interesting and I needed something to do." Actually, while it was a little more circumspect, the employees heard it as "I am here because I need to keep busy". But they also heard a distinct lack of commitment or "skin in the game" and of any empathy for their situation.

It is absolutely critical that as part of your introduction you clearly say why this is the best place in the whole world for you to be working and why your success is clearly linked to the success of the team.

While I am doing this first introduction, I always talk about a few past teams and assure that I give attribution to those who participated. This is especially important if those teams were in the same company. By identifying individuals by name who were part of your success, you are demonstrating that you will share the success and glory with the team.

Finally, I like to talk about what motivates me. I talk about my three work satisfiers as described in Chapter 42 and how I am motivated at a personal level to succeed and evaluate success.

How Do I Manage?

Having a clear expectation of your management style is important. Defining your personal expectations of your team at the first is part of building the early structure for success. Being clear on your preferences for types of management and the styles you generally use can be a great way to structure the team.

In a management training program I went through, they described the concept of developing your non-negotiables. These were described as your philosophical views that you would not bend on. I believe that as a new manager, having a clear set of principles or non-negotiable is very important. For me, absolute honesty is mandatory, as is disagreeing and having adamant discussions, but then all supporting the decision that we come to. I make it clear that no one will ever be censored for challenging me or anyone else on the team during the discussion, but after the decision is made we need to come together as a team and support the outcome. I also make sure that they know that challenges are not personal, they should be based on facts, not random opinions.

I believe telling a story of how your management style and views were developed is important to your new team. I sometimes use the Four Types of Management or the Catholic and Protestant Styles of Management to define how I manage and relate. I also tell a story that for me relates a lot about how I evaluate all of my decisions and actions. This is that story:

After graduating from University, I went to work for GM as a maintenance foreman. I did this job for a year when I was asked to move into the Plant Engineering group and take over the computer and technology side of the plant (this was a 3.5M square foot manufacturing plant with 7,000 employees). As I took the job, I found out that the employee I was replacing had been fired for embezzlement and was facing criminal charges. Over the next few months I was involved with the lawyers and police in unraveling how he had set up contracts so they were awarded to certain vendors and how he received significant kick-backs. As I saw this I realized how easy his path had been from a good employee to one who essentially defrauded his employer. It started with lunches with the vendors, free carpeting from one of the contractors and led to rigged contracts with 6 figure fraud. Through this process I realized that, as an employee, your decisions can only be evaluated in one context: is this a good decision or path for the owner of this company? If you are in a public company, that is the shareholders: in a private company it is the owners: and in a governmental organization, it's the citizens. While it is important to consider other stakeholders (employees, customers, partners, suppliers), in the end, if you ask the simple question. "will the owners see this as the right decision?", you will be on the right track.

This story, which is true, reflects two major views I hold dear, be truthful and trustworthy and evaluate decisions based on what is best for the stakeholders, led by the owners. While I do not expect you to use this story, find the events that have shaped your views and turn them into representations of your style and your philosophical position.

How Do You See the Team

This should be a reflection of how you see the team, remembering that you are often just meeting the team for the first time: often this is not your personal view, but what has been communicated to you. If you are moving within the company, it may be how you and others perceived the team from another position.

The point is not to position this as what needs to be done, but to establish a first set of discussions about where you want to go and what you want to do. A statement about the teams recognized strengths and weaknesses and then a dialog about how the team members perceive this is important.

Establishing a Baseline

Once you have a clear introduction complete, you need to move the discussion to establishing a baseline to begin your next set of activities. This baseline needs to define what you expect in the next 10-30 days from the team. When I do this, I do three things to establish the baseline: begin to create a new team culture and common language, define how I expect the team to relate to me, and define my immediate goals in a larger framework of the goals of the team.

Common Culture and Language

As you will see when you get to Chapter 43 "3 Rules of Work", having fun is important to me. However, just saying that is not really of value, so I believe you should always start with an activity that has an element of fun. I found this in a strange place, in the movie "Bill and Ted's Excellent Adventure" (Herek, 1989). Before you laugh, if you have not seen this movie, it is a movie that operates on two very different planes. There is the plane of slightly banal teen comedy, and then there is the plane of biting business and social commentary. The script of the opening scene (transcribed by: Sonja Kemp) of the movie is representative of tidbits dropped throughout:

(San Dimas, California - 1988)
(Bill's Garage)
(Bill and Ted are playing their instruments in Bill's garage. Ted is video-taping.)
Bill: *I'm Bill S. Preston, Esquire.*
Ted: *And I'm Ted "Theo...(he realizes he's still behind the camera) Oh! Bill, here take it.*
Bill: *Okay. (he takes the camera and begins filming Ted.)*
Ted: *And I'm Ted "Theodore" Logan.*
Bill: *Yeah! (he sets down the camera and faces it so that it's taping both of them.)*
Both: *And we're Wyld Stallyns.*
(They both play their guitars, and they are very bad. They end up blowing out a speaker and they open up the garage door to air out the garage.)
Bill: *Oh, Dude! Let's bail. We blew it. I guess we used too much power. Ted, while I agree that in time our band will be most triumphant, the truth is Wyld Stallyns will never be a super band until we have Eddie Van Halen on guitar.*
Ted: *Yes Bill, but I do not believe we will get Eddie Van Halen until we have a triumphant video.*
Bill: *Ted, it's pointless to have a triumphant video before we even have decent instruments.*
Ted: *Well how can we have decent instruments when we really don't even know how to play.*
Bill: *That is why we need Eddie Van Halen.*
Ted: *And that is why we need a triumphant video.*
(Pause)
Both: *Excellent. (Air Guitar.)*
(At that moment that alarm clock goes off.)
Bill: *Uh-oh. We're late.*
Ted: *For what?*
Bill: *For school, dude.*
Ted: *Oh yeah.*

If you did not see every bad business meeting you have been in represented in this script, read it again. "We need more revenue to support our product development...but without more development we cannot grow revenue...but without marketing..." and so on. The point is that after Bill and Ted agree that they cannot succeed they do an air guitar and exclaim *"Excellent"*.

When I take a team over I ask everyone to go home and rent Bill and Ted's Excellent Adventure and watch it. As people do, they come back and comment about the points they picked up, but they also begin to use the movie as a metaphor for focus and doing the right thing. I think the line from Socrates "True wisdom is knowing you know nothing." and Bill's response "That's us dude." is one that often people recognize. Failure is far more often caused by what you do not know than by what you do.

In one team, after about a month, a group of about 15 people were in a meeting in a heated discussion about a decision. Two of the participants began a lengthy discussion of how something was going to be insurmountable. Almost simultaneously 3 people did an air guitar and said "Excellent". Immediately the team stopped and began to focus on an answer, not on convincing themselves that they were in a corner.

The other point that comes out of this is that it is not OK to go along if you disagree. And any well thought out position can be represented. And that we are a team and now have something that binds us together.

How Does the Team Relate to You

For some readers this is a tough question. Do you manage by fear, respect, or something more akin to love. Are you comfortable being challenged? Can you admit when you are wrong?

I cannot answer these questions for you, but as you move into a leadership position, you need to have a clear answer to these. And, in getting these answers, be truthful with yourself. If you hate being proven wrong, don't tell people you like to be challenged. Someone will challenge you and when you react badly, your entire leadership persona will suffer. If your answer is that you do not like being challenged or proven wrong, think for a moment about PT Barnum. PT Barnum famously said. "You can fool all of the people some of the time and some of the people all of the time, but you cannot fool all of the people all of the time". I believe the corollary to this is, "No one is always right." So if you assume you cannot always right, how can you present this in a way that makes sense, so you can be challenged but respected, not feared, but generally loved as a manager (in a good way).

As before, I cannot tell you what to do, but I will relate what I say to a new team. The first thing I say is that I know I am a reasonably smart person. I got to where I am by being smart. However, I really cannot take any credit for that as you are really defined by your parents, how they raised you and the education you were fortunate enough to get. And then I get to the key point, "While I know I am smart, I know that together, the group of you are smarter than me." The point there is that while I may be both smart and knowledgeable, the sum of 5 or 10 direct reports has more brainpower and knowledge than me (or you). Recognizing this at the outset sets the tone. I go on to say that I will have strong opinions and I will support them and defend them with fervor, but if you convince me I am wrong, I will switch positions. It is more important to be right than proud. And when I do, I will give attribution to you for your thoughts and position.

I then go into my personal version of PT Barnum's line. I will create a number of ideas, but I know they are not all good, sometimes an idea is just that, an idea and on examination is found wanting. The key point is that if you have continuum of ideas and creations, you must accept that some will be flawed: finding the flaws and weeding them out is a good process and not something wrong. The first time you are in a meeting and make a suggestion and someone responds with data that makes it invalid and you agree and move on, you will have gone far to winning your team. And now all that brainpower is focused to succeeding...and you are the leader.

The Plan

Before talking to your new team, make sure you have two things clear: 1. how does this team relate to the greater organization and what is expected of the team to add value, and 2. what is my 30 day plan to assure that everyone is working together to succeed. As these two elements are different for every team in every organization it is impossible to actually do anything that is of value to define them here. However, on this point I would encourage you to actually make a bullet list.

What are the three goals or outcomes that are expected of this team by the rest of the organization. If these are deliverables, what is the timeframe. If they are activities, is there a quantifiable goal?

Assuming you do not have a specific and complete action plan (and even if you do you may want to solicit some input), you need to develop a clear outline of how you intend to use the next 30 days to clarify the plan, how the work will be aligned and managed and what the specific deliverables and goals are.

The Meeting

With this agenda and points now defined it is time for the meeting. Use this time to establish that you are a leader that both listens and can be trusted. Make sure to allow some time for questions in the middle. In many ways, you are the new tour guide and you want to convince the team to follow you on the tour and get excited about the scenery as well as the destinations.

Keep it as brief as possible, but linger afterwards to allow people to express their opinions, both publicly and in confidence. Above all, realize that you will be spending the majority of your time with these people over the next part of your life and this meeting will set the tone for that time.

Strategy

The strategy section is fairly limited, but it has a few essential points on strategy that can be added to the strategic discussion and help in understanding the strategic process. While I considered adding more in this section, I decided to keep a number of advanced topics for a future book.

Chapter 14 Strategy, Vision, and Business Plans

You probably have heard of a business plan. You may have heard about your companies vision or strategy, but how do the three come together? In this chapter the differences between the three will be highlighted, along with some ideas of how to be effective if you are asked to lead or contribute to them. Business plans are the documentation of the execution of a vision and a strategy, so we will start with vision and strategy. It is important to realize that the two are not the same, but are very tightly coupled and, I will argue, both critical to the success of any venture.

I found Michael Hyatt's comments on vision and strategy to be very clear, "Vision and strategy are both important. But there is a priority to them. Vision always comes first. Always. If you have a clear vision, you will eventually attract the right strategy. If you don't have a clear vision, no strategy will save you." He is the Chairman of Thomas Nelson Publishers, the largest Christian publishing company in the world and the seventh largest trade book publishing company in the U.S.

I think he has it exactly right. Vision is where you want to go, and strategy is how to get there. As there have been whole books written on this subject, this chapter will, of course, be fairly high level, but I felt that it was a critical point.

Vision

What is vision? It is not complex. It is your view of where you believe things will be at some point in the future. Vision can be about the market, your products, services you will deliver, the size of your company, profitability, or all of them together. Often your vision is about the impact your company will have. Here are a few examples of vision:

> *Apple:* "To make a contribution to the world by making tools for the mind that advance humankind."

> *FedEx 1973* (when it was founded): "We deliver your package next day by 10:30."

> *FedEx Today:* "FedEx Corporation's vision is a world where goods and information move quickly and seamlessly. A world where

businesses source raw materials and parts globally, then move high-value goods quickly between continents and across time zones. A world where global information and transportation networks can shrink time and distance, creating competitive advantages for customers."

Cisco Systems: "Changing the Way We Work, Live, Play, and Learn."

Pfizer: " Pfizer will strive to achieve and sustain its leading place as the world's premier research-based pharmaceutical company. The company's continuing success benefits patients, customers, shareholders, business partners, families and the communities in which they operate all around the world. Pfizer's mission is to become the world's most valued company to all of these people."

Genentech: "Utilize the science of biotechnology to become a leader in revolutionizing the treatment of patients with cancer, immunological diseases and angiogenic disorders."

General Motors: "GM's vision is to be the world leader in transportation products and related services. We will earn our customers' enthusiasm through continuous improvement driven by the integrity, teamwork, and innovation of GM people."

The core message in each of these vision statements is how the company intends to transform or change expectations by its presence in the marketplace. Also, the vision becomes a clear measure of decisions and directions. Contrast the vision message with what you know of the company. In Apple's vision there is no reference to the company as a leader or its employees. In the GM vision it is all related to the company and its employees, not the customer and change. Which do you think is more inspirational? If GM said their vision was to "transform the way people work and play through new transportation paradigms", is it more visionary?

Vision can also be a goal, though most times it will be a goal that will evolve over time. The FedEx vision when the company started, of delivering your package by 10:30 the next day is clearly a goal. This became the vision of how the company would change the world. Now that vision has changed to become inclusive of the broader capabilities of the company. The interesting thing is that both of the FedEx vision statements do not refer to the company per se, though they are both totally oriented to the business of FedEx.

Vision is not the same as mission. Mission is much more about the results of the vision, often the value that it will create. While often vision and mission are interchanged, they are truly different. The mission is a clear statement of how achieving the vision will change the marketplace and the value it brings to the stakeholders of the company. While mission statements are company specific, vision often includes industry or other outside items. For example, a vision may foresee a dramatic reduction in size of a component, while the mission might use that change to create value for customer. Of the vision statements above, the Cisco one is more mission than vision. The Cisco advertising line of creating the human network is more of a vision. In the past, the Cisco vision of IP as a unifying force that tied the world together was visionary.

A great vision reflects both leadership in thought and believability. Another critical point is that vision will evolve over time, but this happens relatively slowly. As a vision looks forward 5-10 years or even longer, annual changes will be small, reflecting only those new or changed perspectives that occur. As you develop vision, test it with both people inside your company and outside. If your vision is to leverage a change that is coming in your industry, make sure that your stakeholders are bought into the change.

Strategy

With a vision of where you want to go, you can develop your strategy to get there. Too many times I have heard strategy described as the next program or the next product or the next feature. That is not strategy. Strategy is understanding how you are going to make your vision a reality. Without strategy, a vision is only a dream. Strategy is not about tactics. Sun Tzu was a leading general in China and lived in the sometime between 500 and 200 BC. He is credited with writing "The Art of War", an amazing book on the elements of warfare, many of which have been adapted to business today. In the URL links in the back of the book is a link to both a detailed translation of his works as well as additional modern interpretations. As

Sun Tzu wrote in the Art of War, "All men can see the tactics whereby I conquer, but what none can see is the strategy out of which victory is evolved." The point he is making is that the strategy happens before any of the battle is waged. Strategy is about clearly thinking through all of the factors required to win. Another critical point is that while your vision may be more fixed, your strategy will adapt as the terrain changes.

I believe the book, `The Mind of the Strategist: The Art of Japanese Business.' (Ohmae, 1982) It was written in 1975 by Kenichi Ohmae, then a director at McKinsey & Company, and is a great introduction to the thought process required for strategic success. While many of the examples are dated and address early Japanese corporate strategy, his core concept remains relevant today: The purpose of strategy is to maximize competitive advantage and strategy is based on analysis. The "strategic triangle" of customers, competitors, and company is an effective analysis framework for identifying competitive advantage. The key point is that to understand your strategy, you must analyze these three interfaces. In the next section we will discuss a methodology for analyzing the company-competitor interface, so at this point the focus is on the customer.

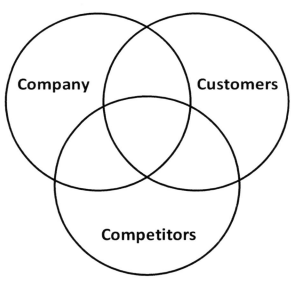

Figure 14-1 Diagram of Strategic Intersection

The relationship to the customer or the marketplace is critical to understanding your strategy. Understanding the changes faced by your customers and how customers will approach solving their problems are critical to developing a strategy. Understanding how your customers and the organizations within your customers respond are critical to how you strategize moving forward.

Another point in the "Mind of the Strategist" is to truly understand the business you are in. The point made is that General Motors is not in the car business, but in the business of enabling people to get where they want to go. Even the GM vision of Transportation Products is somewhat limiting versus "Transportation Systems". Similarly, cable television companies are not in the TV business, but in the business of delivering information content, entertainment and connectivity to homes and businesses. In the end this clearly shows that cable companies would be competing with the telephone companies. It also would show why wireless is a technology that a cable television company should be paying attention to. Make sure you and your team are clear as to the business you are in as it will help in evaluating the transitions in the relationship with your customers and potential shifts in your competitors.

Strategic Imperatives

After defining where you want to go with your strategy, you need to define a set of strategic imperatives. Strategic imperatives are those things that have to happen to make your strategy successful. There should be a small number of strategic imperatives, typically 3 to 5 items that you must make happen to succeed with your strategy.

In the Nortel example above, there were a few strategic imperatives: to get the right relationship with an IT Business Applications vendor (i.e. Microsoft), to develop a message to the market to create a pull for the resulting solution, and finally, to create an offer that would continue to protect the revenue and margin.

When defining strategic imperatives, there are two elements that should be considered: what has to happen, and what cannot be allowed to happen. A good example of an imperative is the successful invasion of Italy in WWII by the allies. This was a fundamental imperative to being able to invade across the English Channel as it diverted significant Nazi troop strength and proved out a number of the techniques later used at Normandy. But there were others that were just as critical. For example, the allies knew that supply and re-supply would be critical and that there was no way to capture a harbor in a reasonable amount of time. Therefore, another imperative became developing an artificial harbor that could be put in place directly off the beach and used for the critical first weeks supply efforts.

Building a Strategic Plan

Using these three elements (vision, strategy and strategic imperative), a strategy can be developed.

Positional Analysis

Firstly, with as much data as possible, define the current position. This should detail your position, its strengths and weaknesses, and how you relate to both the customers and the competitors. Part of this positional analysis can be one or more views on how things are going to change. In the next chapter, the completive box concept is one way to look at changes. In addition to competition changes, be clear about changes in your customers, both existing and new customers. Use any and all sources of data. For example, the US Department of Labor has great data on employment by category and region. In many industries there are analyst reports. Use all of these sources to build a complete view of where you are, how that is changing and what factors might change it for the future.

Pay attention to major shifts in the market. For example, in the late 80s and 90s, the US auto collision industry underwent a huge shift with the advent of the direct repair program (DRP). This program meant that the consumer did not have to get multiple estimates and could just take the car to a shop, where the estimate and the repairs would be done with a guarantee backed by the company. While some auto body shops saw this as a way to reduce their revenue and potentially the quality of the repairs, some shop owners saw this as a major change in the market. They realized that many consumers, potentially the majority, would opt for this easier and faster method versus shopping around and getting money from the insurance company and then managing the repair. Even though it meant a reduction in their revenues, some owners focused on these programs. By 2001 the percentage of collision repairs going through the DRP mechanism was over 34%. By the end of the decade, in some markets and some insurers, over 50% of the repairs were going through these systems. A strategy of focusing on insurance partners that supported DRP, if executed in the early 90s, could have the impact of significantly growing the business.

Alternatively, for a shop not associated with these programs, the available market is reduced by the percentage of repairs going through the DSP.

Finally, the positional analysis should include identification of a set of potential positions/directions. This can then become a set of positional scenarios to use in the development of the strategy.

Define the Strategy

Now that you have a clear view of where you are and , as best as you can develop, a view of the directions that will drive the future, a strategy can be developed. The strategy should define where you believe that you can go, to get maximum advantage and change your position. However, strategy must be defined in an actionable set of steps. In any endeavor there are limitations, these must be taken into account. Sometimes a set a strategic options or scenarios is the best way to define the strategy. By looking at 2-4 options, the best one will come. However, when the strategy is complete, check back to make sure you are moving to your vision.

Strategic Imperatives

As you develop the strategy, the imperatives will come out of the process. Before the process is complete, the imperatives must be analyzed to assure that they are achievable. For example, if there are 5 strategic imperatives and there is a 20% probability of each of them failing, then there is a 100% probability that at least one will not be accomplished. After the imperatives are defined, an analysis of potential outcomes using some level of probability is required.

Business Plans

John Morgridge, the President/Chairman of Cisco Systems through its incredible growth, is often quoted as saying, "Business plans are like peeing down your leg, it gives you a warm feeling but it doesn't do anything for you." The point is that business plans look good, but are not a real measure of success. But, if we start with our strategic imperatives, we can translate that into a set of plans that are focused to getting to the goal, not on documenting a financial plan.

If we translate the business plan into the action plan for driving the strategic imperatives then it becomes a much more effective document.

A clear and precise plan to deliver the strategic imperatives is mandatory. I remember one business planning session where the General Manager got up and said his objective in the business was to grow and his strategy was to grow his market share! In the end, his strategy was no more than to achieve an objective and that was the strategy. What he did not move forward with was a strategy to change his market share, which would of necessity have brought out some questions:

> *Are you going to grow you market share by market growth in new customers or by taking share from your competitors?*
>
> *If you are taking share from your competitors, which ones is the share coming from?*
>
> *How are you taking that share from each competitor? Is it based on selling, products, or price?*
>
> *Are there different programs for different competitors?*
>
> *and so on......*

The point of this is that a real strategy emerges from starting with a firm set of facts in the positional analysis and continually working through the strategy and the imperatives until you have arrived at something that is clear and achievable.

Strategies and Plans Change

An extension of the Morgridge quote is that both peeing on your leg and a business plan start to smell after awhile. This is an absolute fact. Any strategy is only good until the first real battle is joined, but even before that may become an issue. In Chapter 7 "Decisions, Decisions, Decisions", I discussed the Avaya decision of a next generation device and how the lack of a checkpoint meant not only failure for that product, but also a major delay for the iPad version.

A regular review of the strategy is mandatory. Depending on your industry, this might be annually or a little more, but it may be less if you are in an industry where technology is driving change. In order to assure that these changes are being managed, both the positional assumptions and the imperatives must be examined. As you develop your plan, agree on a mechanism for when these will be evaluated in the future.

Finally, I will return again to Sun Tzu. One critical point in your plans is to clearly analyze your advantage (or disadvantage) and make your plans based on that. Sun Tzu is clear of how to measure your capability versus your opponent (taken from www.suntzusaid.com).

> *It is the rule in war, if our forces are ten to the enemy's one, to surround him: if five to one, to attack him:*
>
> *if twice as numerous, to divide our army into two.*
>
> *If equally matched, we can offer battle:*
>
> *if slightly inferior in numbers, we can avoid (watch) the enemy:*
>
> *if quite unequal in every way, we can flee from him.*

I have repeatedly seen the planning process developed in an excruciating way, only to end in what is essentially "a miracle occurs". For example, I once saw a business plan that clearly stated, " With 20% of the Competitor's sales resources, we are going to equal the competitor in volume". In thinking about it, it was clear this was only possible if the product sold itself (in this case it was comparable to the competition), or if we had people that would work 24 hours a day, seven days a week. In the end the great strategy failed as the miracle did not occur.

A Business Rhythm

In Nortel in the late 2000s, a group of executive managers came from General Electric and brought in some GE thinking. This led to Lean Six Sigma and a few other programs, but one area that came with this transition was the creation of a regular rhythm of a strategic conversation. The program that was introduced had 4 defined phases, each was implemented in a calendar quarter. One key point was that each phase started with a review of the previous phases and an open opportunity to discuss the changes that might have occurred. This meant that each session was an opportunity to open a dialog on something that might have changed from another previous session. Obviously over time, the sequencing of this goes away as they blend into a continuum. The four phases were as follows:

Human Capital - this first phase focused on the employees and management required to deliver the strategy, deliverables and budgets as defined in the previous sessions. This is where advancement and cross-training as well as succession planning takes place.

Strategy - This session is focused on exactly what the position and strategy are going forward, all the way to Strategic Imperatives.

Multi-generational Product Planning - this part of the process focused on reviewing the plans for the Strategic Imperatives (though in Nortel's case there was a heavy focus on product development).

Budget - The last quarterly session is the budget. By the time this came around, the 3 previous sessions in the year would make this relatively easy.

The key point of this process was multi-fold: it spread the activities to manage the business strategy and elements into an extended period, but still kept them integrated and sequential. When compared to many other strategic planning processes, this is much better. In many organizations, there is a 6 week effort to do something to satisfy the requirement and then you can go on about what you were already doing. The continual process meant that nothing was a huge short term burden and that progress could be evaluated regularly.

However you do it, the process of strategic planning, review, translation to imperatives and action, needs to be a continual process. Strategy cannot be something that is done once, tied with a ribbon and put on the shelf for all to gaze on. It needs to be the living and breathing translation about how the vision will become reality.

Vision and Strategy are Leadership

Finally, having a clear vision, strategy, and plan to complete your strategic objectives is one of the most important parts of leadership. While you may be able to talk and dance your way for a little while, in the end, your stakeholders will know if you are not on the tight track. As Lewis Carroll said, "If you don't know where you are going, any road will get you there." Without the clear elements of vision and strategy, any idea that comes along is a good one, the result often being a set of things that do not hang together and can be attacked individually in the market.

Finally, Jack Welch, of GE fame said, "Control your destiny! Or … someone else will!". Always be clear and brutally honest in this process. Make sure you are clear about how the competition and the customers are changing and how your position will be impacted. Only by having a clear view and process, based on data that is not filtered or "optimized" will you generate a winning strategy.

Lest you think that this is easy, Sun Tzu is very clear at the end of the first chapter of the Art of War that planning is hard work, but the only way to succeed: "Now the general who wins a battle makes many calculations in his temple ere the battle is fought. The general who loses a battle makes but few calculations beforehand. Thus do many calculations lead to victory, and few calculations to defeat: how much more no calculation at all! It is by attention to this point that I can foresee who is likely to win or lose." Sun Tzu is clear, the success of the endeavor can be directly correlated to the effort and thought put into the planning. If the goal of planning is to generate a few slides so that the board or the executive management stops asking questions, then a simple effort to get that done is all that is required. However, success will only come to those who have clearly defined the path and understand all of the elements of success.

Chapter 15 The Competitive Box

In the late 80s I was charged with doing strategic planning in a mid-size networking company. The process was data driven and required an analysis of how our company interacted with the competition. Out of that thought process came a tool that I believe can be used in many industries and companies to model the company relative to its competition. This applies as much to the business planning as to the strategic planning process.

Introduction

The basic Competitive Box is shown in Figure 15-1. In the middle is the company to be analyzed (e.g your company), and around that box are the competitive interfaces that define the competitive position. Each of the competitive positions are defined by how they relate to the analyzed company. The companies on either side of the analyzed companies are companies in the same "space" and are impacted similarly by the upper and lower competitors.

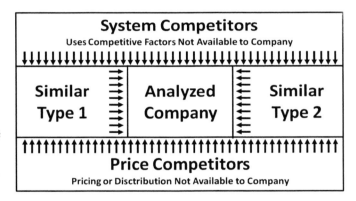

Figure 15-1 The Competitive Box

System Competitors

Systems competitors use factors unavailable to space players, monetizing value in different areas. An example is a company that offers the same capability as the analyzed company as part of a larger portfolio. In general, the systems competitors squeeze the space from the top and remove a percentage of the market. In the example of the auto body repair, repair shops that are part of a DRP would limit the market available to a non-DRP shop through a system competitive factor of being part of the DRP.

Similar Competitors

These are companies that are similar to the analyzed company in competing in the same space. They will often be similar in product portfolio, distribution, etc. In this space the comparisons are very clearly drawn on defined values and capabilities. In the audio industry, there are a number of companies that make Blu-Ray players. Comparing a Blu-Ray player from Sony or Panasonic or Samsung is a clear comparison of features, price, and perceived performance/quality. The Sony Playstation 3 that includes a Blu-Ray player would be defined as not being part of this space, but would rather be part of the systems competitors above.

Price Competitors

Price competitors represent a fundamental discontinuity to the traditional space above them. In recent years the emergence of open source software has defined a new price-based competition in many technology spaces. In the DVD world, low price non-brand name competitors have defined a very low cost point in the market. Sold in Wal-Mart, these players often have price points 70% or 80% lower than their brand name competitors. Another potential low end disruption is access to a channel that changes the market. In many segments, direct marketers have emerged that use the lack of a channel to create a new price point. Existing competitors often cannot sell directly at competitive price points without impacting their existing distribution/reseller/retail channel. An example of this is Visio, which used Costco as a low-markup/high volume channel to create a pricing point significantly below that of their Japanese and Korean competitors. Visio accomplished what many thought was impossible, creating a new American television company.

Building the Competitive Box

Figure 15-2 shows a chart for Genesys, a company in the contact center space. Contact Centers are the sites that host the annoying phone agents that call you or answer your calls. The equipment to run these systems is highly specialized. Genesys is a mid-size competitor in the contact center space that is positioned with a highly functional offer that is relatively high priced.

Genesys has a set of direct competitors, which break into two distinct camps. On the left are competitors that only sell contact center equipment and do not sell traditional voice or PBX systems. On the right, Cisco and Avaya sell contact centers, but also sell the core PBX.

Oracle and SAP sell complex business management software, including Customer Relationship Management (CRM) and are delivering more and more of the contact center functionality in their offer, so they are limiting the market as the systems competitors. On the bottom, a new set of cloud-only based offers at

	• Oracle, • SAP 3%		
• Aspect • Interactive Intelligence • Other **21%**	Genesys **10%**		• Avaya • Cisco **60%**
•Cloud based CC (Five 9's) •Web Self-Service •Unstructured Chat Environments **6%**			

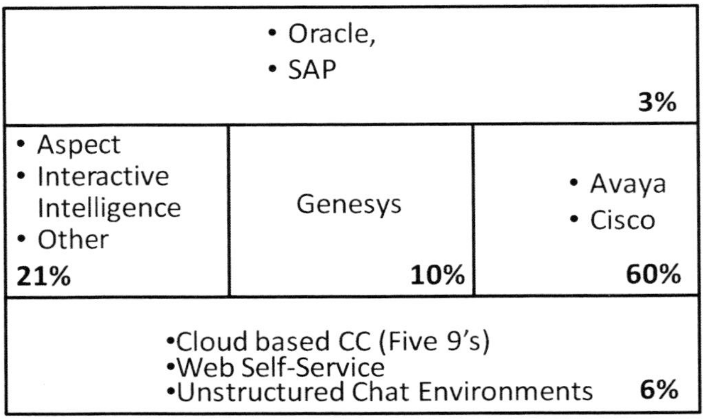

Figure 15-2 Genesys Competitive Box

significantly reduced price points as well as web self service and chat built into web sites is also reducing the market as Price Competitors. Note that this market assumes that the middle players will all have some form of cloud (or hosted) offers, so this represents offers from companies that are exclusively cloud-based. As this market evolves, the cloud percentage will be much larger than the share of the exclusive cloud providers.

This box clearly indicates the four challenges that Genesys faces in the market. In addition to the competitors, the relative market share of each box is shown as well (this is only for illustration in this example - the numbers are not actual for any given year). Later we will scale the boxes to competitor market share size, but for this part of the process, merely knowing the relative share is sufficient.

To build a box for your company, start with putting it in the middle of the box. Figure 15-3 is provided to enable you to do this exercise.

System Competitors 1. ____ 2. ____ 3. ____ ___%		
Similar Type 1 1. ____ 2. ____ 3. ____ ___%	Your Company ____ ___%	1. ____ 2. ____ 3. ____ Similar Type 2 ___%
Price Competitors 1. ____ 2. ____ 3. ____ ___%		

Figure 15-3 Competitive Box Template

Start by writing your company in the middle. Now think about your direct competitors, the companies that sell the same products as you, in the same channels or geographies. There are two areas for similar competitors, because often these types of companies may fall into two different camps. For example, if your competition is regional, one might be the US competitors and the other those in another geography. Alternatively it may be driven by product mix. For example, if you were Panasonic, you might want to put Sharp on one side as they make televisions, but not stereos and DVD players, and Pioneer on the other as they make stereos and DVDs and do not make TVs. You will notice that I just left room for 3 for each category, if there are more, just fill them in, though, if you start getting more than this number the market is looking very competitive or very fractured.

The next step is up to you. If you can clearly define the systems competitors, start entering them. You may find that the system competitors are a much smaller number, especially if you are a mid-size company. You can often recognize a systems competitor as someone that wins because they are providing a broader product set and services beyond your capability. I was talking with an IBM salesperson recently, and he made the point that they only win when the customer is looking for capabilities that the traditional vendors do not have. Typically this is around integration and a system value. For those vendors who would lose to IBM in that scenario, IBM is the system competitor.

Similarly, begin to enter your price competitors. You can generally identify these as the competitors who, when you hear they are being considered, would cause you to change your strategy and emphasize value and capability and stop selling if the customer indicates that the lower value of the price competitor meets their needs.

After entering the competitors in a way that makes sense, add up the market share of the competitors in each box and enter it on each line where the percentage is as well as yours. The total of the market should be 100%. Generally, the others in the market will fall into one of the direct competitive boxes to the right or left of the analyzed company.

Competitive Pressure

The Competitive Box defines four competitive interfaces. Using this you can define how your company competes on each of the interfaces. Each competitive interface has a combination of pressures. Some will be greater than others today, some will change in the future. If we use the Genesys example from the previous figure, we can map where the greatest competitive pressures come from. In Figure 15-4, competitive pressures are added, represented as a number of arrows forcing in, squeezing the Genesys market share. The more arrows, the larger the competitive pressure and threat. One way to look at competitive pressure is to see it as defining

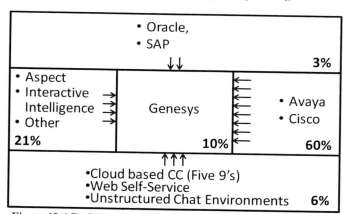

Figure 15-4 Defining Competitive Pressure

where the company is losing revenue and market share to a specific competitor group.

Another factor to consider is the market size of the competitor and where share can be grown. In this example, both the top and bottom competitors, while introducing a change in the market, are relatively small market share today. Even a significant win or growth in those spaces will have little impact on the company from an overall revenue perspective.

This chart demonstrates that the largest competitive threat comes from Avaya and Cisco as part of a total communications solution. The similar contact center only solution players are second, while the emerging cloud solutions and web/self service are third. Finally, the systems companies are the smallest threat. You can use the space around the center box in Figure 15-3 to add arrows around your company box.

Competing on the Interfaces

Now that the interfaces have been defined, it is possible to define a general strategy for competition on each interface. Competing on an interface can be done in one of four ways:

Grow - an interface where the company will focus to increase market share and take share form one or more of the competitors on that interface

Defend - an interface where the company will not focus to grow/take share, but will focus to assuring that share is maintained versus this competitor group

Ignore - In some cases one of the interface may be appropriate to ignore as it represents a relative low threat due to market conditions

Partner - this is an interface where the company sees partnering as the right answer to co-opt the competition. Generally partnering only happens on the upper and lower interfaces, not the horizontal ones. One critical point of partnering is that it often becomes an exchange of allowing the partner to have a certain percentage of share (or another view is wallet share) in exchange for advantage on the other interfaces.

It is interesting to contrast the 4 ways of competing with the five allocations of troop strength as suggested by Sun Tzu (see Chapter 14). The determination of which interfaces to focus on are a balance of the opportunity to grow and the ability to compete. Figure 15-5 shows a

Philip Edholm

potential plan for Genesys to compete on the interfaces.

In this case, none of the interfaces are to be ignored, Trying to compete equally on all interfaces is generally not a plan to succeed. It is better to have a couple of clear focuses.

On the system competitor interface, Genesys should focus on partnering with the large software vendors to optimize their mutual customers. By focusing not on growing, but on retaining share

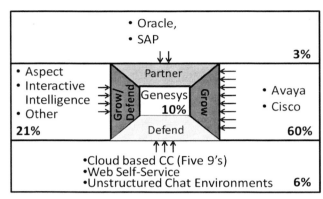

Figure 15-5 Defining a Strategy in the Competitive Box

through partnering, this is the tight path. This partnering can be leveraged on other interfaces to create affinity in customers using these software elements.

On the lower side, cloud and Web/Chat, the goal is to defend by offering a cloud-based solution and to incorporate chat into the product. Rather than focus on opportunities where web or chat is the predominant requirement, Genesys could focus on the larger solutions that give it advantage and on extending its offer through a cloud service.

Obviously Avaya and Cisco, with 60% market share between them, are the major focus for growth and expansion. While these are the most powerful competitors, they represent the only opportunity for significant growth.

The last interface is the one on the left with similar companies that do not sell the underlying communications systems. This is an interface that needs to be analyzed carefully because each individual competitor is smaller that Genesys and may be focused on segments that may or may not be approachable. If resources are limited, this may be best treated as defend, or, if weakness is seen in the competitors, it could be a grow.

In Figure 15-7 you can define your situation for the competitive interfaces. As with the discussion of Genesys, consider each of the boundaries and where you would focus your energy to maximize your growth and market share and to minimize erosion.

Competitive Factors

The next focus is to include the competitive factors that will enable success on each of the interfaces. These can be either strengths of the company or weaknesses. They can be based on any factor that will generate advantage (product, technology, channel, price, etc). Each interface becomes an analyzed model of how to compete based on both the interface and the

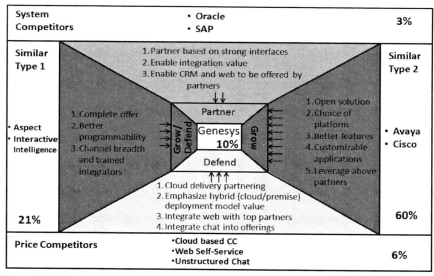

Figure 15-6 Competitive Factors

competitors and your decision as the level of competitive focus to give it. While a single chart can represent a high level view, a compete SWOT (Strengths, Weaknesses, Opportunities and Threats) analysis should be done for each interface. For illustrative purposes, Figure 15-6 shows a completed Competitive Box for Genesys.

Added into the previous information is how each competitive interface is to be addressed, albeit at a high level in this view. The inclusion of all of the data from the earlier analysis enable as a complete view of the competitive environment in a single diagram. In Figure 15-7, all of the information you have built can be entered. As with the other charts in the book, the URL

Philip Edholm

references in the last Chapter will enable you to download the figures in PowerPoint format.

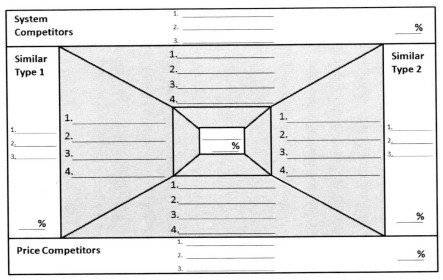

Figure 15-7 Complete Competitive Box Template

Mapping Share with the Competitive Box

The completive box can be used to map the share using an area mapping also. Area mapping makes the size of each of the boxes equivalent to something, in this case it is set to be equivalent to market share. So any box will have an area equivalent to the market share percentage, so a competitor equal to the compared company will have the same area, one with double the share will have double the area. This is of most interest as it can be used to demonstrate how transitions in the market will impact the competitive landscape in the future. It can be a powerful tool in scenario analysis. For example, if we map the Genesys competitive box and assume that this is the box for 2012, it would appear as shown in Figure 15-8.

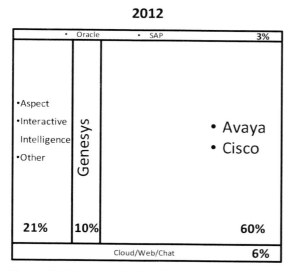

Figure 15-8 Mapping Market Share onto the Competitive Box

The next step is to build a set of assumptions about what will happen in the market and use these to modify the market share areas as the assumptions occur. Generally, a time frame of 4 or 6 years will make the most sense for this analysis. If you choose a 4 year window, then there will be three maps, today, +2 years and +4 years. For example, if we make a few assumptions about this market:

Oracle and SAP will grow their share of capabilities and functions currently sold by the contact center companies so they will get 12% market share in 2016.

The dedicated cloud vendors and the Web/Chat functions will continue to grow and attack the market from a price and new function and will grow to 15% share by 2016

Cisco and Avaya are both vulnerable due to their size and churn in the installed base that will make many customers available over the next 3 years. This will result in a loss of share to 48% by 2016

The goal for Genesys is to grow market share by 4 points by the end of 2016.

With these four assumptions, the map of the market progression shown in Figure 15-9 was created. It maps the changes assumed above and then

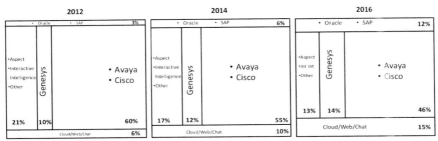

Figure 15-9 2012 to 1026 Share Maps for Genesys

shows the assumptions of how the market will need to progress for Genesys to achieve its goal.

As you can see from the analysis, the only way to achieve the goals if the market assumptions are correct is to essentially have the other vendors on the left lose half their share. If we map an alternative where we make the same assumptions about the encroachment from above and below and assume that the middle companies retain their positions, Figure 15-10 is what the scenario map looks like for Genesys.

As can be seen from these scenarios, having a clear view of how to take

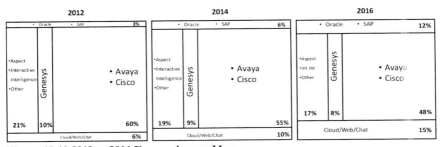

Figure 15-10 2012 to 2016 Encroachment Map

market share from the similar competitors is the only way to grow.

The Competitive Box is a useful tool in defining your strategy and should be used to build a model of how your actions and assumptions will drive share and revenue going forward.

Chapter 16 Death in the Middle

The concept of death in the middle is a simple one. The premise is that the market always embraces either high capability/high price or lowest capability/lowest price and does not allow products or offers in the middle to succeed. There has been significant work close to this area in many business schools, in "Competitive Advantage: Creating and Sustaining Superior Performance" by Michael Porter, he talks about being outside of the norm, but does not clearly talk to why failure in the middle is virtually guaranteed.

Defining the Middle

The middle is the group where you are neither a price or capability leader. Figure 16-1 shows a popular mechanism of mapping offers to price.

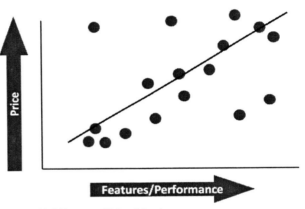

Figure 16-1 Feature/Price Matrix

This clearly shows the challenge that emerges. The line here represents an average of capabilities versus price. Many times Product Management will try to be on this line. The result is shown in Figure 16-2. What emerges is a band of products/offers that are acceptable to the customer. Above this band

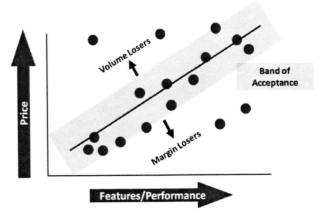

Figure 16-2 The Band of Acceptance

the price/capability ratio reduces volume, below it reduces margin and profit. Assuming that the cost to produce and develop a product has a correlation to the price, then the market ends up being arrayed in this manner. However, within a defined product space, the market actually transitions to what is shown in Figure 16-3.

What happens is that the majority of the customers (this is not always true, but seems to be generically true) buy the lowest cost product or offer that will effectively meet the needs. A smaller segment buys the highest functionality (or the premium brand in marketing parlance), regardless of price. The reasons for these two purchases are based on a variety of human motivations. The low end buyers are motivated by a basic need, the high end buyers by other factors such as prestige, avoidance of replacement, etc. In Chapter 24 "Finding Pain", the concept of why buyers buy different offers will be investigated, but for this section, suffice it to say there are really bipolar buying patterns.

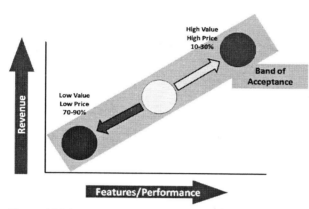

Figure 16-3 Death in The Middle

The challenge is that finding buyers in the middle becomes very difficult. You have to find buyers that want your specific set of incremental features/capabilities and are willing to pay an incremental price for them. Unless you can find a differentiated market space where your position is either at the top or the bottom, the result will be either:

      Exit the space
      Invest to move to the top
      Fall to the bottom
      Redefine the Market

How Death in the Middle Occurs

Each of the four death modes above can be identified through excellent examples.

Exit the space

One potential option is to exit the middle ground. This can either be done by exiting the market altogether or exiting only that part of your product portfolio or offers that are in the middle. This allows you to clarify the positioning of your top and bottom offers. In the late 90s, Sony had three CRT based projectors for video/television in the marketplace. While the lamp based projectors had come into the market, for quality, using CRT tubes (using three beams - red/blue/green) was still the only way to have a really good picture. Sony had three models: the G50 was designed in a relatively small chassis with 7 inch tubes, the G70 was a large chassis with 8 inch tubes and the G90 was a chassis essentially the same size as the G70, but with larger 9 inch tubes. The result was a clear low end product, but the G70 was essentially a G90 with slightly smaller tubes. From a price perspective, the G50 was about $12K, the G90 about $35K and the G70 was in the middle at about $25K. The result was that consumers bought the G50 for home theaters and businesses bought the G90 for boardrooms. The consumers would not pay the $13K upgrade, even though the quality was noticeably better, and no one wanted to save $10K on a boardroom upgrade and risk the quality not being perfect. As a result, the G70 never sold in volume and was discontinued years before the other models.

Invest to move to the top

Investing to move to the top is a dramatic strategy that can be successful. Essentially it requires the company to decide that it is better to be at the top rather than leave the market or be driven to the bottom. A good example of this is Smirnoff. Originally Smirnoff was positioned as a premium brand of vodka. However, Smirnoff faced competition from two sides that ended up putting it in the middle, Low cost brands and house brands defined a new price floor that was below Smirnoff and satisfied the needs of the "drinking for effect" buyer, while new "premium brands such as Stolichnaya and Absolut came into the market. The result was putting Smirnoff in the middle. The response was not to actually move the Smirnoff brand above the premiums, but to introduce a new brand that was intended to be positioned even higher (Ketel One). In the end the

Smirnoff brand moved to the bottom of national brands. Other cases of investing in a product to move it up market, either by product improvements or brand investments have been successful.

Fall to the bottom

The last impact is generally what will happen if neither of the above paths are taken. The middle product/offer will suffer from both low-margins, because it is being discounted to compete with the low price products, and under-investment against the top end products that are generating both equal or higher volume and more margin for investment. The result is essentially self-fulfilling. The product is discounted to win a percentage of the low price space, effectively reducing margins. In an effort to preserve margins, the investment is reduced. In the Smirnoff example above, the Smirnoff brand is now positioned as the low price non-generic and does not try to compete at the premium level. In Nortel, between 2004 and 2006, the data portfolio underwent a significant reduction in capability versus the Cisco premium offer, resulting in a 40-50% relative price premium for the Cisco brand over the Nortel brand. The result was that the investment available made it virtually impossible to keep up with the Cisco investment (this was also driven by the extremely high Cisco customer loyalty). The end result was a loss in market share to both Cisco at the high-end and low end competitors.

Redefine the Market

The other way to change this positioning is to actually redefine the market so that a new space is created. This is a challenging proposition as the new market must be highly isolated, not just a sub-segment. Taking the Vodka example, flavored vodkas can be thought of in this way. Another real change is the creation of the pre-mixed drinks like hard lemonade or the Smirnoff Ice. In this case, the change was from selling actual vodka to selling a pre-mixed drink, that is bought by a very different customer, often a beer buyer looking for a change.

The challenge in redefining is that there is often an attempt to make it based on features or some other customer factor. This is often represented when someone says, "customers will buy our product because we have X and Y, but cost less than the competition that offers Z and A".

Applying Death in The Middle to Technology

The concept of death n the middle can be applied in other areas as well. This is an example in technology and the tablet world. In the world of devices, there are three form factors for devices that can be carried easily other than a traditional PC. One is the pocketable smart phone, the second is a device with a 5 to 7 inch screen, and the third is a device with a 9-11 inch screen. While the later two are called tablets, together they represent three distinct spaces, with the 5-7 inch tablet clearly in the middle. Figure 16-4 show why this is a big issue in the enterprise tablet market.

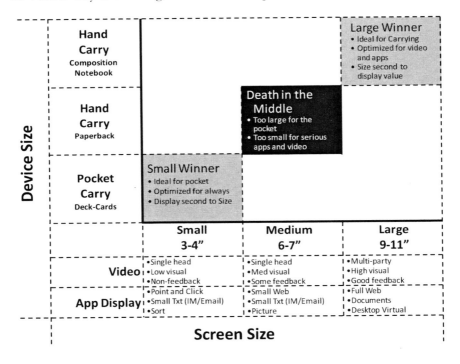

Figure 16-4 The Middle for Tablets in the Enterprise

As can be clearly seen, the combination of screen size and device size lead to a clear segmentation that creates the "Death in the Middle". In screen size, screens 7 inches and smaller are limited to a single head video versus multi-party video, are not large enough to truly see visual expressions, do not have true windowing, do not enable text reading for page views of forms or documents. They also will not enable desktop virtualization in a meaningful way as they are just too small to replicate in any way the experience on a 15-25" PC monitor. To see this effect, using a cut out window of paper will show how little of your PC screen can be seen at 7 inches. It is critical to remember that usable screen is the square of the diagonal measure, so a screen with 9.5" has twice the area of a 7" screen. This is critical as displaying multi-party video or seeing real response expressions in video requires a minimum size. Note that all of the iPhone video screens shown are a single headshot......conversely, any screen larger than about 4" precludes the device from being small enough to fit into a pocket easily. So, devices with both mid and large size screens are relegated to being carried versus being a pocketable device. Figure 16-5 shows a comparison in a video environment of a 7" to a 10.5" screen.

10.5" screen device
UI Screen and Multi-Party Video Conference

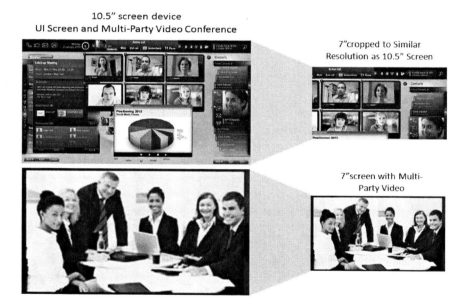

7"cropped to Similar
Resolution as 10.5" Screen

7"screen with Multi-
Party Video

Figure 16-5 Comparison of Different Tablet Sizes versus Delivered Screen Value

It is clear from this view that the 10" screen is much more effective. While a 7" or 4" screen can be used they will not provide the content or visibility. This is why Steve Jobs said that 7" tablets were "dead on arrival" in the company's Q4 2010 earnings call.

Was Goldilocks Wrong?

In the children's fairy tale, Goldilocks decides on the porridge that is in the middle, the smallest chair (which she breaks, indicating that she should have chosen the middle chair), and the medium softness bed. The message of

---

The Story of Goldilocks and the Three Bears

Once upon a time, there was a little girl named Goldilocks. She went for a walk in the forest. Pretty soon, she came upon a house. She knocked and, when no one answered, she walked right in.

At the table in the kitchen, there were three bowls of porridge. Goldilocks was hungry. She tasted the porridge from the first bowl. "This porridge is too hot!" she exclaimed. So, she tasted the porridge from the second bowl. "This porridge is too cold," she said So, she tasted the last bowl of porridge. "Ahhh, this porridge is just right," she said happily and she ate it all up.

After she'd eaten the three bears' breakfasts she decided she was feeling a little tired. So, she walked into the living room where she saw three chairs. Goldilocks sat in the first chair to rest her feet.

"This chair is too big!" she exclaimed. So she sat in the second chair. "This chair is too big, too!" she whined. So she tried the last and smallest chair. "Ahhh, this chair is just right," she sighed. But just as she settled down into the chair to rest, it broke into pieces!

Goldilocks was very tired by this time, so she went upstairs to the bedroom. She lay down in the first bed, but it was too hard. Then she lay in the second bed, but it was too soft. Then she lay down in the third bed and it was just right. Goldilocks fell asleep. As she was sleeping, the three bears came home.

"Someone's been eating my porridge," growled the Papa bear.
"Someone's been eating my porridge," said the Mama bear.
"Someone's been eating my porridge and they ate it all up!" cried the Baby bear.
"Someone's been sitting in my chair," growled the Papa bear.
"Someone's been sitting in my chair," said the Mama bear.
"Someone's been sitting in my chair and they've broken it all to pieces," cried the Baby bear.

They decided to look around some more and when they got upstairs to the bedroom, Papa bear growled, "Someone's been sleeping in my bed,"

"Someone's been sleeping in my bed, too" said the Mama bear
"Someone's been sleeping in my bed and she's still there!" exclaimed Baby bear.

Just then, Goldilocks woke up and saw the three bears. She screamed, "Help!" And she jumped up and ran out of the room. Goldilocks ran down the stairs, opened the door, and ran away into the forest. And she never returned to the home of the three bears.

THE END

---

this story, beyond the silliness of the bear's house, is that the middle ground satisfies. If Goldilocks had chosen the middle chair it would not have broken. Author Christopher Booker (Booker, 2005) characterizes this as the "dialectical three", where "the first is wrong in one way, the second in another or opposite way, and only the third, in the middle, is just right."

Booker continues "This idea that the way forward lies in finding an exact middle path between opposites is of extraordinary importance in storytelling". This message, that the middle is the right path, may be true in politics, but it will always fail if the two ends have adequate and distinct choices. In fact, the real world argues just the opposite, people either prefer their porridge hot or cold, not in between, and their beds soft or hard, and the smallest chair was the best if it had just been built right.

The message is that we have been led to believe that the middle ground allows the best coverage, when, in the real marketplace it is generally the cemetery of thoughtful ideas.

Chapter 17 A Real Strategic Analysis

I am including in this book the actual strategic planning data that was developed and used in Nortel Enterprise group in the 2006 time frame to define and justify the relationship that Nortel built with Microsoft and was in place until the Avaya acquisition of the Nortel Enterprise Business unit at the end of 2009.[1]

In 2006, Nortel was in a difficult position in the PBX/IP PBX market (telephone systems owned by businesses). The company had a reasonable installed base, but was not winning in new accounts. The convergence of voice and data had created a difficult position in how the company was competing with Cisco. But a big part of the issue was within the customers' organizations. The challenge was that in the IT departments of most organizations, the group that was using and therefore representing the Nortel products was in a weak position. In

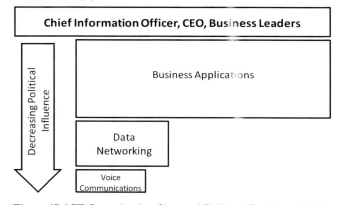

Figure 17-1 IT Organization Size and Political Position - 2006

Figure 17-1, the positions of the three major groups in IT (relative to the Nortel offer) can be seen. The figure shows two dimensions. The distance from the top, where the CIO and Business Leaders are, represents the

---

[1] As Nortel went bankrupt in 2009 and has ceased to operate as a product company and after Avaya acquired the assets of the Nortel enterprise business they decided not to extend the relationship, all of the information presented herein is moot and therefore can be made public without violating any company privacy agreements. As all of the planning that was part of this analysis was through 2012, any proprietary data is now irrelevant.

relative political power of the organization. As you can see, the Business Applications group is driving the business, so the teams that deliver them have the greatest power. The Data Networking group, which has evolved to be the basis for delivering business apps and mobility is less powerful, but is still more powerful than the Voice Communications group. The problem is that the latter has become a utility by this point, reflecting that it had moved through all three of the phases discussed in Chapter 35 "The Three Phases of a Technology".

The other dimension is the size of the box. In a typical organization, 80% of the spend in IT was going to Business Applications, 15% to the network, and only about 5% to the Voice Communications. Cisco was working hard to convince the Data Networking teams to position that they should provide the voice and converge using Cisco for voice and data. In the next chapter, "The Competitive Box", we will discuss this positioning a bit more. As the data investment was 3 times that of voice, if faced with making a decision, any either/or decision would naturally favor the larger and more politically connected group in the customer organization. The challenge for Nortel was to develop a strategy that would change this balance. That was done by partnering with a larger vendor in the Business Applications space (Microsoft) and changing the game. This partnership, announced in 2006 as the Innovative Communications Alliance, led to a 2 point gain in market share (over a 12% base) and generated almost 20% of the revenue for the

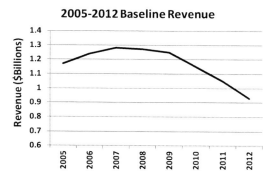

Figure 17-2 Original 2005 to 2012 CS1000 Product Family Revenue Plan

Nortel voice business in 2008. The fundamental change was not in technology, but changing the relationship with the customer. This is a description of how that strategy was arrived and sold to senior management and the board.

The problem that Nortel faced was that the transition from separate voice systems to a converged system that put the voice communications on top

Philip Edholm

of an underlying IP data network had changed the market. While Nortel was retaining its market share versus the traditional competitors, Cisco and new entrants were winning a larger percentage of the new customer opportunities. Figure 17-2 was an actual projection of the revenue in the voice communications business as projected by the Product Management team at the beginning of 2006. This revenue did not include any contact center, SMB, or data networking, but was limited to the voice/PBX solutions called the CS1000 Family.

Analyzing the Market, the Competition and the Customers

Early in 2006, an analysis was done of a number of potential options for changed investment and potential acquisitions. Due to the financial state of the company, it was not realistic to define a strategy based on a major acquisition, therefore the strategy had to be based on investing primarily organically.

One clear point that was seen in the market was that the traditional voice communic ations system, which had converged with the data infrastruct ure, was now beginning to converge

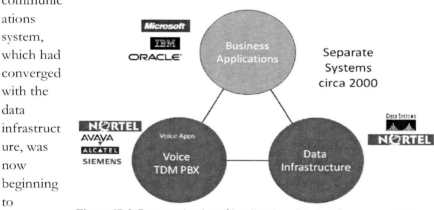

Figure 17-3 Communications/Applications Market Structure - 2000

with the information systems. Figure 17-3 shows what the markets and key players in the three areas of Business Applications, Data Networking Infrastructure, and Voice Communications were in 2000.

As convergence occurred, the Data Infrastructure and the Voice solutions came together as shown in Figure 17-4. Cisco had used the dominant position in the data infrastructure to drive into the VoIP space and was approaching 12% revenue market share. But the big challenge that was

156

coming on the horizon was the convergence of communications and the business applications. For knowledge workers who used computers as personal productivity tools the advent of having communications directly integrated into those tools was a powerful concept. Web conferencing products and IM with presence was beginning to demonstrate the value of bringing these together (what became known as Unified Communications and Collaboration over time). In addition, the advent of web services and SOA was opening the door to enabling business process applications to use communications to have significant impacts on streamlining business process. What became clear was that this was

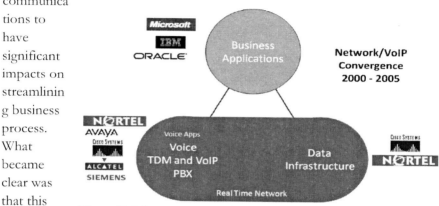

Figure 17-4 Communications/Applications Market Structure - 2006

pointing to another convergence: business applications and communications. What was clear in the industry in early 2006 was that this was going to be a significant area of change for the industry and that the decision about who would own all of the functionality between traditional communications and the business applications was in question. Cisco, intent on growing their share of the overall IT spend had launched a set of plans and standards to make their network the basis of the next generation architecture. Meanwhile, both IBM and Microsoft, along with Oracle, were putting in place frameworks to deliver much of this new middle ground in their portfolios. In question were services such as IM, presence, SOA frameworks, etc. In meetings with the business software companies, it became clear that they, especially Microsoft, saw Cisco as a threat and wanted to reduce the network to a transport, not a control point.

In the end we saw two market scenarios going forward, one where the network would be dominant, and one where the business applications would be dominant. Figure 17-5 shows how we looked at the comparison

157

Philip Edholm

of these two options.

As we analyzed the two options, it became clear that the upper option was not achievable for Nortel. An outline of a strategy to enable the

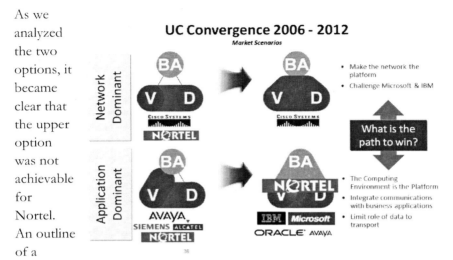

Figure 17-5 Nortel Strategic Options - 2006

business applications vendors to provide a set of intermediate components would have three key strategic values:

By aligning with the applications vendors, we would be changing the game for decisions. As was discussed in Figure 14-2, while the relationship map favored Cisco in the convergence of the voice and data, the investment and relationship favored the applications vendors in the convergence of voice/data and business applications.

Cisco was in a position to out-invest Nortel by at least 2-5 times and with their ability to acquire companies this was even greater, potentially 10 to 1. A strategy that focused on big partners would minimize this advantage. The business applications vendors would become System Competitors if we did not make them into partners and this would further limit the market opportunity.

With this in mind, we proceeded to an analysis of what the market would look like from 2006 to 2012 and how a relationship could change that positioning.

Using the Competitive Box

After defining how that the transformation was occurring in the market, we used the Competitive box to project how this would impact Nortel, first if we did nothing and then if we developed a strategic partnership with Microsoft. The first step was to project how the convergence of business applications and communications would be adopted. This was a major forecasting exercise that segmented both companies and users into groups based on their use of computing and the adoption. The US Department of Labor statistics was used t o develop detailed adoption models that enabled projecting how the market would change. There is not space her for a detailed review of this process, but it dew some basic conclusions. Figure 17-6 shows the Nortel Competitive Box as of the beginning of 2006.

The traditional PBX/voice competitors are on the left, and Cisco, the new entrant is on the right. As Nortel had a data infrastructure product,

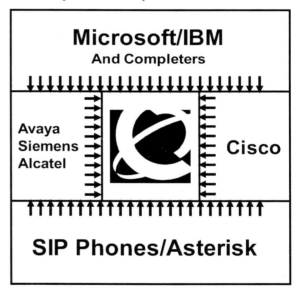

Figure 17-6 Nortel Voice Competitive Box - 2006

Cisco could be considered equivalent. At the top was the new emerging companies of IBM and Microsoft. Microsoft had announced an IM based adjunct to its Office suite called OCS that was also moving to be voice enabled. IBM had announced a collaboration platform called SameTime that had IM and a number of other features. The reference in the figure to completers was a clear interpretation that Microsoft and to a lesser extent IBM were creating a platform and expected others in the marketplace to provide the wrap around of products and services to deliver their vision. for example, Microsoft had engaged a small number of companies to build desktop telephones for their OCS system and was actively seeking services organizations to enable deployments. At the bottom, there were emerging a number of new entrants into the market. Open Source products like Asterisk were enabling very low cost deployments and a number of companies were talking about delivering telephony devices using SIP and other standards.

As the analysis progressed, a scenario emerged that the management team believed was the scenario that Nortel needed to plan to. The scenario had a few salient points:

Cisco was going to be able to exploit their data infrastructure position to a leadership position in VoIP through 2012. The team projected that Cisco would get to between 20 and 25 points of share by 2012. In fact, Cisco reached 30 percent share in early 2011.

The Open Source and SIP telephony based solutions would evolve to 20% share in 2012. While this is not completely come to pass, it is generally viewed that the non-traditional voice systems, including cloud using open SIP phones is now about 10-15% of the market.

Finally, Microsoft and IBM would change the market by taking significant share. It was anticipated that by 2012 35% of the revenue would be driven to these vendors. What is less clear in the models is that the overall revenue is changing. Where in 2006 the revenue was limited to voice and communications, now this market includes the IM, web conferencing, and other elements, even extending to video and document collaboration. When looked at in that larger light, the share that Microsoft has is much larger than only its share in voice. IN fact, over 70% of enterprises today have adopted some form of Microsoft communications system.

By applying these assumptions to the Competitive box, based on 2006 market shares and the projections, Figure 17-7 shows what could happen in the market and what would be required to maintain a 15% market share.

For Nortel to maintain its 15% share, essentially all the traditional competitors would have to almost go out of business. Even at that point,

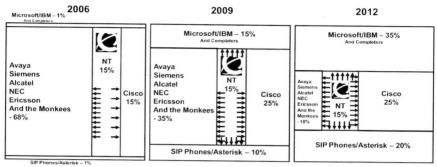

Figure 17-7 2006-2012 Nortel Voice Market Share Analysis

Nortel would only be a 15% share holder and would not be a significant force in the market.

However, based on the work outlined earlier, by creating a deep partnership, Nortel could change the boundaries. Figure 17-8 shows how, by partnering to become a "completer" of the total Microsoft solution and driver of a major business application like Microsoft, Nortel could dramatically change the market. Such a partnership would have three impacts in the competitive box: It would dramatically improve competitiveness against Cisco, resulting in Nortel taking share that would have been won by Cisco.

It would be a knock-out punch against the other competitors in the space by aligning Nortel with the key strategic partner of almost 60% of the enterprises.

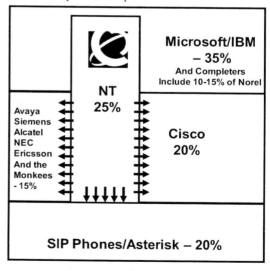

Figure 17-8 Growing Nortel Through Microsoft

It would open the door to Nortel being the preferred vendor for Microsoft real-time, enabling Nortel to get a significant percentage of the revenue that was in the new top quadrant.

However, the strategy was not without risk. A rapid adoption of the Microsoft solution would reduce Nortel revenues in the future years. Figure 17-9 shows the actual revenue modeling presented in the executive review of the strategy.

The baseline data here was the same as predicted by the Product Management team and shown in Figure 17-9. The solid black line shows the pre-strategy revenue prediction from the product team. The lowest line shows the anticipated revenue erosion of the partnership. The next line up labeled Microsoft additional shows the anticipated revenue line with additional revenue from the new quadrant. As can be seen, while it is significantly better than the baseline, it is still not aggressive. comparing the plans, the increase of $100-200K of revenue would be a 1-2 point increase in share in the $8B market.

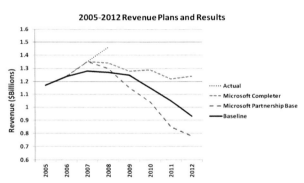

Figure 17-9 Nortel 2006-2012 Revenue in Strategic Plan

Based on this strategy, in July of 2006, Nortel entered into a partnership with Microsoft that was positioned as the most significant partnership for Microsoft next to HP (their largest partner by far). In the announcement of the Innovative Communications Alliance (ICA), Steve Ballmer enthused about how the companies would transform the industry, The result was dramatic. Overnight Nortel was acknowledged as the leader in the new space. Customers that had not considered Nortel before as a vendor to work with as part of their strategy to leverage their huge Microsoft investments came to see Nortel as the preferred vendor. Over the next two years, the momentum moved from a few hundreds of deals to thousands.

In 2008, the ICA relationship and Microsoft were critical in fully 20% of the Nortel enterprise revenue. Nortel market share grew over 2 points due to the ICA and its impact by the end of 2008. This growth is shown by the top line on Figure 17-9 that ends at 2008. Nortel's bankruptcy in 2009, caused not by the enterprise business, but by a variety of other factors, interrupted the story, but the strategy was well on the way to success.

Conclusions

The strategy described above is one that takes a cue from the book "The Innovators Dilemma" by Clayton Christensen (Christensen, 2003). His premise is that innovative companies often miss the next change and transformation as they try to protect their installed base and products. The strategy by Nortel to embrace the Business Applications vendors, particularly Microsoft was both bold and dangerous. While the short term results were very positive, the question remained, what of the longer term impact? Many times I was asked by customers, partners and analysts why this was the right strategy to pursue.

To answer this question, I would often relate two stories that capture, for me, the danger of thinking that you can resist change and how thinking about change in the old paradigm can influence your view of the future.

The first is the "story" of the company that made buggy whips at the end of the 1800s. With the advent of the automobile, the son was trying to convince his father, the company founder, that they needed to move from making buggy whips to steering wheels. In keeping with the concept of knowing what business you are in, the son saw a logical progression from buggy whips to steering wheels as advanced control mechanisms for vehicles. After much cajoling, the father decided to try out the new steering wheel for himself. The next day, after thoroughly using the steering wheel himself he declared, "well it works pretty well, but the horse is really bruised."

The second story comes from the early days of the technology business. In 1984, one of the larger computer companies in the industry was Wang Laboratories, a company that made word processing systems. Wang had taken the concept of a desktop system and optimized it to be used with a shared printer, primarily to replace typewriters. for groups like lawyers, offices, and others that typically produced lots of specialized documents and reports, the word processor was a boon. Wang was very successful at the time with over $3B in revenue and 33,000 employees. However, by 1986, the PC, led by IBM. Microsoft and Apple was changing the industry. It was becoming clear that a word processing software package could easily run on the PC. Imagine for a moment you were a senior executive at Wang at the time and one of the strategy team came and proposed that Wang should sell its word processing software on the PC. As a business leader concerned with short term revenues and outlooks, the obvious answer was "NO". The result was catastrophic, as Wang went bankrupt in 1992. Imagine an alternative if the management team at Wang had accepted that the world would change and they could not stop it. If Wang had introduced the Wang word processing software directly to the IBM PC then they would have instantly been the leader in that segment. By talking to customers, they would have seen that "suite" of applications was desired. Both Lotus and Harvard graphics were within a few miles of Wang. By acquiring these products and paying attention to what was coming on the Macintosh. Wang could have created its own API As the combination of the three most popular apps at the time would have meant that Wang would have been the dominant desktop productivity vendor, the Office suite from Microsoft might not have happened. If business apps vendors choose to build to the Wang "Panes" interface instead of the Microsoft version (as Wang Panes would also run on Unix), one could see a very different market today where Wang is a $30B company, and Microsoft is $5B and going out of business being relocated by Linux and Android.

The point of both of these stories is simple, not understanding the changes that are coming and are beyond your control will kill any business. If you do not define the future, other will and the result will not be pretty. Think outside the box and find the future.

Sales

I once worked for a salesman who had become president of the company and he often said "nothing happens until you get an order". His point was that the art and act of selling is crucial to a enterprise. While I would suggest that all other areas of business are equally important, the selling area has a number of critical points and some of these lead into marketing as well.

Chapter 18 Three Rules of Sales

Many years ago, I went into sales at the suggestion of the Sales VP in a company who told me that you could not understand how it is to be a salesman unless you have actually carried a bag. While my heart lies in technology and strategy, I became the number one salesman in the company and later ran a North American sales force that exceeded goals. Through the years I have run into a large number of managers that are in positions to manage and influence sales, but who have never had the experience of having their livelihood directly dependent on their own selling efforts. These Three Rules have been my way of communicating the core values necessary to understand and evaluate activities around sales organizations. They have withstood the test of time and have been effective for many years. I regularly talk to salespeople about this topic using the Three Rules and have had universal agreement that they do, in fact, describe sales and the sales management challenges accurately.

Rule 1: Sales People are Like Amoeba

Amoeba are simple creatures, they move towards food and flee from pain. Sales people are exactly the same, they do things to optimize their financial rewards and minimize getting yelled at or having problems with management. As with amoeba, when the sugar and pain are aligned so they both move the amoeba in a specific direction, all works well. The problems arise when the sugar and pain begin to be at different angles. Then the motion becomes much less defined and more random. The worst thing you can do is to get the sugar and pain aligned opposite each other so that when the amoeba moves to the sugar it receives pain. The amoeba will eventually quiver and die: the salesperson goes and plays golf. Some refer to this as salespeople being "coin operated", but I believe there are other factors that influence behavior in many cases beyond pure money.

The ramifications of this rule are profound. Given two products, one easy to sell and one hard, absent any encouragement, the salesperson will always focus on the easier. For example, in the mid-2000s, Nortel had a great voice communications product and a challenging data networking product. For the company, the greatest value was when both were sold, but it was far harder to sell data, so the salespeople would revert to making the easier sale. As there was no incentive to sell the harder product, the sales team focused where they could optimize the money. The result was a significant loss of share in the data networking space.

Another critical challenge is the transition from an installed base sale to a new product area. In this case, the installed base sale will generate short term volume, but the new evangelical sale is critical to the company's long term success. If the new product does not take off in the market, the company will lose its position and shrink significantly. The salesperson who sells an evangelical product and achieves the company goal, but misses his overall quota has failed and will soon be out of a job. On the other hand, the sales person who focuses only on the existing products can be seen as being a great success in pure revenue numbers. Aligning all elements of the compensation and rewards range to driving the sale force to achieving the overall goals is complicated and hard work, but is essential for success. Just booking revenue is not enough, the combination of product, customer, geographic, and vertical mix must match the longer term strategy of the company.

Aligning these elements requires two major considerations: 1. can this be achieved within a singular group of salespeople or 2. does it require creation of a separate sales group. Key considerations in this analysis are whether there is a strong correlation between existing customers and the new offer (which tends to drive towards having a singular customer interface) and how challenging the difference in skills are between the offers. One way to manage this is to have a focus group in the new product area that serves as an overlay. However, even an overlay requires motivation built into the compensation system to assure a level of focus in finding new opportunities.

One clear way to define this process is to clearly lay out the goals of the sales team beyond a basic revenue number. Then define the incentive mechanisms to assure that the results are clearly defined in the steps to achieve the goal. For example, if the goal is to have 2 customers for the new product for each salesperson, defining a plan where the accelerators of income can only be achieved if the goals of having 2 new product customers have been achieved.

Philip Edholm

Rule 2: Sales People Live in Mortal Fear of the Funnel

For most sales people, their funnel is the dominant aspect of their lives. If you have one that is well defined and working, you are in heaven: if you do not, you have to get one. If you ask a salesperson about their funnel and they say it is great with clear visibility, they are saying that they know where their income is coming from. The key is that a salesperson with a visible funnel is very hard to "move" from their role. If a salesperson has a good funnel and gets a recruiting call, they generally know that the new company will not give them a funnel: they will have to build it. And building a funnel is hard work and is made more difficult through the rejection and stress of building the relationships. Companies should evaluate changes in the organization and structure of the sales organization to understand the psychological impact of funnel changes built into any action.

For example, in 2000 the organization I was in moved from a geographic sales organization model to one totally built on vertical industry categories. The result was that the entire sales force was reorganized into teams around verticals (Manufacturing, Financial, Education, Healthcare, etc.). The goal of the exercise was to make the salespeople more relevant to the customers by giving them clear focus in a vertical industry. This would assure that the salespeople were familiar with the business requirements of the vertical and would be more effective at linking the products they were selling to clear business value to the customer.

However, in the planning of this exercise, there was little thought given to the funnel for the salespeople. A typical geographic salesperson in for example Cleveland Ohio, would have had 5-10 accounts within a reasonable distance of Cleveland. After the reorganization, that same salesperson might have become part of the financial vertical and have financial accounts in Cleveland, Cincinnati, Indianapolis and even Chicago. From a funnel perspective, this resulted in many of the salespeople losing 80-90% of their funnel accounts. In the 9 months after this change, there was over 30% attrition in the sales force, and to make things worse it tended to be in the top performers.

While it is not directly tied to the funnel, this reorganization also had two other impacts that had a significant negative impact on both revenue/earnings and morale. First, just as the funnels had changed, so had the faces that were calling on the customers. The same 80-90% churn that was seen in the funnel applied to the customers, as the salesperson they dealt with every day were reassigned. While the transition of an account from one to another salesperson is common, it is rare that over 80% of the accounts transition in a short period. The result is a huge strain on both the sales force and the customers and generally results in some lost customers and lost relationships. This can result in lost customers or deals and orders being pushed out as the customers builds confidence in the new relationships. Another less obvious change is the increase in travel resulting from the new vertical focus. For example, the Cleveland salesperson, who previously did very little travel, is now travelling 1-2 days per week. The result is an increase in cost of travel and a decrease in effectiveness.

Rule 3: All a Salesperson Controls is Their Time

Salespeople do not control the company, the products, the customers, the budgets, the economy, or the phases of the moon. The only thing they really control is their time. How they allocate their time is the largest control they have over their success (in addition to their own skills). The average salesperson can do 1-3 sales calls per day. This is dependent on the territory, the customer type, etc. In New York City on Wall Street it may be 3+: flying between customers in Kansas, it may be only 1. There are about 150 selling days per year (after removing vacations, office, training, sales meetings, and other events). This means the average salesman can make between 150-450 face to face "calls" per year. For purposes of analysis, let us assume 350 calls per year. If we further assume that 75 of the 350 calls are to be made prospecting for new customers, following up new leads, qualifying opportunities, etc., this means there are about 275 real sales calls per year. In the marketing section of the book, this is defined as dis-qualifying customers, that is the time and activities that are spent deciding that a prospect is not worth spending the time trying to sell. The next is to identify how many calls are to be spent selling to prospects that do not become customers. If we further assume that this is another 75 calls, then we are left with 200 calls that actually generate revenue. By dividing the quota of the salesperson by the number of calls, we can calculate the revenue per call. For example, with a quota of $4M and 200 calls, each sales call has to generate $20,000 in revenue to achieve the goal. A customer that the salesperson calls on each week for an average of 45 weeks would need to generate revenue of $900K for it to be in line with goal achievement.

This rule allows a very simple way of understanding revenue generation and territory planning. It also can be used to understand how to manage account time (if the account described above is only buying $250K, the salesperson can only visit once per month). Another key insight is that the goal of optimizing sales calls is a companywide activity. In many companies I have heard the phrase "everybody sells", and this is true in two ways. Everyone should know and be ready to sell to the customer, but equally (and maybe more) important, everybody impacts the number of sales call your teams can make. If you expect the sales team to generate their own presentations, proposals, etc., the result will be fewer sales calls. Unless they are superstars, the end result is less revenue. A continual improvement program of defining and optimizing the number of sales calls per representative is critical to sales success.

Applying the Three Rules

If you are a sales professional, the three rules discussed here should be clear. However, if you are not a sales professional and you have responsibility for programs or events that have to be driven by a sales force, use these rules to analyze the potential effectiveness of what you are asking of the sales team. Use the rules to think through how to accelerate your sales teams effectiveness.

Chapter 19 Time Based Sales Management

This chapter builds on the third rule of sales, the only thing a salesperson controls is their time. With this as the basis, then it is clear that managing and allocating time to the task of the sales process is potentially an effective way to manage a sales organization.

In the late 80s I took over a sales organization that was in significant distress. The team was not only dramatically missing their goals, but was missing forecasts by 30-50% within a quarter, or even a month. In working through the challenges, it became clear that we had no clear mechanism to define how we were investing our time versus the required outcomes to meet our overall goals. I instituted a clear process for each salesperson to work with their manager and define how they were going to spend their "time" represented as sales calls. They started by defining their stretch goals for growth in their installed base accounts and then proportioned the remaining calls to achieve the necessary flow of new business. This becomes a combination of direct calls for "disqualifying" leads and for actual selling. This process should be tightly linked into the Market flow process defined in Chapter 26.

Figure 19-1 shows a methodology for using this planning for three different typical large sale business opportunities. This is for large sales where the annual quota is high, such as in the information technology area or large equipment. The values could be easily changed to reflect other business models as well. The "Explanation Ref Number" correlates to the descriptions below that define how each value is defined and used. Each example reflects a slightly different business model or state of the territory. Example one is a mid-size sale predominantly with the installed base. Example 2 is a slightly smaller scale sale with a relatively larger growth component in new sales. Example 3 is a larger sale with a relatively large installed base and large revenue/low volume sales. Comparing the examples demonstrates how focus in sales changes with different revenue/business models using these techniques.

The model assumes that some things are givens: the quota goal, the number of sales calls, the mix between new and existing customers, the ratios of success in disqualifying and selling new customers, and the average revenue for sales. These are all assumed for this analysis, to do the same for another situation requires developing those assumptions.

Annual Revenue Planning Examples					
	Explanation Ref Number		Example 1	Example 2	Example 3
Basic Data	1	Annual Quota	$ 4,000,000	$ 2,500,000	$ 3,500,000
	2	Planned Direct Sales Calls	300	200	350
	3	Required Disqualifications per sales opp	5	5	5
	4	Sales Call per disqualification	4	4	4
	5	Revenue effectiveness (calls/$New / calls/$Existing)	0.75	0.75	0.75
Existing Account Planning	6	Existing Annuity Accounts	10	5	6
	7	Average Stretch Revenue per Existing Account	$ 250,000	$ 200,000	$ 300,000
	8	Total Revenue Plan from Existing Accounts	$ 2,500,000	$ 1,000,000	$ 1,800,000
New Account Planning	9	Revenue from New Accounts	$ 1,500,000	$ 1,500,000	$ 1,700,000
	10	Average Revenue per New Account	$300,000	$250,000	$500,000
	11	Required New Accounts	5	6	3
	12	Required Disqualifications/Lost Opportunities	25	30	17
	13	Required Disqualification/Lost Sales Calls	100	120	68
Sales Call Allocation	14	Available Selling Calls	200	80	282
	15	Relative value of new revenue based on effectiveness	$ 2,000,000	$ 2,000,000	$ 2,266,667
	16	Total "equivalent" revenue	$ 4,500,000	$ 3,000,000	$ 4,066,667
	17	Average revenue per sales call	$ 22,500	$ 37,500	$ 14,421
	18	Average sales calls per existing customer	11	5	21
	19	Average Sales calls for new customers (plus effectiveness)	18	9	46
	20	Actual revenue per sales call for new customers	$ 16,875	$ 28,125	$ 10,816

Figure 19-1 Revenue Planning Types

Explanations by Ref Number:

1 - Annual Quota - this is the total revenue that the sales role is expected to produce. If there is a desire for a cushion this can be greater than the actual quota.

2 - Planned Direct Sales Calls - this is the number of direct face to face calls the specific salesperson is committed to doing in the course of the year. This should be derived off the calculated selling days based on the other activities in the company.

3 - Required Disqualifications/lost opportunities per sales opportunity - As discussed in the market based business planning, this is the number of face to face calls required to get to a new sales opportunity that is actually closed. This includes both the disqualification and initial selling to lost opportunities.

4 - *Sales Call per disqualification* - These are the number of sales calls made on lost opportunities as well as calls made on accounts that are determined to not be qualified. They are lumped together her as an average.

5 - *Revenue effectiveness (calls/$New / calls/$Existing)* - This is a representation of the relative ration of effort to get a new sale to a new customer versus selling to an existing account. The relative 75% shown in this analysis says that it takes 75% of the effort to get a $ of revenue from an existing account as from a new account (or the new is 33% harder...). As in 4 and 5 above, these numbers need to be based on experience in the specific market, but once derived they are easy to understand.

6 - *Existing Annuity Accounts* - the number of existing accounts that are planned to generate revenue in the quota year.

7 - *Average Stretch Revenue per Existing Account* - the planned average stretch revenue target for the above annuity accounts that this salesperson supports.

8 - *Total Revenue Plan from Existing Accounts* - the total revenue (#6 x #7 above) that is planned to come from existing customers.

9 - *Revenue from New Accounts* - The revenue required from new customers to meet the goal. This is calculated by subtracting the existing revenue (#8) from the total revenue goal (#1).

10 - *Average Revenue per New Account* - This is the estimate of the average revenue that a new account will generate based on the specific products the company sells.

11 - *Required New Accounts* - this is the required new account revenue (#9) divided by the average revenue per new account (#10).

This is the number of new customers that must be won to meet the quota goals.

12 - *Required Disqualifications/Lost Opportunities* - This an estimate of how many accounts will have to be met with or sold to some level to get to the actual wins described above. It is a combination of disqualifying meetings and lost selling opportunities. In the words of one salesperson, these are the frogs that must be "kissed" to get to the prize.

13 - *Required Disqualification/Lost Sales Calls* - this is an assumption of the average number of calls to either: disqualify an account or go through the selling process far enough to actually determine it was lost. Note that this is an average. In some cases a single call will disqualify a potential prospect, in some cases the loss may come late in the selling process. This number should be derived through an active feedback loop in the sales process where every sales person is required to feedback their level of effort in every opportunity that has direct selling.

14 - *Available Selling Calls* - this is the total number of sales calls available to actually close revenue based on subtraction the Disqualifications/Lost (#13) calls from the total available (#2). These are the sales calls that have to generate actual revenue.

15 - *Relative value of new revenue based on effectiveness* - this is an "artificial" increase in the new revenue value for the sales value calculation that reflects the relative difficulty in the new customer revenue versus existing. It essentially increases the relative time spent on new customers by artificially raising the amount of "revenue" there.

16 - *Total "equivalent" revenue* - this is the sum of the existing revenue (#8) and the "inflated" new revenue (#15). This is used to determine the revenue per sales call that is required

17 - *Average revenue per sales call* - by dividing the total "equivalent revenue (#16) by the available calls to actually generate revenue (#14), the actual required revenue per sales call can be calculated.

18 - *Average sales calls per existing customer* - based on this set of data, this is the average revenue that each customer call must generate in an existing account. It is calculated by dividing the average revenue for an existing customer (#7) by the average revenue per call (#17). As can be seen, for this set of data, the average ranges from 11 to 21 calls per year.

19 - *Average Sales calls for new customers (plus effectiveness)* - This is the calculation of the number of sales calls available to close new customers. It is calculated by dividing the average new customer revenue (with the effectiveness increase - #10/#5) by the average revenue per call (#17). As can be seen, for large relative deals, this can be a large number of calls as in Example 3, while for smaller deal flows it is relatively less.

20 - *Actual revenue per sales call for new customers* - This is the actual revenue generated by each new sales call after the "increase is removed. It is calculated by dividing the actual new account average revenue (#10) by the number of calls (#19)

As can be seen, this simple analysis enables the sales manager to effectively plan and manage the resources utilization. By starting at the macro level across the organization it is an effective way of assuring a match between resources and goals. Using these techniques, I was able to dramatically change the sales performance and within 9 months the sales team was within 3% of actually achieving the goal. A key message here is not to spend all of your time selling to your comfort zone, but to get to where the money is to be made.

Another way of using this technique is to manage time spent within a customer. If we look at Example 1 from the above analysis, the salesperson must generate $22,000 per sales call and has 11 calls per average customer. However, human behavior often causes this to not work. For example, I often have gone with a salesperson to an account. On the drive out the salesperson will enthusiastically say that this customer is by far his/her best customer: they love the company's products, they buy every year, and they are a great reference. I ask the salesperson a simple question: what is the annual revenue and how often do you call on them. Often the answer is "I see them every week at least once, and they booked over $500K last year!!!". Obviously, with at least one call per week and a few extras, the salesperson is seeing this account 50 times in the course of the year. With a target per call revenue goal of $22,000, the customer would need to generate $1.1M to meet the requirements. By spending 25 additional calls on this customer beyond those justified by the revenue model, this salesperson is actually falling behind. It is interesting how many times the salesperson who is selling to his/her comfort zone is the 80% producer....because they wasted time on the defined return.

Finally, analyzing sales time use also helps understand the critical role the overall company plays in achieving sales effectiveness. The company needs to do everything possible to maximize the number of calls made. Anything that reduces the calls per year is bad: anything that increases them is good. If we assume that the average revenue rate per call is $20K, if you can increase the calls from 300 to 400 per year, and increase the "selling" calls from 200 to 300, then the revenue goes from $4M to $6M. Conversely, if the salesperson can only make 100 "selling" calls per year, then either they have to generate $40K per call to make the $4M quota or the actual revenue will be only $2M. The company needs to focus on systems, processes and tools that minimize the time a salesperson spends outside of making sales calls. This can be accomplished by providing tools, selling materials, inside sales help, etc. In one company I was in, the reconciliation of revenues to an account was difficult as the revenue went through channels and the channels did not credibly report the actual end customer. This required the salespeople to "register" their revenue. An analysis showed that salespeople were spending 20% or more of their time on this process. Obviously this reduction in sales calls has a commensurate impact on the productivity and the outcomes. If you reduce the number of sales calls in any of the models shown, you will instantly see that the revenue per call has to go up by a commensurate amount.

Conclusion

With these Three Rules (ameba, funnels and time) and particularly focusing on the third, the process of effectively managing a sales force can be simplified. Also, whenever an action or program is planned, it is simple to just review the Three Rules and make sure that you are not creating a situation where you will violate one of them.

Chapter 20 Value Add Selling Model

The concept of layered value in the sale of products is an extension of Chapter 5 on value add economies. It is taking the same concept and applying it to how people evaluate their purchases, allowing us to better understand how to manage marketing and value messages for the products or services an organization is delivering. In the case of value add selling, there are three layers of selling as shown in Figure 20-1. The key differentiation is what is being sold. The pyramid on the left is the number of products available in each level, while the inverted pyramid on the right is a measure of how long a product must be used and the probability of change requiring it to be discarded. So products with short life cycles and low probability of change are at the bottom, while products with long life cycles and higher probability of change are at the top. For example, products that have long use cycles and low probability of change (for example an electrical outlet) are at the bottom, as are products that have short duration of use (a consumable like soap or toilet paper). This bottom level, where purchases are made based only on physical attributes dominates most consumer products. Purchases at this level are made based purely on features and price.

The second level is service-based purchases. For products that have a probability that some form of service will be required during their use, the consideration of how that service is provided will become a critical factor in the purchase. At this level are cars, appliances, etc.

Finally, the top level is where vision becomes important. This is generally not required in consumer products, with the exception of some computing

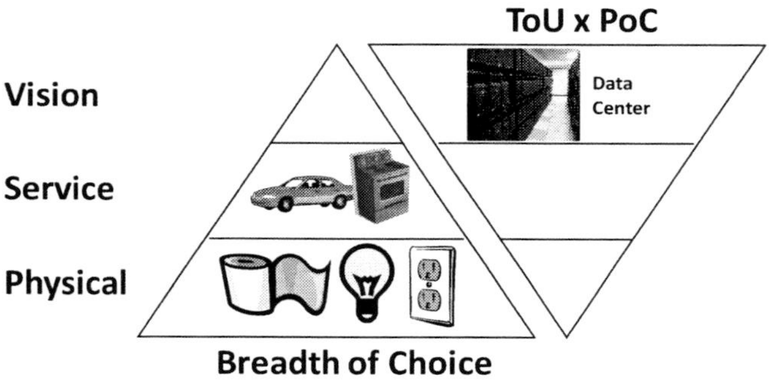

Figure 20-1 Value Added Selling Model

products (Apple's vision for iTunes was critical in the success of the iPod as was the app store for the iPhone). However, for enterprise or business purchases this becomes critical, In technology, for systems that will have an economic life of 5-10 years, the probability of change is high, so the vision of the vendor to how change will be accommodated is critical.

Within the value selling model there are two important concepts: a winning proposition at a higher level cannot overcome an overwhelming advantage at a lower level and higher level propositions cannot be applied to products that do not meet the criteria of probability of change times time of use.

Physical Level Products

Physical level products are purchased without regard to higher level values. When going to the store to buy toilet paper, no consumer is looking for an 800 number for technical support on how to use the toilet paper. The concept of service for toilet paper is not a buying consideration. Similarly, when buying toilet paper vision or future innovation is not a consideration. Regardless of your purchase (even the really big package at Costco), you are never more than 1--15 rolls away from a new buying decision. The fact that someone might invent the perfect toilet paper (incredibly soft/never tears) tomorrow is not a consideration in our purchase. This points out the time of use which is also a length of the use time of the investment is a critical factor in defining products that are purely physical.

As noted earlier, in the market the sheer volume of physical products is overwhelming. Whether the items in a grocery store or in the local hardware store, it is vast. The challenges of rising above this morass to make your product succeed are ?????

Service Level Products

When making a purchase that has longer time of use and higher probability of needing service, the value of service can become a differentiator in the purchase. A great example of this is an automobile purchase. Consumers generally understand that a new car purchase that is to be used for 2-4 years will require a variety of service and maintenance during that period. The convenience and cost of these services can become a critical factor in a final buying decision. However, very few people will buy based only on services: the basic car, design, performance, and cost will be critical factors. Once service becomes a critical buying factor, it can be approached in a range of

179

ways. At the lowest level, assuring the customer that they can buy with confidence of support enables the completion of a purchase based on physical preference. In the car business a simple 36K/36 month warranty and a close dealer would be the basics.   Extending the warranty time is another option, though this appeals only to those planning to keep the car for an extended period. However, additional steps can be taken to make service a larger value in the decision. In the auto world, bundling of consumable maintenance items (oil changes, brakes, etc.) for the first number of miles is an example. Both of these have the impact of reducing the Total Cost of Ownership (TCO) of the buying decision. In fact looking at TCO is a critical step that can be taken, if the physical value makes differentiation of products difficult.   In the enterprise world, this has become common for many types of hardware and other systems.

Vision Level Products

Finally, there are certain products for which having a vision of the future is critical, since change is inevitable during the life time of high-priced product . While there are some examples of this in the consumer world (when HD televisions were first introduced the tuner system reflected the coming HD broadcast system), vision is generally restricted to buying in the enterprise or corporate space. While it may be interesting to see the designs that a given car company is showing for its future products, it is not a critical factor in a current purchase. If you see a really interesting concept car at the Audi display, it may cause you to look at the Audi cars, but generally consumers will not ask to see future car designs before making a current purchase.

In the enterprise technology market, vision becomes critical for hardware and even software. Whether it is in technology or even in areas like real estate, buyers realize that their decision will have long term use and the vendor having a clear vision of the future and how the products that are sold today fit into that future is critical to the purchase. This concept of vision can manifest in many ways. A vision may show how new technologies and capabilities will be included in the future. Or it may demonstrate insights in how the vendor sees changing the market.   Often vision or direction is the factor that seals the deal for a purchase today.   A good example of this was when Ungermann Bass (UB), and early networking company, embraced a new standard called MAP that was being pushed by the manufacturing industry. Even though UB did not have any products that were compliant with the standard, the mere vision and commitment of support won the company the lion's share of manufacturing network revenue. In many cases a vision of the future and clarity of how a company sees its own and its customer path to that vision can become the clear differentiator, if the physical and services values are similar.

Finally, vision may be very important to services companies. If the service being offered is not just maintenance, but is one that will change over the use cycle, the vision of the services company may be critical to a long term commitment. This is true in fields such as outsourcing, where it is a complete function that is being sourced to an external vendor.

Clear Differentiation is Critical

The value add selling model provides a clear framework for defining value to the customer. To start, you must have clarity on which value levels are going to be critical to your customers. If it is not clear how purchase decisions are evaluated, conduct some simple interviews, either before purchasing or right after to determine which level of buying decision was included.

Use this information to have a clear view of how your offer is differentiated from your competitor at each level. This is a critical point. If the buying decision in your market space is not heavily based on the physical attributes of the product other than price, but service is critical, a clear understanding of the buying preferences in the service level may enable you to tailor your offers in a way to both win and optimize your revenue/margin. Similarly, having a clear definition of your vision that is used in selling is critical, if your customers are buying into your support of the uncertainty of a longer term purchase.

In any case, clearly defining these values is critical. Write them down and make sure that all of the team understands how you are positioning and differentiating at each level. Do a SWOT analysis on your overall offer at each level, including how it influences your customers' buying behavior. While it may take a special presenter or meeting to check off the vision requirement, not covering this for customers that are concerned about your company's vision, will open you up to sales losses without understanding why. If your service offers are not well positioned and communicated versus your competitors', this can result in similar losses.

Chapter 21 How Small is too Small? Or...why a channel?

One critical area that is often misunderstood in the market is the relationship of total annual revenue from a customer and how to sell to that customer. Obviously in sales there are many kinds of transactions: a single transaction that is either in a retail setting or at the clients location: an annuity sale that is relatively low interaction: and finally an ongoing sale that requires continual interaction to get business. This section deals predominately with the latter, but the concepts can be applied in a simpler form to the former cases.

System Sales

A system sale is one that requires ongoing relationship between the seller and the buyer. While this is very common in large technology, it applies to many other businesses as well. In the computer business, a typical buying company will maintain a multi-year purchase relationship with a vendor. To maintain this relationship, we can think of it as being a "strategic selling" relationship (no specific reference to any sales tools using that name). The point of a strategic selling relationship is that it requires the vendor salesperson to have ongoing knowledge of the customer, how they use the products, and what their plans are. It also generally implies that the customer is getting future product information from the vendor, as well as advice and assistance with transitions, integration, and planning.

Obviously, a strategic relationship is very valuable to creating ongoing revenue and repeat business. Whether through support, expansion, or adjacent revenue, a strategic selling relationship enables significant enhancements to future revenue. The challenge is to align revenue with interactions to assure that the revenue can cover the time spent.

In the previous chapter "Three Rules of Sales", a model to derive revenue per customer was developed and can be used to define individual sales activities. This same model can be applied to how to sell to different classes of customers, based on their anticipated annual revenue.

Defining Who Owns the Sales Relationship

If we aggregate the cases in Chapter 19 Time Based Sales Management, an assumption of $20,000 of revenue per sales call is reasonable, though we can vary this down dependent on the type of product or service and the margin. Another critical factor is how many times you have to call on a customer to maintain a "strategic" relationship. While this may vary across industries and products/services, a good rule of thumb would be every 4-6 weeks. Think back on relationships you have had a professional level. If you do not interact with the person for 3 months, do you think of it as an ongoing or a "new" interaction? In a 2011 Newsletter to the New York Society of Association Executives (Brown, 2011), George F. Brown, Jr., CEO and cofounder of Blue Canyon Partners Inc. ,observed that a characteristic of all good strategic relationships are a minimum of quarterly executive meetings. If this is combined with just a pre-meeting or a follow-up, and even if it is only 2-3 times per year, it is clear that a minimum for a strategic relationship is 8 face to face meetings per year, and 12 is probably required in many cases. If we use our $20,000 per meeting revenue goal, this comes to $160K to $240K per year. If we drop the revenue goal to $15K, then this number drops to $120K to $180K.

If we use a number of either $100K to $200K, it is now possible to establish the floor where a vendor can have a direct relationship with the buying company. Below that level, the revenue generated will not justify the salesperson's time and the salesperson will not make quota. If 30% of the opportunities across the entire sales organization fall 5% below the floor, the company will not meet its targets.

The next key question is what percentage for the market of the product or service is below this floor. If we assume that the revenue that the vendor derives is tied to employee headcount (one measure of some product types), then a simple formula will tell us:

Required Sales Call Revenue
_____   **<= Number of**

Employees
Annual Revenue per Customer Employee

For example, if the revenue per customer employee is $200 and the Required Sales Call Revenue is $160,000. then the organization must have

800 employees that use the product/service. It is easy to see how this model changes. If we talk about healthcare insurance, the average revenue per employee may be $12,000, so the same value may apply to an organization with only 15 employees (though the margins in healthcare may make this impractical).

Through this analysis, the direct strategic relationship "floor" can be established. Then, by using industry data, the percentage of the market that is below that floor can be identified. For example, in the US small businesses (SMBs)are often defined as less than 250 employees. Using the current US Dept of Labor information from Q42011 (US-DoL, 2011), about 40% of total US employment is in companies of under 250 employees. If we raise this to 1,000, it is about 54%. What this means is that without an economic path to this customer segment, it will not be available to your organization.

Channels are the obvious way to get to these segments. What the channel does is two-fold: 1. by aggregating your products with other adjacent requirements, they increase the revenue per employee to achieve a more viable level, and 2. by geographic concentration they increase the sales call density significantly. As the number of companies in the SMB space are 10 fold those in the larger space, within a specific density of calling, there are many more opportunities.

Modeling Scale Versus Channels

With these techniques it is possible to define a layered model of sales calling. Figure 21-1 shows how all of these factors come together in a model for an organization selling at the $200 per client level.

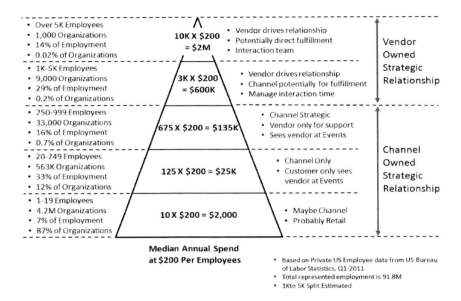

Figure 21-1 Channel Strategy Map

A few notes on this model. It is based on the US Department of Labor, Bureau of Labor Statistics (BoLS) data for Q1 2011. It uses the non-seasonally adjusted employment data as a basis. In Figure 21-1, all non-government employment is included for a complete view. A different BoLS report , reported total government (state, federal, and county) employment is listed at 22,259,000 in December of 2010, so that the 91,803,000 of private employment in these tables represents over 80% of US employment. The model in 21-2 eliminates the 1-19 employee businesses. As these typically spend less than $2,000 per year, strategic relationships are impossible for items other than potentially healthcare and other large ticket items. As government organizations tend to be larger, the model depicted in Figure 21-2 is probably better from a percentage perspective to evaluate total opportunity for a product or service.

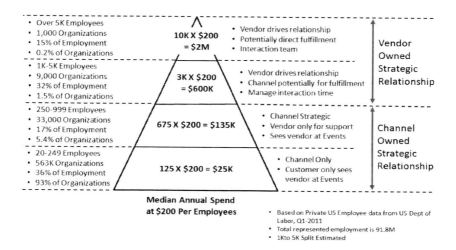

Figure 21-2 Over 20 Employee Businesses

In this model the line has been drawn at 1,000 employees as the point where it is uneconomic al to sell with a direct strategic relationship below that line. As can be seen, almost 54% of employment falls below that line. By not having a valid business plan to reach this market economically, the potential size of the business opportunity will be severely limited. In fact, the BoLS shows that the under 20-499 segment represents almost 35.6% of employment if we eliminate the under 20 segments.

While there may be product differences required to address these smaller firm markets, , having a clear plan for how to market and address this segment is critical. In the section of this book entitled "Protecting Margin From SG&A", there are additional thoughts on critical factors around channel engagement and marketing.

Conclusions

In this chapter and the previous, the critical relationship of sales time to revenue and channel structure have been described. The models presented here to enable a business to define the relative mechanisms of sales and how to align revenue by customer category to channel and who owns the strategic relationship.

Finally, we can bring this back to the first Rule of Sales, salespeople are like amebas. Given the opportunity and a quota, salespeople will naturally pursue any opportunity, regardless of size or detriment to their achieving a larger goal. To this end, clear rules of engagement, that have clear lower limits of size that vendor salespeople can sell to directly, are critical. This has two very desirable impacts: it keeps the direct vendor salesperson from using selling cycles where it is impossible to have a true strategic impact, and it prevents the chasing of channel opportunities by the direct salesperson. Clear lines that define when a direct salesperson will be compensated as a strategic seller are critical. As the channel is going to be paid for the selling effort in this case, also paying a direct salesperson will invariably result in a negative business model.

Chapter 22 The Customer Always Lies

At the beginning of this chapter I want to be clear, I love customers, both as customers and as individuals, but the point of this chapter is that customers often have significant motivations to lie. The problem is that if we want them to continue to be customers, we cannot call them liars, we have to learn how to work around their predilection.

To start, when did you last lie as a customer? Was it when you walked into a store to look at a product you knew you were going to buy on the web and let the salesman spend time selling you? Or did you lie with the time honored phrase, "Just looking." Or, when looking at cars and having the salesman show you the top model, saying that you preferred the smaller because of the size, while not mentioning the real reason was that the larger was out of your budget?

I remember looking at the Lotus Elise, a small (very small) sports car. I was looking at the car and the salesperson came over and actually looked at me a bit askance as I am over 6 feet and fairly large. I said I wanted to try the car out, so he got the keys, After opening the door he indicated there were two ways of getting in the car: feet first or sitting on the wide sill and dropping into the seat and then twisting in the seating position. He assured me the foot first method generally resulted in injury and visits to a chiropractor. So I sat on the door sill. It is about a foot off the ground and the seat is about 3-4 inches lower. When I sat down the roof actually hit my back about 3 inches below my neck. But being the trooper I scrunched down and slid into the seat. Once there I swung my legs in and by pulling my knees to my chest I actually got into the car. In the driving position I realized that I could not move more than one inch in any direction. While this might have been great for time at the track, it would have made a 45 minute commute a nightmare. So I proceeded to extract myself from the car by repeating the process. I was now looking at the car and needed a way to say that I could not spend $70 thousand on a pure toy, so I said, "Well, I love the car, but I know my wife will never get in it in a dress and that makes it a no-go." In reality, my wife is about 30% smaller than me, would have easily gotten in and out, but I did not want to say the reality that this was not a car for larger males.

The point is that we all lie in sales situations, to protect ourselves, to protect others, to minimize conflict, and for myriad other reasons. The point of this chapter is that when you understand and accept this, then you can use a variety of techniques to get to a sales opportunity. A key value of understanding this is to know when to not waste anymore time. As the three rules of sales covered, reducing time in non-winning situations is critical to meeting sales goals.

The Missing Feature

After reviewing the product the customer comes back to the salesperson and says the product or service is great, but it is missing the one key feature that they need. Generally the outcome of this is a note to the head office that this is a critical feature that is required and resulted in a lost business. However, often this is not the case. Assume for a moment I am your competition and the customer has decided that they are going to buy from me for some reason (could be anything, we play golf together). The next question the customer asks is what feature do I have that is not in your product. Every company and every sales person has this list of unique "lock-down" features. So I tell him that he needs to reference the "reverse squiggly feature" that only my product has. When he meets with you he indicates that without the reverse squiggly feature they will have to go with the competition. Obviously, if your company spends the time and effort to build the reverse squiggly feature it will have no impact on the deal, there will always be another feature requirement.

The customer does this because they have learned that it is easy and the losing salesperson doesn't protest. It is much harder to say, "I don't like you and really would prefer to not have you coming to see me for the next five years". Or to say, "I don't trust your company and your financial situation." The challenge then is to try to see if this is really a problem or not. The next chapter has some additional techniques on objections, but one easy way is to say something like "You know, I think that feature is in our next release. I need to call the office to make sure, but if we had it in _____ (pick an appropriate time frame), would that change your mind? If the answer is, "Well, I know that was important, but there are other features you are missing as well", you now know that this is not a feature based decision.

Early in my career, in Sytek, the CEO would always use the same line "You know, I think we have that running in the lab", and then drive to see if the result was a change in the decision. In the majority of cases, the customer would immediately back-pedal to another topic or issue. However, on more than one occasion this resulted in a frantic call to the development team to get a feature done to meet the demand that actually generated an order.

The Price is Too High

This is another place we all lie. Unless the product or service is uniformly priced across channels and vendors, there is always room to use price as a decision to not buy, whether or not the price you have proposed is the lowest price. The challenge with a price lie is to really understand if it is a real objection or part of a negotiation. In many ways the process of negotiation is a set of respective lies, "I could not sell that for less than X". "I could not buy that for less that X-Y". And the result of each of us realizing that we are "lying is agreeing to a price of X minus half of Y.

It is Always Your Fault

Another area where customers routinely lie is in affixing blame for a problem or issue.   If I am operating your product and for some reason there is a failure or a problem, it is a lot easier for me to tell my boss it was because your product failed rather than saying I made a mistake. This is a general fact of human nature. It extends to your channels that sell your products as well. If your channel mis-configures your product and it causes their customer an issue, they are far likelier to tell the customer it was an issue with the product, not that they made a mistake.

While we can all agree that taking responsibilities for each of our actions and the outcomes and consequences is the right and noble thing to do, we all know the real world is not that way. Many, if not most, human beings will always try to minimize their culpability, and generally if they are customers, that will result in moving the responsibility to you. A good example of this was in the configuration of network routers (the switches in the Internet that move the data packets around) as a cause of network system failure. Independent tests showed that up to 50% of the failures in the late 90s were due to operator mis-configuration. However, when talking to an engineer/operator at a customer they would vehemently say this never happened. This was because they had positioned themselves as the experts and this fact would make them look less capable.

As a vendor (or channel partner), you have to decide how to manage this situation. Do you put capabilities for automatic logs to demonstrate who caused a failure? Or do you live with the outcome as it keeps the customer happy? This is a challenging situation that exists in every business situation and needs to be clearly defined and analyzed.

Finally, while the preceding is about the customer lying, in the case of the channel partner, it may be the vendor that is lying about the partner. If the product does not work, the vendor may be telling the customer that the problem is with the channel's configuration and service. Conversely, the channel partner may blame their configuration errors on the vendor.

A Grain of Salt

The point of this chapter is simple, every customer preference or comment needs to be clearly analyzed as to its accuracy and truthfulness. This is not intended to be a condemnation of all of us, but merely a recognition that people will be people and people lie to make things easier, to protect themselves and for other reasons. Unless you clearly analyze data and information with other inputs and feedback, relying on the truthfulness of customers will get you in trouble.

Chapter 23 Objections

This and the next chapter were highly influenced by training I received in a program called Sandler selling. While it may not be the right selling approach for a every situation, I found it to be very good for sales professionals. In this course, objections were seen as two things: 1. a red flag that needed to be removed or 2. a real indicator that the sale was not going to happen. The key learning is that an objection that is not addressed or eliminated can and probably will derail a deal, so all selling time from when the objection is known forward is probably wasted. As each salesperson has a limited amount of time (see Chapter 18: The Three Rules of Sales", getting past an objection or recognizing it as a no-go is critical.

In many ways, objections are one of the most difficult parts of managing the relationship with your customer or prospect. The reason is very simple: an objection can either be real or be raised for an entirely different purpose. In other words, an objection can be very truthful, or a lie. For example, saying that I cannot buy a 2 seat sports car because I have two children may be a valid objection, but if I have another car and this car is only for special occasions it may not matter. I may not want the car for other reasons, but that is a convenient objection. Similarly, features, price, size, anything that is an objection can be both valid or be put forward for other reasons.

The key is to have a clear view of how to validate an objection before deciding to try to meet it. When presented with an objection, you have to think through the validity of the objection in the greater construct of the sales relationship. Is the objection one that you can meet, or is it one that you cannot? IF you cannot meet it, do you know if your competition can? For example, a request to sell a product at a price where it is not profitable is a deal killer. But how do you know if it is a deal killer?

The only way to do this is to acknowledge the objection and test how fixed the customer is to the point. For example, if your customer wants to buy 10K widgets and says they cannot pay more than $10 each, if your pricing for 10K widgets is $12, then you have an issue. Remembering that a discount of $2 may eliminate all of our profit, you know that you cannot meet this abjection to your price. The first step is to acknowledge that the

Philip Edholm

objection is an issue, as in the following dialog:.

> **Salesperson: "As you know, our widgets are top quality, and for a volume of 10K, our lowest price is $12 each."**
>
> **Customer: "Well, I can't pay over $10"**
>
> **Salesperson: "Are you willing to accept less features or quality?"**
>
> **Customer: "No"**
>
> **Salesperson: " We have a problem then as I cannot meet your price."**
>
> **Customer: "I guess not."**
>
> *Salesperson: "Oh well."*

At this point it appears that the objection means the two parties are far apart. The salesperson has two options: 1. he can stop selling and walk away, or 2. he can proceed to try to make the sale by convincing the customer that the $12 price is worth it. But, if the $10 price was a real limit, then that is a waste of time. But there is a third option, as taught in the Sandler classes. That is to stop selling and the do what I think of as a Columbo technique (Columbo was 1970s television detective who would always ask just one last question just as he was to leave that would trip up the suspect). The Columbo routine goes like this from the previous conversation:

> **Salesperson: "Well, I guess there is no way we are going to make this deal happen, you are at $10, I am at $12"**
>
> **Customer: "Yep"**
>
> **Salesperson: "Well I guess it is over then. It was great talking to you today and I look forward to working on your next deal."**
>
> **Customer: "Thanks for trying"**

Salesperson stands up to leave: "By the way, how is your son doing in football this year?"

Customer: "Really great, he is the new quarterback"

Salesperson walking to the door: "Outstanding, I guess he will be throwing against my boy in a few weeks."

Customer: "See you then."

Salesperson, now at the door turns as if something is bothering him: "Can I ask one question?"

Customer: "Sure"

Salesperson: "I have been a widget salesperson for going on 20 years, and I know our prices for widgets are equal to anyone else, I just was wondering how you were getting widgets for $10 each?"

Customer: "I don't really know, we haven't found any at that price."

Salesperson: "But if you can't get them at $10 you will not buy any then?"

Customer: "No, we have to buy them, $10 is the budget we have."

Salesperson, turning around: "O Well then I probably should make sure you know our quality metrics as we can meet those needs."

Customer: "Sure, I can look at those

And the sale continues.....

The point is that the salesperson allowed the objection to essentially kill the selling process, but then used the Columbo technique to validate that if the objection could not be met, then the customer would not buy at all. The result was realizing that the customer had a budget issue in that he planned to pay less than the market, but still needed to buy, regardless of achieving his goal.

By being clear about objections and testing to see if they are real, you can avoid wasting selling time and "leaving money on the table" by allowing an objection that is really a goal becoming the driver of the deal.

Chapter 24 Finding Pain

Another concept in the Sandler sales training was the concept that people only spend money when they are in pain. Find the pain and you can get the money. While this seems a simplistic concept, it is amazing how many times a salesperson totally misses the fundamental requirements of the prospect.

For example, two people set out to buy a car. One is a 20 year old part-time college student earning just over minimum wage. The other is a 55 year old manager, recently divorced. While they are both looking for a car, the pain that they are solving with a car purchase is very different. The 20 year old needs a car because riding the bus is logistically impossible where he lives. The 55 year old is making himself feel better and is hoping to get more dates.

The point is that if you tried to sell a basic economy car to the 55 year old you would fail, while the 20 year old will have little interest in an exotic Italian sports car. Similarly, understanding what the motivation of your buyer is critical.

A critical way to evaluate this is through two mechanisms. The first is Maslow's Hierarchy of Needs as proposed by Abraham Maslow in his 1943 paper *A Theory of Human Motivation*, and detailed in his 1954 book *Motivation and Personality*. The hierarchy is

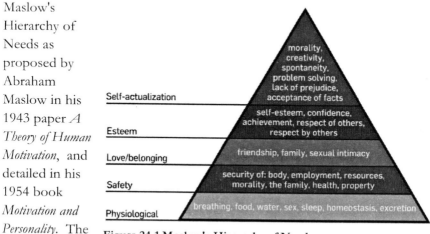

Figure 24-1 Maslow's Hierarchy of Needs

shown in Figure 24-1 (Wikipedia, 2012). What Maslow opined was that needs could be layered, with the most fundamental at the bottom. The lower needs relate to existence, but the higher needs relate more to the individual relation to others and self-expression. It is clearly possible to evaluate buyer pain as a need. The 20 year old was fulfilling what is essentially a Physiological need in today's cities, while the 55 year old was purchasing for Esteem. By clearly considering the purchase in this type of framework, you realize that some purchases are driven by necessity and some by desire, but all are driven by pain. Even the trip to the shopping mall to purchase something is a pain. It may be the pain of boredom and a lack of self-esteem, or it may be an expression of belonging, but it is a pain, but not necessarily the pain of a specific product.

Another way to look at pain is through the lens of Chapter 20: Value Added Selling Model. In that model, the

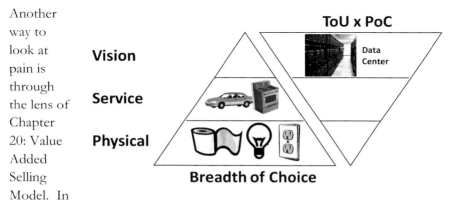

Figure 24-2 Value Added Selling Model

products in the physical category are purchased because of a basic need or requirement. This can be met by a physical product or a "service" that meets the need. Physical valued items can be sold to meet the needs in Maslow at all of the levels. The need can be well defined. In the Services segment the purchases may be made out of fear of problems or failures. Selling service is like selling life insurance. The company selling the insurance is betting that you will not die, you are betting that you will. Since none of us either wants to die or really believes we are going to die, the purchase of a life insurance is purely fear avoidance. It is a Safety need in the Services category. Finally, vision is a pain of fear of long term change. In fact, the relationship of pain to time changes at the upper levels of both Maslow and the value models.

Throughout the business process, from strategy to planning to execution, it is worthwhile to ask, "What is the customer's pain? Do we understand it?

Do we understand how to assuage it? Does the customer see a clear path to relief?" By clearly answering these questions, you have a clear path to getting money for your pain solution.

Chapter 25 You Can Lose Them All

In the movie "Pleasantville" (Ross, 1998), there is a scene in the barbershop after the High School basketball team loses its first game ever, where someone says the line "you can't win them all" and the mayor responds " but they do win them all". The point of the line is that in a movie of a dream world you can win them all, but in the real world you eventually have to lose. In Pleasantville the dream world of 50s television is changed (corrupted?) by two teenagers from the 90s, resulting in altering the world so you cannot win them all. The challenge that this thinking leaves is that you can always lose some and win some. If you cannot win them all, then we assume you cannot lose them all. So, if you try long enough, you will win some by default.

The reality is that you can, in fact, lose them all. The old salesman's tale of kissing 9 frogs to find the prince, of how "the law of averages" will definitely work in proving that you cannot win them all, but it does not in any way prove that you cannot lose them all.

Early in my career I worked as a Systems Engineer with a salesperson that I have come to recognize was one of the best strategic salespeople I ever met. He really understood how to identify both the customer's and buyer's needs and manage the sales process. He closed deals that I thought would have been impossible to close. This was early days in the Local Area Networking industry and he decided to position our company's products into the large 3echnology firms in Palo Alto in the Silicon Valley. He decided to have a breakfast seminar and invite a reasonably large group. He invited about 75 potential attendees and had over 43 responses indicating attendance. Traditional marketing wisdom would say that you should expect about 25-50% fall-out in an event like this where there is no "skin in the game", so the expectation was for 20-25 attendees to actually show up. To increase the odds, he did follow-up calls (this was before wide-spread email if you can imagine).

On the day of the event we went early to the hotel where the suite was set up. I set up the demo and we waited for the prospects to arrive. And waited. And waited. In the end, not a single prospective customer showed up. We had indeed "lost them all". In fact it might actually have been worse if only one showed up. The salesperson took advantage of the misses to call people and set up meetings, which was the real goal of the event, but the fact is inescapable, you can lose them all.

I spent quite a bit of time in telecommunications companies in the 90s that were in markets where the overall market growth was relatively flat. In this type of market, there are two major revenue sources: the upgrades and expansions of your customer base and the "churn". This is explained in the Chapter 28 "Killer Churn". In this type of market, the key aspect to future survivability is not upgrades or retaining you customers, it is how many of the customers churning from your competitors you win. While this may not be a large number, without it you are losing installed base share and losing the next stages of revenue. I remember a distinct call when a senior Product Marketing leader responded to a question about "Greenfield" (or new customer accounts) by saying that really wasn't important as the company did not win many of those. In fact, he was stating the obvious, the company was essentially losing them all, but as it was making the current sales number without those wins there was complacency. In this case the company had actually accepted that they could not win, while not accepting the obvious, that without those wins the company installed base was shrinking and eventually this would lead to failure.

So we can lose them all. And we can even see that we are losing them all and if it is not an immediate problem we can avoid acting on it. So why is this important? Because you always need to think and plan as if you can, and will, lose them all. Believing that somehow you can win based on the law of averages will result in outcomes that are not acceptable. Because if you know you can lose them all you will always think about how to win some..and then more.. and more.

Focus to Win

In any process, the first step is to focus on the area where there is the highest probability of winning. In "Crossing the Chasm", Geoffrey Moore postulates that a company needs to focus on a single market to get across the chasm. Without this focus on a pragmatic adapter of technology for a true business purpose, the company can be caught in the chasm. In other words, if you do not find that niche, you will lose them all.

If we think about every endeavor in the same light, we realize that we always need to think about how to get the first win. The key is to look at the target outcome and analyze the options or segmentation to get to a view that gives you a single win. When the business plan is being written, the revenue is almost always based on a percentage of the available market or customers, blah..blah..blah. But now it is time to really get focused on which is the best opportunity for the first win.

When a team is behind at the end of the first half, you often hear the coach talk about focusing on just the next score. Or, after coming back from a major deficit, the coach says that all they focused on was the next play. The point is that percentages are a great indicator of the overall game, but they do not accurately predict the outcome of the next play. Each play needs to take into account the players from both teams, their skills, and other factors such as whether the referees are calling the game closely or loosely. Then each possession becomes a separate event and an opportunity to maximize the probability of success, or you can lose them all.

One Win at a Time

A simple view of getting each win one at a time will begin to drive the process of wining overall. While the first win is hard as the factors may be known, but unproven, a key to the next win is being really clear about why the previous win(s) happened.

A good example of this occurred in the sales of data networking equipment in the mid 2000s. Cisco was the dominant player in the data networking space with 95% share in the routers used to connect the different site together and 65% share in the switching equipment used to distribute data networking inside the campus. The company I was with had much better share in the European markets and even more share in the Middle East. While the worldwide share of switching was at around 7%, the European share was at 15% and the Middle East was over 30%. The senior management team asked the question why the share was so much higher in these markets. The answer was that our sales teams and technology teams were better there than in North America. However, when really examining the facts, it became clear this was not the factor. In North America, the common practice was for the telecommunications carriers to sell raw data paths and for enterprises to buy routers and manage the data over those paths themselves. As the probability was that these routers would be from Cisco, it became an easy sale for Cisco to sell the campus distribution that would attach to these routers and would have common management and support. Selling an alternative solution for the campus was hard, if not impossible. But in Europe, almost half of the routers were not owned by the enterprises, but were owned and operated by the telecom and sold as a managed service. In fact, in the Middle East the local telecom so controlled the market that it was almost 100% managed routers. Without the Cisco router presence in the buying process it was much easier to win selling an alternative brand. In fact, when you looked closely at the Nortel American market, you found that the segments where the company was winning were either ones that did not have multiple sites (hospitals, universities), or organizations where the purchase of the campus was organizationally separated from the site routers (US Army, large multinationals).

The problem is that without really understanding this, it is easy to misread the win. By clearly understanding that focusing on accounts where the router decision is clearly separated from the local distribution decision dramatically increases the probability of success. It also leads to a strategy of how to increase the percentage of managed routers as an overall business strategy.

To get that first win, analyze your target space in two dimensions: 1. what are the positive buying drivers that will influence the purchase, and 2. what are the negatives. A positive buying driver is a factor that would cause a purchase from you and a negative is one that would make it more difficult. For example, if the customer has a specific type of system and your product or service works well that is positive, or if they have something that is not compatible that is a negative. Consider other factors such as investment readiness, etc. The next step is defined by your market. If your market is a smaller set of target customers, review each customer against the criteria and rank them. This should give you the focus. If your market is larger, you have to do some segmentation,. This will enable you to focus.

Don't Be Complacent

The key message of this section is that complacency and expectation are fatal. It is absolutely critical that you always work as if you can lose them all. By assuming that each win is critical and you cannot count on anything, you will focus on the factors you need to succeed. And always remember, in Pleasantville, you can win them all.

Marketing

Before you can sell, you have to have your marketing bases covered. The focus of this section is to clarify a few key areas: how marketing and sales relate, what are the elements in a marketing plan based on transactional volume, and a few key concepts that have continually been used by winning teams.

Chapter 26 The Side Funnel or Defining Customer Acquisition

This chapter discusses a model of how to think about the process of marketing and customer acquisition. Figure 26-1 shows the two axis of customer acquisition: the horizontal is the customer's needs as a match to your offer, the vertical is your relationship with the customer.

At the bottom are potential customers you do not have any relationship with. As you build your relationship they move up in the model. On the horizontal is the relative value of your offer to the prospective customer. For some, there will be little or no value, while for others it will be high value with an absolute fit

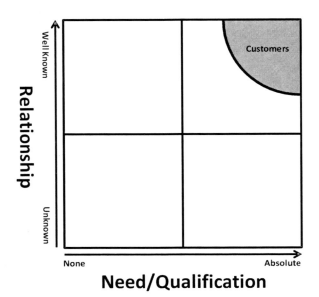

Figure 26-1 Qualification Versus Relationship to the Prospect

to their needs. The goal is to get to the upper right and acquire the suspect/prospect as a customer. For this to happen, two things must occur: 1. you must build a relationship with the customer and 2. your offer or solution must meet a need for which they will give you money. This chapter is how to think about that process in a structured way.

Figure 26-2 shows the basic concept of this model for how customers are acquired. It defines 4 basic steps to acquiring customers: the Universe of Unknown Suspects, Known Suspects, Qualified Prospects, and finally customers. The following are the definitions of each category:

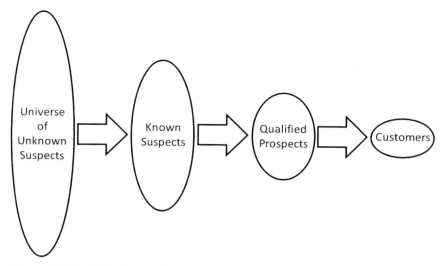

Figure 26-2 The "Side Funnel" for Marketing

Universe of Unknown Suspects

The Universe of Unknown Suspects (Universe) is all of the potential people or organizations that you could potentially sell your product or service to. The Universe is generally large and often precludes direct contact. For a Universe there is limited detailed information, and often it is not possible to actually get the information. For example, a mailing list of subscribers to a magazine may not be directly available, but will represent a Universe based on the magazine.

Known Suspects

Known Suspects (Suspects) are identified individuals/organizations with whom direct communications is now possible. These may have responded to a mailer or called a number or favorably answered a telemarketing call. Generally, the Suspect has indicated a desire to learn more about how your product or service can be used by them.

Qualified Prospects

The Qualified Prospect is someone or some organization that meets a set of criteria that are good indicators that they will buy something that you have to sell. The qualifiers may be financial: do they have the money? Or they

Philip Edholm

may be around existing things they have. For example, selling water skis to someone who does not have a boat or access to one is unlikely, so being qualified as having a boat is key to selling water skis.

Customers

Finally, the process ends up in a customer, someone who has decided to give you money for the product or service.

The key point of this is that customer acquisition is a process and needs to be well defined. If we combine the thoughts of the matrix of relationship and the funnel process, we can see how each step represents a change in the matrix as shown in Figure 26-3.

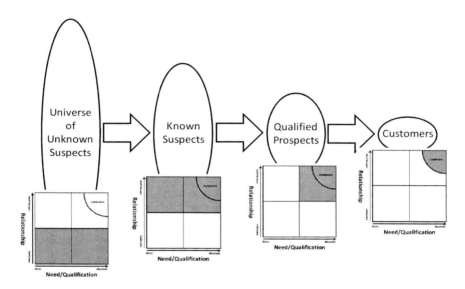

Figure 26-3 Moving Customers Through The Funnel

At the beginning, we only have unknown suspects, the Universe of Unknown Suspects. At the Suspect stage some portion of these are now identified and known. At the qualified prospect stage the Suspects have been reduced to those who are qualified, and then finally some percentage of these become customers.

208

It is obvious that we can define the transitions in each stage and give them names. Figure 26-4 defines the names for each of the process steps.

Each of the steps is different in what is being done and needs to be clearly thought as part of a linear process.

Lead Generation

The first step in the process is Lead Generation. This is about getting some percentage of the Universe of **Unknown** Suspects to become known. The easy way to think about it is to realize that in any group that could buy your products, some of the people are going to be interested in what you have to

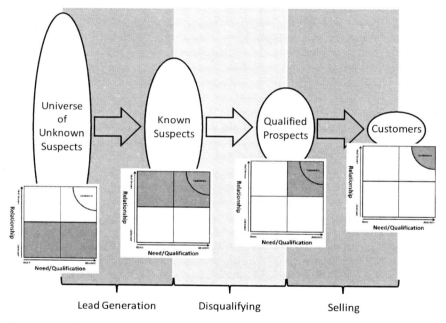

Figure 26-4 The Three Processes of The Funnel

sell. The goal is to get them to raise their hands.

Lead generation uses many different tools. The item that you put out there to get someone to raise their hand may come in many forms. It can be a direct mailer, an advertisement, even a mention in an article. It can be through an advertised link on a search engine page. All of these can be thought of as the trigger that you have set to generate a Known Suspect.

The moment someone triggers one of these by revealing to you their contact information, they are no longer part of the great unwashed Universe, they move to the Known Suspect category.

We have some piece of information that has two critical components: 1. the suspect has reason to believe that he or she is interested in knowing more, and 2. has provided you with some level of contact information. For example, to get a white paper on a web site you need to leave your contact info. The act of taking the white paper indicates interest in a topic that might lead to a purchase, and leaving a contact name and address makes you known.

When you define your lead generation step, having clarity about how both of these triggers are managed is important. Leads that have been "gathered" without a clear interest that is translatable into value for your product or service, are no better than choosing randomly out of the telephone book. An example of how Known Suspects can be poorly acquired happened to me in a marketing campaign at a trade show in Las Vegas in the 90s. The company I was with had a small staff, so we hired a local contract person (often known as a "booth babe") to work in the booth. When deciding on the person from a book of head shots, we picked a young lady that was closest to being "normal". While being attractive she was not a showgirl or that type: we wanted her to appear as if she could be an employee. When she showed up, we had her dress in a company golf shirt and khaki slacks and man the front desk. We were giving away a small pin with LED lights that blinked and if you gave us your contact info you could get a pin. Within minutes we had a line of 50 men waiting to get their pin. When we tried to use the leads, we found they were worthless as the leads reflected the desire to have a cute young lady pin on a pin versus an interest in our product.

When designing a lead generation campaign, you must consider two factors: 1. a method to rise above the noise and 2. a clear message as to why the suspect should raise their hand. It is important to realize that these may be different. Another time I did a direct mailer to a large (30 thousand) mailing list of potential resellers of a product. As the product was a board that plugged into a server and our competitors were selling server products, we had done some early positioning as the "Naked Switch". This mailer continued that theme in a classy way. The trifold mailer had pieces of men's and women's clothing lying on the floor on the first two folds and them opened to a page where there was a clear message that the "Naked Switch" could improve their business revenue and profitability if they responded to see how to become a reseller. The external positions, while loosely tied to the internals was only there to get the recipient to open the mail, but the clear message was to only respond if you wanted to learn more about a clear offer.

As you formulate your lead generation, keep both of these concepts in mind. You always need to think about how to rise above the noise, but be really clear when you move someone to a suspect that they are in fact signaling a need. It is important to understand that all of this is part of the process, as the next steps will show.

Qualification or Disqualification

The challenge with known suspects is that we primarily know them on the vertical axis of relationship: there is no real measure of their need. The next step in the process is to find the qualified suspects, but it is often much easier to define those things that would disqualify a suspect.

The point of disqualification is to identify key attributes that are indicators that a suspect will probably not complete a purchase. For example, a key disqualifier is not having an allocated budget. Obviously another way to think of this is to ask if there is a budget, but the key point is that having a budget is not, in of itself, reason to qualify a suspect, but not having budget is a clear disqualifier. Generally this is true of disqualifiers: regardless of what other factors there are, a disqualifier is an absolute barrier that will eventually block a sale.

The point of disqualifying is to not spend selling time on suspects that will never buy. A suspect asking about car accessories for a car they do not own is an example of someone who probably will not buy.

The process of disqualification must be well thought out. Start by writing down all of the critical factors in your winning. Look at your recent wins and losses to build a list of factors. List reasons you lost a deal and reasons you won. When this list is complete, begin to look at each point you wrote and understand if it has value as a disqualifier. Some will be obvious: for example every time a prospect had a box from company X, in the end the prospect did not buy your solution. First examine why this is and then you may find that having a box from X is a disqualifier. Consider other factors:. For example, who were we selling to, organization structure, public versus private, in other words identifiable factors tied to winning or losing.

If you see key winning factors that are in most or all of your wins, ask if there is an opposite factor that was absent in all of those. If you only win when someone has a specific product or situation, then not having that may be a disqualifier.

The key point is that the suspects are the frogs of the old nursery rhyme: you have to kiss them to see if they are a prince, but the kiss needs to be well thought out. The success of customer acquisition is truly driven by this step. If you qualify too many suspects, you will waste time selling and the close ratio will drop and the sales effectiveness will be reduced, ultimately leading to failure. If you disqualify potential prospects and do not try to sell them, you limit your revenue potential.

In many companies, I see this step as being poorly defined and managed. For example, the company gathers leads through a lead process and then, without any disqualification, throws all of the leads to its channel partners. The channel partners/resellers then complain that the leads were worthless. The point there is that neither organization has clearly thought through disqualifying. The vendor generating the leads has left that to the channel and the channel assumed the leads were prequalified. Having clarity of who owns this process is critical. I have seen the same process issues in organizations with direct sales. The leads were sent to sales without any disqualification or any training on the steps and criteria for disqualification. Do not ignore this step in the process or the result will be a reduction in efficiency or revenue. Don't sell until you have qualified.

Selling

The final stage of the process is obvious. We now have a qualified prospect that has a problem we can solve, money to spend and does not have any of the specific issues that would prevent us from winning. The next step is to sell your product or solution against the other options that are being considered.

If you are lucky, the previous processes yielded a qualified prospect that has a problem you can solve and is not going to look at other options, but the reality is that most times there are alternatives. So the selling process is a combination of two things: 1.justifying the value versus cost of your product or solution and 2. contrasting to you competition. It is also about building the relationship with the prospect.

Marketing Versus Sales Roles

Often people outside of Marketing and Sales (and even sometimes within those organizations) have problems understanding the difference between Marketing and Sales. The key difference is that marketing manages the program part of the process and sales manages the customer interaction side. The role of marketing is to do the positioning and to implement them through programs. As a rule of thumb, every marketing person should have at least twice their salary in budget for programs. In other words, a marketing person without a budget is...a salesperson, without specific customers.

In the customer acquisition process, both marketing and sales have defined roles. Figure 26-5 shows the relative role as the process progresses.

For each step in the process, each organization should have defined roles, but some specifics need to be identified and agreed upon for success.

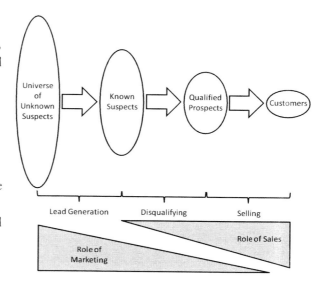

Figure 26-5 Marketing and Sales Roles Through the Funnel

Lead Generation

In this step, Marketing has all the responsibility. Whether building the program, executing it or getting feedback (how many of the suspects actually became qualified prospects), the marketing team is responsible.

Disqualification (and Qualification)

This is where the most challenges exist in defining the relative roles. I believe that marketing should take responsibility for defining the disqualifiers and the criteria for qualification. This should be a specific process that generates a clear template for the salesperson to use.

The big question is who manages the disqualifying process itself. Generally this is a sales task, but it may be a marketing process, especially if the first step of disqualification is done by phone in a call center. If this group is not designed to be involved in the sales process, but is only doing disqualification, it may make more sense to have it in the marketing group. In this case the disqualifying process may be in two parts: 1. an initial contact by an inside sales team to eliminate some percentage of the suspects and 2. a direct call on the remainder to decide if they should be moved forward into the selling process. The inside sales team that uses telephony (or video) as the only way to reach the customer is much more efficient, but ultimately, a direct face to face meeting may be required.

When the disqualification process is done by the same staff that will ultimately have a role in the sales process, it should be in sales. However, there needs to always be a clear demarcation of stages and effort. For example, if the disqualification process is assigned to an inside sales team that also does sales work, whether independently or in conjunction with an outside sales team, then there needs to be a clear mechanism for allocating time between the disqualifying process and the selling process.

Selling

In the selling phase the major activity and the management of the prospect is left to the sales team. While often this stage is left solely to the sales team, the marketing team plays a crucial role in providing the tools to both minimize issues in the sales process and to maximize the time the sales team has to sell.

The marketing team should have a clear view of each step in the sales process, by creating differentiated product and competitive positions, and having appropriate tools for the sales teams to use. A successful marketing team anticipates most/all of the issues and prepares responses before they come up. However, it may be even more important to use rapid feedback to generate tools and material based on the real on-the ground-experience. Then the key is to document this information for the broader sales team.

Instrumenting the Process

Regardless of where each step is done, a clear set of process steps to instrument the process is critical. Not only should there be a mechanism for tracking each lead as it moves through the process, tracking the time associated with each step, either universally or tied to each lead, is crucial. This allows each step to be analyzed for effort and effectiveness. Tracking the disqualification factors and other factors is also critical. Finally, keeping a clear view on these steps enables a continual improvement of the process.

Chapter 27 Transactional Business Modeling

A number of times in my career I have been asked to create a business model for a new product or company. These models need to incorporate revenue, customers, expenses, etc. into a cohesive whole. While often using percentages and abstraction can provide an estimate of the market and opportunity, the customer acquisition from the previous chapter provides a ready framework to build a complete business model on.

The first step in the model is to look at each of the three steps and plan the step from three dimensions: effectiveness , cost, and time. Figure 27-1 shows these factors on the process discussed previously. Each of these factors becomes an assumption in your business model and will have an impact on how the model drives the process. All of the data used herein to demonstrate the process is fictitious and

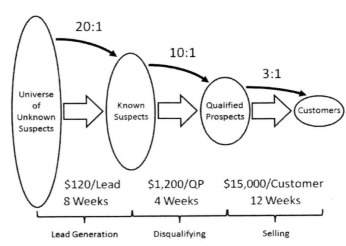

Figure 27-1 Modeling Transactions in the Funnel

only for reference. The assumption is that this is a business that sell something to the customer at a value of $100,000 and there is a single purchase for that value.

Each stage then has a model of the input, the activity and outcomes and the cost and timing to complete the activity. The following are the explanations of the stages shown.

Lead Generation

In Lead Generation, the three factors are easy to define. Time is how long it takes to cycle a lead generation campaign from the start to having the Known suspects identified. If the campaign is a repeat with older material and a new suspect pool then this may be shorter. If you have to develop the lead materials, then it is longer. A critical second factor is the touch-to-lead ratio. For example, if you send out a 20,000 piece mailer, how many responses do you get? If you get 1,000 of your 20,000 mailers to respond, then your response is 20:1 or 5%. Finally the cost per Known Suspect lead can be calculated: this can thought as the cost of each touch, that will be the ratio times the cost per suspect lead. In the data shown on the figure, an average lead costs $120. This means that the all in cost for each touch to generate a lead is $6 as the ratio is 20:1 between touched and suspects. So for our campaign to touch 20,000 in the Universe, we will spend $120,000 and get 1,000 Known Suspect leads. It is important that the costs should also include any internal employees dedicated to this task as their cost is part of this process as is the overhead and management dedicated to this area.

Generally lead programs will generate from 2-7% returns on touches. As you build you business model, this is an important assumption that you will need to define along with the timing and the cost of each suspect lead. The timing in the lead generation process is the time from when the investment is committed to when the leads are passed on to the qualification/disqualification process.

Qualification/Disqualification

This process has similar factors. The first is the ratio between the number of Known Suspects at the beginning and the number of Qualified Prospects coming out the other end. In this model it is assumed that the suspects can be disqualified in 4 weeks at a cost of $1,200 per resultant Qualified Prospect and the ratio is 10:1.

The ratio is obviously a critical factor here. The challenge is that it is not related directly to anything in market share or other processes because this includes suspects that were never suspects. For example, I was at a CIO magazine event as a presenter with a vendor. After the session, all of the attendees were given a list of the attendees. I received a call from a different vendor company about my interest in their product. They had moved me to being a Known Suspect based on that list. It was a short call, as I was one of almost half of the "suspects" were immediately disqualified as they were vendors. The remaining names that were passed on would not include someone that was not even a suspect.

As we discussed in the previous chapter, having a clear view of the investment in disqualifying is very important, most organization do not understand this, but the ratio is even more critical.

For this discussion I have limited this to a single average process stream, in an organization, there may be different ratios for different lead sources. If you use this process to operate a larger construct, tying lead sources to effectiveness throughout the process is critical.

The qualification process assumptions are the time it takes on average from when a suspect lead is received to it being identified as a qualified prospect. This time may include both an inside phone call to the suspect and/or a physical visit to the person. In the chapter on Time Based Sales Management, the topic of what percentage of sales time should be dedicated to disqualifying was discussed. It is important to remember that if 30% of the salespersons time is going to be spent disqualifying, 30% of the cost needs to be allocated here (including fringe and variable compensation). Also included in this cost should be the marketing time to maintain the disqualifying factors and any inside sales or telesales time. Also, internal costs should include all burden (benefits, office space, travel, etc.) and management overhead.

Finally, the ratio is very specific to an industry, a product, and the lead generation mechanism. While I have used a ratio of 10 to 1 here, this could be much lower or much higher. As you develop a model of this type, document a clear set of logic for the ratio selected.

Selling

The final part of the process is the actual sales process. As in each of the others, the ratio from Qualified Suspects to Customers is critical. In this model I have used a 3 to 1 ratio or assumed that 33.3% of the qualified prospects turn into customers. From experience, if your disqualifying process is well built this is a reasonable assumption. If you are in a relatively limited competition market this may be 2:1 or even less, while if you have 3 or more competitors in the space it may be higher. Obviously your market share must be less than the result of your close rate. If you are selling to all of the customers that actually buy and you win 33% then your

market share should be 33% or less.   If you win 1 out 2 Qualified
Prospects, your market share would be 50%, only if you knew all of the
Qualified Prospects and had the capability to sell to them.   If your lead
generation and qualification processes miss customers who buy from your
competitor then you have lost share. The time spent in this step and the
associated investment are also important. The time spent is the time it
takes to get to a yes from the one customer the ratio defines will buy. The
cost associated with the selling in the model here is $15,000 per closed
customer. The cost is all of the costs, including the sales management and
other cost like travel and sales materials.

Selling

The final part of the process is the actual sales process. As in each of the
others, the ratio from Qualified Suspects to Customers is critical. In this
model I have used a 3 to 1 ratio or assumed that 33.3% of the qualified
prospects turn into customers.   From experience, if your disqualifying
process is well built this is a reasonable assumption. If you are in a
relatively limited competition market this may be 2:1 or even less, while if
you have 3 or more competitors in the space it may be higher. Obviously
your market share must be less than the result of your close rate. If you are
selling to all of the customers that actually buy and you win 33%m then
your market share should be 33% or less.   If you win 1 out 2 Qualified
Prospects, your market share would be 50% only if you knew all of the
Qualified Prospects.   If your lead generation and disqualifying miss
customer who buy from your competitor then you have lost share. The
time in the step and the investment are also important. The time is the time
it takes to get to a yes from the one customer the ratio defines will buy.
The cost associated with the selling in the model here is $15,000 per closed
customer. The cost is all of the costs, including the sales management and
other cost like travel and sales materials.

Plan in reverse

By having a clear view of the process, we can build a plan in reverse. For
example, if we want get $1 million in revenue in a specific month of doing
business and all of it will come from new customers that are identified
through this process, we can use the assumptions above to build a model.
If the average customer spends $100,000 then we have to have 10
customers to achieve the goal. To get 10 customers, we will need 30

qualified prospects and 12 weeks before the revenue goal date so the sales team can close on the revenue. To get 30 qualified prospects we will need 300 Known Suspects and 4 weeks before the required start of selling or 16 weeks before the revenue goal date. Finally, we will need to touch 6,000 Unknown Suspects and 8 weeks to get our 300 Qualified Prospects. So the entire process from initiating the Lead Generation to having customers in this model is 24 weeks or 6 months, so the revenue actually occurs in the 7th month.

Figure 27-2 shows the total picture including the ratios, numbers and timing

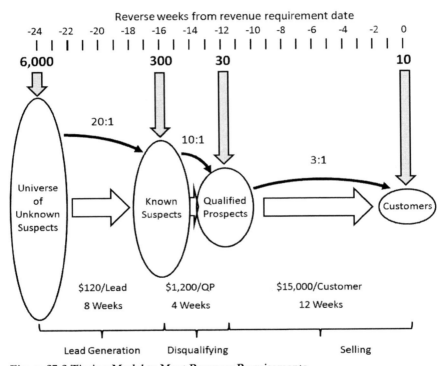

Figure 27-2 Timing Model to Meet Revenue Requirements

for the model. However, in addition to modeling, it is possible to calculate the cost of the process. With 10 customers, we will spend $15,000 each for the sales stage, resulting in a total of $150,000. Disqualifying costs another $36,000 (30 Qualified Prospects * $1,200). Lead Generation costs another $36,000 (600 * $120). So for our theoretical model, the total cost of customer acquisition is $222,000 or 22.2% of the $1 million of revenue.

This is probably high for some businesses, but if it is a new product with a 65% margin, this leaves $428,000 for R&D, G&A, other marketing and profit. Note that this number does not include other marketing costs such as branding.

This chapter is focused on the acquisition modeling process, but it is clear how this data can be included in the P&L models in earlier chapters to analyze the business financials and with the Time Based Sales Management to manage the sales activity.

Creating a Plan

Now that we have a clear view of the structure of the customer acquisition, we can build a simple spreadsheet to show all of the elements. This becomes a time-based waterfall. Figure 27-3 is the model with only one month of business shown for clarity.

Month	Customer Data				Revenue	Costs			
	# of Suspects Touched	# of Known Suspects	# of Qualified Prospects	# of Customers		Lead Generation	Dis-qualifying	Selling	Total
1	3,000					$ 18,000			$ 18,000
2									
3		150					$ 18,000		$ 18,000
4			15						
5									
6								$ 75,000	$ 75,000
7				5	$ 500,000				
8									
9									
10									
11									
12									
Annual Totals	3,000	150	15	5	$ 500,000	$ 18,000	$ 18,000	$ 75,000	$ 111,000

Assumptions	
Lead Ratio	20
Disqualifying Ratio	10
Selling Ratio	3
Lead Timings (Weeks)	6
Disqualifying Timings (Weeks)	4
Selling Timings (Weeks)	12

	Outcome	Investment
Lead Cost per	$ 120	$ 6
Disqualifying Cost per	$ 1,200	$ 120
Selling Cost per	$ 15,000	$ 5,000.00
Revenue Per Sale	$ 100,000	

Figure 27-3 One Month Business Plan

The model becomes a two dimensional model showing time on the vertical and the process on the horizontal. To make the time modeling easy, this assumes a period of 12 months with the time for each event turned into months: 2 months for Lead Generation, 1 month for Qualification and 3 months for Selling. Obviously a more detailed or a quarterly model could be used.

In the customer data we see the input of our activities. In the first month there are 3,000 Unknown suspects touched. That results in 150 Known suspects (3,000/20) 2 months later. That results in 15 Qualified Prospects 1 month later (150/10). Finally, after an additional 3 months there are 5 customers (15/3). Based on our revenue of $100,000 per sold customer we have $500,000 of revenue in month 7. In a more sophisticated model these could be front loaded by putting the expenses ahead of the revenue, but the totals will be the same. Also if this is converted to a quarterly view as is done later, this is even less important.

At the bottom are the assumptions that drive the model, and on the right, the outcome investment used to drive the costs. If each lead generated has a cost of $120 and we need to have 20 touches to generate that lead, then each touch costs $6. This is a reasonable cost for a two-mailing program with a tri-fold mailer and including postage and the name/address purchase. Similarly, both the end cost of Qualification and Selling can be changed to a cost per suspect or Qualified prospect. This is identified as the investment column. This allows the cost to be built in when the activity starts. So the cost of lead generation occurs when the mailing happens. The cost of Qualification happens in the month of the activity. For sales, the cost is shown in the second month instead of the third as this activity goes over 3 months.

To convert this to a rolling plan, it can either be built as this plan was, starting from the number of suspects touched, or by working backwards from the revenue. Figure 27-4 shows the model with the rest of the year revenue added and the required acquisition back to lead generation and the associated costs.

Month	Customer Data				Revenue	Costs			
	# of Suspects Touched	# of Known Suspects	# of Qualified Prospects	# of Customers		Lead Generation	Dis-qualifying	Selling	Total
1	3,000					$ 18,000			$ 18,000
2	3,000					$ 18,000			$ 18,000
3	3,600	150				$ 21,600	$ 18,000		$ 39,600
4	3,600	150	15			$ 21,600	$ 18,000		$ 39,600
5	4,200	180	15			$ 25,200	$ 21,600		$ 46,800
6	4,200	180	18			$ 25,200	$ 21,600	$ 75,000	$ 121,800
7		210	18	5	$ 500,000		$ 25,200	$ 75,000	$ 100,200
8		210	21	5	$ 500,000		$ 25,200	$ 90,000	$ 115,200
9			21	6	$ 600,000			$ 90,000	$ 90,000
10				6	$ 600,000			$ 105,000	$ 105,000
11				7	$ 700,000			$ 105,000	$ 105,000
12				7	$ 700,000				
Annual Totals	21,600	1,080	108	36	$ 3,600,000	$ 129,600	$ 129,600	$ 540,000	$ 799,200

Assumptions		
Lead Ratio	20	
Disqualifying Ratio	10	
Selling Ratio	3	
Lead Timings (Weeks)	6	
Disqualifying Timings (Weeks)	4	
Selling Timings (Weeks)	12	
	Outcome	Investment
Lead Cost per	$ 120	$ 6
Disqualifying Cost per	$ 1,200	$ 120
Selling Cost per	$ 15,000	$ 5,000.00
Revenue Per Sale	$ 100,000	

Figure 27-4 Extension to In Year Starts

As can be seen, we now have all the costs of running the business if is started at the beginning of the year, but only for the revenue that came from the new activity. The assumption in this model is that the number of customer acquisitions is increasing by 1 every 2 months. So in the 7th month, the total closed customers is 5, and then in the 9th month that goes to 6 and in the 11th month to 7.

To extend the model for the full year, we can project forward and back. For both we will assume the same growth in customers and the requisite revenue and investment. Figure 27-5 shows how this is then extended.

Month	Customer Data				Revenue	Costs			
	# of Suspects Touched	# of Known Suspects	# of Qualified Prospects	# of Customers		Lead Generation	Dis-qualifying	Selling	Total
1	3,000	120	9	2	$ 200,000	$ 18,000	$ 14,400	$ 20,000	$ 52,400
2	3,000	120	12	2	$ 200,000	$ 18,000	$ 14,400	$ 40,000	$ 72,400
3	3,600	150	12	3	$ 300,000	$ 21,600	$ 18,000	$ 45,000	$ 84,600
4	3,600	150	15	3	$ 300,000	$ 21,600	$ 18,000	$ 60,000	$ 99,600
5	4,200	180	15	4	$ 400,000	$ 25,200	$ 21,600	$ 60,000	$ 106,800
6	4,200	180	18	4	$ 400,000	$ 25,200	$ 21,600	$ 75,000	$ 121,800
7	4,800	210	18	5	$ 500,000	$ 28,800	$ 25,200	$ 75,000	$ 129,000
8	4,800	210	21	5	$ 500,000	$ 28,800	$ 25,200	$ 90,000	$ 144,000
9	5,400	240	21	6	$ 600,000	$ 32,400	$ 28,800	$ 90,000	$ 151,200
10	5,400	240	24	6	$ 600,000	$ 32,400	$ 28,800	$ 105,000	$ 166,200
11	6,000	270	24	7	$ 700,000	$ 36,000	$ 32,400	$ 105,000	$ 173,400
12	6,000	270	27	7	$ 700,000	$ 36,000	$ 32,400	$ 120,000	$ 188,400
Annual Totals	54,000	2,340	216	54	$ 5,400,000	$ 324,000	$ 280,800	$ 885,000	$ 1,489,800

Assumptions			
Lead Ratio	20		
Disqualifying Ratio	10		
Selling Ratio	3		
Lead Timings (Weeks)	6		
Disqualifying Timings (Weeks)	4		
Selling Timings (Weeks)	12		
		Outcome	Investment
Lead Cost per		$ 120	$ 6
Disqualifying Cost per		$ 1,200	$ 120
Selling Cost per		$ 15,000	$ 5,000.00
Revenue Per Sale		$ 100,000	

Figure 27-5 Complete Year Activities

We now have all the data we need for customer acquisition to feed into a complete year business model for this business. It is important to note that the annual cost of customer acquisition as a percentage of revenue is actually 27.5% because the growth causes spending to occur before revenue. This is one of the reasons that doing this type of model is so critical, as it will give a true idea of what the business will look like.

Integrating into a P&L

To show how the above data can be integrated into an annual P&L, here is a modeled P&L, shown as Figure 27-6.

	Q1	Q2	Q3	Q4	Total Year
Revenue	$ 700,000	$ 1,100,000	$ 1,600,000	$ 2,000,000	$ 5,400,000
Cost of Sales (35%)	$ 245,000	$ 385,000	$ 560,000	$ 700,000	$ 1,890,000
Gross Margin	$ 455,000	$ 715,000	$ 1,040,000	$ 1,300,000	$ 3,510,000
Gross Margin %	65%	65%	65%	65%	65%
R&D Cost ($)	$ 150,000	$ 190,000	$ 230,000	$ 270,000	$ 840,000
R&D %	21%	17%	14%	14%	16%
SG&A Cost ($)	$ 359,400	$ 528,200	$ 674,200	$ 828,000	$ 2,389,800
SG&A (%)	51%	48%	42%	41%	44%
Core S&M ($)	$ 75,000	$ 100,000	$ 125,000	$ 150,000	$ 450,000
Core S&M (%)	11%	9%	8%	8%	8%
Customer Acquisition	$ 209,400	$ 328,200	$ 424,200	$ 528,000	$ 1,489,800
Cust Acq %	30%	30%	27%	26%	28%
General and Accounting ($)	$ 75,000	$ 100,000	$ 125,000	$ 150,000	$ 450,000
General and Accounting (%)	11%	9%	8%	8%	8%
Gross Profit (pre-tax $)	$ (54,400)	$ (3,200)	$ 135,800	$ 202,000	$ 280,200
Gross Profit (pre-tax %)	-8%	0%	8%	10%	5%

Figure 27-6 Year P&L Based on the Plan

In this model there are some assumptions about the rest of the business. It is assumed that the R&D group is growing from $150K per quarter to $270K over the year and the Core S&M (that part not associated directly with the customer acquisition) and the G&A are both growing from $75K per quarter to $150K per quarter through the year. Both the revenue and customer acquisition costs come from Figure 27-5 and are 3 month summations into each quarter.

So now we can actually see how our theoretical business would perform. As you can see, the growth is dramatic, from only $700K of revenue in Q1 to $2M in Q4. That drives a significant transition in profitability from a loss in Q1 to a 10% profit in Q4. Obviously this is just an example, but hopefully you can use the concepts to model your business or a new growth area.

Using this model for customer acquisition enables you to define the overall business plan and then establish the next set of requirements to complete the plan. For example, in this plan, in the 7th month there are 210 Suspects of which 18 would become qualified prospects.   Assuming that this takes on average 45 minutes per suspect, then we need to have budgeted 157 hours for this task. The budget is for this to be done for about $25,000, so this is probably one person at a $70K salary. If that is not correct then the model needs to change. The customer acquisition rate in Q4 is a spend of about $1.5M, which is an annual rate of $6M, with an average cost per sales head of $300K (including benefits and travel) and a sales manager at $400K, this means we need about 9 sales staff. This is how integrating this type of modeling with the other elements of the business can build a complete business plan.

Chapter 28 Killer Churn

Churn is the loss of customers to other vendors or solutions, and includes business failures. The reason I call it killer churn is that it can be the difference between a profitable and a non-profitable business. The problem is that many companies do not actively understand why they are losing customers and work to actively reduce churn.

In the cellular industry, annual churn sates of 20% or higher are common, predominately in Europe, with the UK being the highest. In the VoIP Communications as a Service (CaaS), a major company stated their churn in 2011 was 2.1% per month, or over 25% per year. While these are different markets, in both, the churn defines a major part of the business model. As there is reduced growth in net new customers. In the wireless market today, the major change driver is adoption of data services and smartphones. This naturally causes churn as customers consider their options. In the CaaS market there is significant growth, but churn is still an issue. While churn in the cellular space is almost always to another carrier, the CaaS churn has 50% attribution to business failures in the small businesses that typically use the products at that time.

In both cases, the cost of churn is very high. In the cellular case, attracting 30% or more "new" customers every year becomes a dominant issue. In 2011, the consulting group WPS reported that average margin was reduced by over 3% when churn went from 2.5% per quarter to 5% per quarter. In the same report they indicated that the average cost of a new customer was $250, just for the equipment, not including advertising and sales.

In the Communications as a Service (CaaS) business, a large player, the company 8x8, Inc reported in late 2011 that they had 26K customers and were growing at about 14% per annum and had 2.1% churn per month. This means that they would need to acquire 6,500 new customers to replace the 25% lost to churn plus an additional 3,500 new customers for the growth in the next year. Based on this volume and their reported SG&A, each customer costs about $2,500 to capture and takes about 18-22 months to break even. This has a major impact on the profitability of the business. A 50% reduction in churn would more than double the profitability of the business, and the resulting growth would be dramatic. If the same number of customers were captured, after 5 years the customer base would be

87,000 instead of only 53,000 with the higher churn. Based on the customer installed base size and value, this should almost double the value of the company.

Churn Impact in Mature Businesses

Even in a mature market space, churn can have a dramatic impact over time. This is especially true in markets that are low growth and where there is one or two large players. Unless the market is a true monopoly like the PC Operating System has been, the market reaches a point where customers can choose between vendors. Then installed base size and churn drive the market.

The enterprise voice systems market is interesting because it is relatively slow moving and has long term commitments. For purposes of this analysis, let's assume that company A has 30% installed base market share. Voice systems typically are bought with a 5-7 year depreciation cycle. During that time they are generally upgraded at a software level at least once, either through a subscription or an upgrade purchase. At the end of the depreciation period the customer IT department typically either upgrades the system with the existing vendor in a major capital program or does a Request For Proposal (RFP) for a new system, typically to both the existing vendor and their competitors. Occasionally a system is pulled out for other reasons, such as after a merger, where the new company uses a different vendor. During the time between the major purchases there are small expenditures for expansions. Using these assumptions about how the market operates, a model of how churn impacts a business can be built.

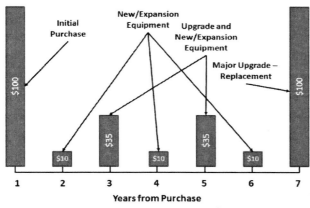

Figure 28-1 Typical Equipment Purchase/Upgrade Cycle ($000)

Figure 28-1 shows a model of a voice customer from an equipment only perspective. The customer makes a major purchase in year one, for ease of view this is set at $100K. For each of the next five years, the customer spends $10K per year on new/expansion equipment. In years 3 and 5, the customer spends 25% of the original purchase for a software upgrade (this is based on the software being 50% Of the purchase and upgrades costing 50% of the original price). In those years the average spend is $35K. In the 7th

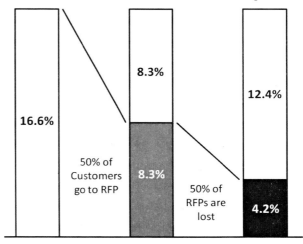

Figure 28-2 Outcomes in New Equipment Buying Cycle - Year

year the customer either does a major upgrade or a replacement. The result is shown as spend in each of the 6 years. The total spend is $200K, or an average speed of $33.33K average per year. For the 5 years where the customer is not doing a major upgrade or transition, the average spend is $100K, or $20K per year. This means that the spend in the 5 years between major upgrades or transitions is the same as the spend in the upgrade/transition year. This data can now be used to understand how churn is impacting the business.

In the 7th year the customer reaches the end of the amortization of the original purchase. Based on the 6 year use cycle, 16.6% of the installed base will be in each year of the cycle, including the new/upgrade purchase year. Figure 28-2 shows how the customers decide to move forward. The assumption is that 50% of the existing customers decide to upgrade from their current vendor without doing a competitive RFP. This means that about 8.3% of the installed base will go to RFP every year. The next assumption is that 50% of the RFPs are lost to a competitor, resulting in 4.2% of the installed base transitioning over to a competitor every year. If we increase this to 5% due to non-RFP transitions, such as mergers or acquisitions (M&A), we now have a 5% annual transition rate. Another way to look at this is that a 5% transition rate equates to the average customer staying with the vendor for 20 years before changing, making this a reasonable number. Even though this is a much lower number than the 20-30% for some other industries, the impact on the business and installed base will be significant.

Figure 28-3 shows the results of this on the installed base market. As shown in the column on the left, Company A has a 30% installed base and

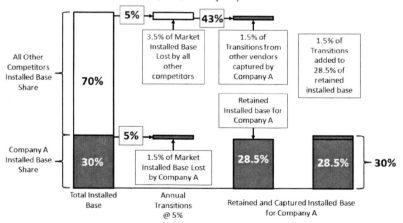

Figure 28-3 Installed Base Churn Modeled

all other competitors total 70%. Each year 5% of Company A's 30% share transitions to a different vendor as shown. This is 1.5% of the total installed base. If the market is relatively stable, the other vendors also have 5% transitions from their 70% of the installed base, for a total of 3.5%. If Company A is going to maintain its installed base, which is critical to maintain revenue going forward, it must replace the 1.5% from the 3.5% or win about 43% (42.857% exactly) of the transitions from its competitors. As Figure 28-3 demonstrates, when the 43% of the competitors transitions are added to the Company A's installed base the original 30% is set for the next year.

Using this model, it is now possible to predict what will happen to the installed base of Company A over time based on different percentages of capture of the transitions form its competitors. Figure 28-5 shows how different capture levels impact installed base share over a 7 year period. The 43% is the level of capture to stay at a constant 30% installed base. At less than that, the installed base share declines, at more in increases. For each category, the model shows the beginning Installed Base (IB) share for

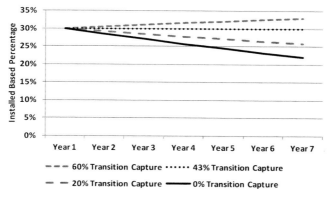

Figure 28-4 Graph of Impact of Transaction Capture on Installed Base

Company A and the sum of all other competitors. The transitions for each are shown based on the 5% assumption. Then the percentage of the other transitions to Company A are modeled and the transitions from Company A to another competitor. The result is a clear share model for the 7 year period. As can be seen, a 60% capture, which is a very dominant competitive position, results in a growth to over 33% installed base (IB) share in the period. Conversely, if Company A only focuses on the installed base, it will drop to under 21% installed base share, a loss of almost 1/3 of its customers. Figure 28-4 is a graph of the gain or loss of Installed Base share from the model.

231

Transition Capture			Year 1	Year 2	Year 3	Year 4	Year 5	Year 6	Year 7
60.00%	All Other Competitors	Beginning IB Share	70.0%	69.4%	68.8%	68.3%	67.9%	67.4%	67.0%
		Transitions	3.500%	3.470%	3.442%	3.417%	3.394%	3.372%	3.352%
		Percentage to Company A	2.10%	2.08%	2.07%	2.05%	2.04%	2.02%	2.01%
		Percentage to another Competitor	1.40%	1.39%	1.38%	1.37%	1.36%	1.35%	1.34%
		Percentage from Company A	1.50%	1.53%	1.56%	1.58%	1.61%	1.63%	1.65%
		Ending IB Share	69.40%	68.85%	68.34%	67.87%	67.44%	67.05%	66.68%
	Company A	Beginning IB Share	30.0%	30.6%	31.2%	31.7%	32.1%	32.6%	33.0%
		Transitions Out	1.50%	1.53%	1.56%	1.58%	1.61%	1.63%	1.65%
		Transitions in	2.10%	2.08%	2.07%	2.05%	2.04%	2.02%	2.01%
		Ending IB Share	30.60%	31.15%	31.66%	32.13%	32.56%	32.95%	33.32%
			Year 1	Year 2	Year 3	Year 4	Year 5	Year 6	Year 7
42.86%	All Other Competitors	Beginning IB Share	70%	70%	70%	70%	70%	70%	70%
		Transitions	3.500%	3.500%	3.500%	3.500%	3.500%	3.500%	3.500%
		Percentage to Company A	1.50%	1.50%	1.50%	1.50%	1.50%	1.50%	1.50%
		Percentage to another Competitor	2.00%	2.00%	2.00%	2.00%	2.00%	2.00%	2.00%
		Percentage from Company A	1.50%	1.50%	1.50%	1.50%	1.50%	1.50%	1.50%
		Ending IB Share	70.00%	70.00%	70.00%	70.00%	70.00%	70.00%	70.00%
	Company A	Beginning IB Share	30%	30%	30%	30%	30%	30%	30%
		Transitions Out	1.50%	1.50%	1.50%	1.50%	1.50%	1.50%	1.50%
		Transitions in	1.50%	1.50%	1.50%	1.50%	1.50%	1.50%	1.50%
		Ending IB Share	30.00%	30.00%	30.00%	30.00%	30.00%	30.00%	30.00%
			Year 1	Year 2	Year 3	Year 4	Year 5	Year 6	Year 7
20.00%	All Other Competitors	Beginning IB Share	70.0%	70.8%	71.6%	72.3%	72.9%	73.5%	74.1%
		Transitions	3.500%	3.540%	3.578%	3.613%	3.646%	3.677%	3.707%
		Percentage to Company A	0.70%	0.71%	0.72%	0.72%	0.73%	0.74%	0.74%
		Percentage to another Competitor	2.80%	2.83%	2.86%	2.89%	2.92%	2.94%	2.97%
		Percentage from Company A	1.50%	1.46%	1.42%	1.39%	1.35%	1.32%	1.29%
		Ending IB Share	70.80%	71.55%	72.26%	72.92%	73.55%	74.14%	74.69%
	Company A	Beginning IB Share	30%	29%	28%	28%	27%	26%	26%
		Transitions Out	1.50%	1.46%	1.42%	1.39%	1.35%	1.32%	1.29%
		Transitions in	0.70%	0.71%	0.72%	0.72%	0.73%	0.74%	0.74%
		Ending IB Share	29.20%	28.45%	27.74%	27.08%	26.45%	25.86%	25.31%
			Year 1	Year 2	Year 3	Year 4	Year 5	Year 6	Year 7
0.00%	All Other Competitors	Beginning IB Share	70.0%	71.5%	72.9%	74.3%	75.6%	76.8%	77.9%
		Transitions	3.500%	3.575%	3.646%	3.714%	3.778%	3.839%	3.897%
		Percentage to Company A	0.00%	0.00%	0.00%	0.00%	0.00%	0.00%	0.00%
		Percentage to another Competitor	3.50%	3.58%	3.65%	3.71%	3.78%	3.84%	3.90%
		Percentage from Company A	1.50%	1.43%	1.35%	1.29%	1.22%	1.16%	1.10%
		Ending IB Share	71.50%	72.93%	74.28%	75.56%	76.79%	77.95%	79.05%
	Company A	Beginning IB Share	30%	29%	27%	26%	24%	23%	22%
		Transitions Out	1.50%	1.43%	1.35%	1.29%	1.22%	1.16%	1.10%
		Transitions in	0.00%	0.00%	0.00%	0.00%	0.00%	0.00%	0.00%
		Ending IB Share	28.50%	27.08%	25.72%	24.44%	23.21%	22.05%	20.95%

Figure 28-5 Impact of Transition Capture on Installed Base Share

Using the revenue numbers for each period, it is possible to now model the revenue from each scenario. The revenue for an existing customer is $29K while upgrading customers spend $100K. The percentage of the market that upgrades in any year is 16.6% from the earlier model. To make the model simple, the share percentages have been converted into customers on an assumption there are 100 total customers in the market (makes the math easy to understand). The analysis table n Figure 28-7 shows a model for the revenue versus Market Share and Installed Base. The first section of the model is the total market revenue based on the 100 total customers. 16.7% upgrade and 83.3% just spend that average annual revenue of $20K. The result

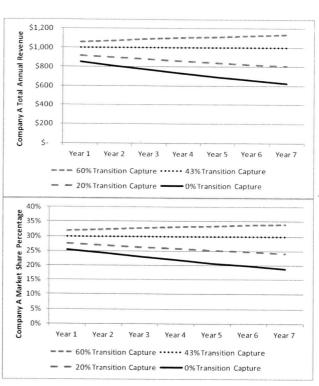

Figure 28-6 Revenue Impact of Transition Capture

is to be expected, half of the revenue comes from upgrades and half from annual purchases (they were set to be equal earlier). Then the annual revenue for Company A is modeled. For the 43% model that retains Installed base share, Company A maintains a 30% market share by having 43% of the transitions. However, if Company A falls to only 20% of the transitions, it loses 17% of its revenue by the 7th year and has lost almost 6 points of Market revenue share. If it does not get any transitions, by the 7th year, revenues are down 38% and market share is almost reduced by half. Figure 28-6 is a graph of the data from the model in Figure 28-7.

		Year 1	Year 2	Year 3	Year 4	Year 5	Year 6	Year 7
Total Market Revenue	Number of Customers	100	100	100	100	100	100	100
	Numbr of Major Upgrades	16.7	16.7	16.7	16.7	16.7	16.7	16.7
	Non Upgrading Customers	83.3	83.3	83.3	83.3	83.3	83.3	83.3
	Revenue Per Upgrade	$ 100	$ 100	$ 100	$ 100	$ 100	$ 100	$ 100
	Annual Purchase Revenue	$ 20	$ 20	$ 20	$ 20	$ 20	$ 20	$ 20
	Total Upgrade Revenue	$ 1,667	$ 1,667	$ 1,667	$ 1,667	$ 1,667	$ 1,667	$ 1,667
	Total Annual Purchase Revenue	$ 1,667	$ 1,667	$ 1,667	$ 1,667	$ 1,667	$ 1,667	$ 1,667
	Total Market Revenue	**$ 3,333**	**$ 3,333**	**$ 3,333**	**$ 3,333**	**$ 3,333**	**$ 3,333**	**$ 3,333**
		Year 1	**Year 2**	**Year 3**	**Year 4**	**Year 5**	**Year 6**	**Year 7**
60% Transition Capture	Beginning Number of Customers	30.0	30.6	31.2	31.7	32.1	32.6	33.0
	Transitions Out	1.5	1.5	1.6	1.6	1.6	1.6	1.6
	Upgrades	3.5	3.6	3.6	3.7	3.7	3.8	3.8
	Transitions In	2.1	2.1	2.1	2.1	2.0	2.0	2.0
	Total Upgrades	5.6	5.7	5.7	5.7	5.8	5.8	5.9
	Total Annual Purchases	25.0	25.5	26.0	26.4	26.8	27.1	27.5
	Revenue Per Upgrade	$ 100	$ 100	$ 100	$ 100	$ 100	$ 100	$ 100
	Annual Purchase Revenue	$ 20	$ 20	$ 20	$ 20	$ 20	$ 20	$ 20
	Total Upgrade Revenue	$ 560	$ 565	$ 570	$ 574	$ 578	$ 582	$ 586
	Total Annual Purchase Revenue	$ 500	$ 510	$ 519	$ 528	$ 535	$ 543	$ 549
	Total Revenue	**$ 1,060**	**$ 1,075**	**$ 1,089**	**$ 1,102**	**$ 1,114**	**$ 1,125**	**$ 1,135**
	Market Share	*31.8%*	*32.3%*	*32.7%*	*33.1%*	*33.4%*	*33.7%*	*34.0%*
		Year 1	**Year 2**	**Year 3**	**Year 4**	**Year 5**	**Year 6**	**Year 7**
43% Transition Capture	Beginning Number of Customers	30.0	30.0	30.0	30.0	30.0	30.0	30.0
	Transitions Out	1.5	1.5	1.5	1.5	1.5	1.5	1.5
	Upgrades	3.5	3.5	3.5	3.5	3.5	3.5	3.5
	Transitions In	1.5	1.5	1.5	1.5	1.5	1.5	1.5
	Total Upgrades	5.0	5.0	5.0	5.0	5.0	5.0	5.0
	Total Annual Purchases	25.0	25.0	25.0	25.0	25.0	25.0	25.0
	Revenue Per Upgrade	$ 100	$ 100	$ 100	$ 100	$ 100	$ 100	$ 100
	Annual Purchase Revenue	$ 20	$ 20	$ 20	$ 20	$ 20	$ 20	$ 20
	Total Upgrade Revenue	$ 500	$ 500	$ 500	$ 500	$ 500	$ 500	$ 500
	Total Annual Purchase Revenue	$ 500	$ 500	$ 500	$ 500	$ 500	$ 500	$ 500
	Total Revenue	**$ 1,000**	**$ 1,000**	**$ 1,000**	**$ 1,000**	**$ 1,000**	**$ 1,000**	**$ 1,000**
	Market Share	*30.0%*	*30.0%*	*30.0%*	*30.0%*	*30.0%*	*30.0%*	*30.0%*
		Year 1	**Year 2**	**Year 3**	**Year 4**	**Year 5**	**Year 6**	**Year 7**
20% Transition Capture	Beginning Number of Customers	30.0	29.2	28.4	27.7	27.1	26.5	25.9
	Transitions Out	1.5	1.5	1.4	1.4	1.4	1.3	1.3
	Upgrades	3.5	3.4	3.3	3.2	3.2	3.1	3.0
	Transitions In	0.7	0.7	0.7	0.7	0.7	0.7	0.7
	Total Upgrades	4.2	4.1	4.0	4.0	3.9	3.8	3.8
	Total Annual Purchases	25.0	24.3	23.7	23.1	22.6	22.0	21.6
	Revenue Per Upgrade	$ 100	$ 100	$ 100	$ 100	$ 100	$ 100	$ 100
	Annual Purchase Revenue	$ 20	$ 20	$ 20	$ 20	$ 20	$ 20	$ 20
	Total Upgrade Revenue	$ 420	$ 411	$ 403	$ 396	$ 389	$ 382	$ 376
	Total Annual Purchase Revenue	$ 500	$ 487	$ 474	$ 462	$ 451	$ 441	$ 431
	Total Revenue	**$ 920**	**$ 898**	**$ 878**	**$ 858**	**$ 840**	**$ 823**	**$ 807**
	Market Share	*27.6%*	*26.9%*	*26.3%*	*25.7%*	*25.2%*	*24.7%*	*24.2%*
		Year 1	**Year 2**	**Year 3**	**Year 4**	**Year 5**	**Year 6**	**Year 7**
0% Transition Capture	Beginning Number of Customers	30.0	28.5	27.1	25.7	24.4	23.2	22.1
	Transitions Out	1.5	1.4	1.4	1.3	1.2	1.2	1.1
	Upgrades	3.5	3.3	3.2	3.0	2.9	2.7	2.6
	Transitions In	0.0	0.0	0.0	0.0	0.0	0.0	0.0
	Total Upgrades	3.5	3.3	3.2	3.0	2.9	2.7	2.6
	Total Annual Purchases	25.0	23.8	22.6	21.4	20.4	19.3	18.4
	Revenue Per Upgrade	$ 100	$ 100	$ 100	$ 100	$ 100	$ 100	$ 100
	Annual Purchase Revenue	$ 20	$ 20	$ 20	$ 20	$ 20	$ 20	$ 20
	Total Upgrade Revenue	$ 350	$ 333	$ 316	$ 300	$ 285	$ 271	$ 257
	Total Annual Purchase Revenue	$ 500	$ 475	$ 451	$ 429	$ 407	$ 387	$ 368
	Total Revenue	**$ 850**	**$ 808**	**$ 767**	**$ 729**	**$ 692**	**$ 658**	**$ 625**

Figure 28-7 Model of Revenue Impact of Transition Capture

This exercise demonstrates that churn is not just an issue for the companies experiencing high churn, it impacts even the relative slow moving businesses. It is worse the larger your market percentage.

For example, assuming that Cisco had a 70% market share in Ethernet switching from the beginning of the market through to 2010, it is a reasonable assumption that their Installed Base Share was also 70%. Prior to 2010, the data networking market had two characteristics: it was dominated by large replacement growth and expansion, and did not have other major competitors. Over the 2009-10 period this changed. The market began to reach port saturation, as new expansion was in wireless Ethernet, replacements slowed as the Gigabit technology proved to be sufficient for the desktop (See Chapter 40 Edholm's Law of Bandwidth), and three strong competitors emerged,

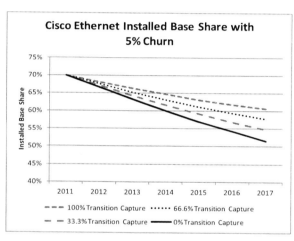

Figure 28-8 Cisco Installed Base Share Loss with 5% Churn

each with strategic competitive positioning (HP, Brocade, and Juniper). The result is that by 2011, the Ethernet switching market, especially in the campus, became a churn market. If we use the same models as done before with a few changes, it is possible to predict what will happen. As before, the assumption is that the market is a static size. If the market increases in size that can be applied to the outcome. The changes in assumptions are:

Cisco starts 2011 with a 70% Installed Base share.

The revenue for an upgrade is $100, while the 5 year revenue for annual average is $150, or $30 per year, reflecting more intermediate investment.

Philip Edholm

The churn/transition rate is left at 5%

To understand the problem, if Cisco has 70% share and loses 5% to transitions, even if it wins all of the transitions from its competitors it can only get 1.5% of the total base. This will not replace the 3.5% lost, essentially guaranteeing a 2% loss in installed base in that year. Using these assumptions, Figure 28-8 is the modeled Installed Base share assuming Cisco captures either 100%, 66.6%, 33.3% or 0% of the transitions from its competitors. As you can see, the prediction is that Cisco Installed Base will drop from 70% to somewhere between 51% and 61% over a 7 year period. The fact that the Cisco Installed Base share will drop by 9 Points even if it

is successful in capturing 100% of the transitions out of its competitors is a major challenge. If the Churn/Transition rate is dropped to 2%, this creates a much better picture as shown in Figure 28-9 , but it requires that customers stay for 50 years before leaving.

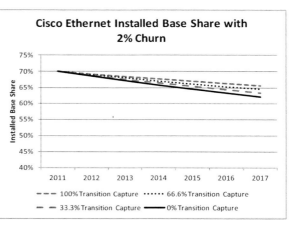

Figure 28-9 Cisco Installed Base Share Loss with 2% Churn

Using the revenue numbers in the assumption, it is possible to convert the installed base losses into revenue and market share impacts. Figure 28-10 shows revenue and market share graphs for the 5% and 2% churn scenarios. The revenue has been normalized to the reported 2011 Ethernet market size of $21.134 Billion as reported by Del'Oro (Jim Duffy, 2012). The revenue numbers generated by the model reflect the actual amounts in 2011, where Cisco had 64% market share for the year, again by Del'Oro.

If the model assumptions are correct, for Cisco to maintain the revenue of its L2/L3 business over time, two factor must happen:

Cisco must reduce churn to a low level.

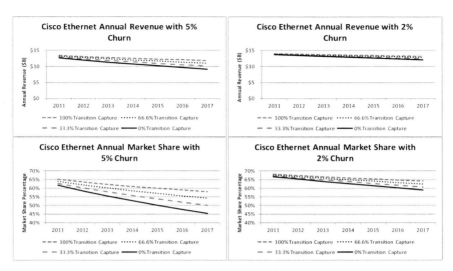

Figure 28-10 Cisco Market Share Projections for 5% and 2% Churn Scenarios

The market needs to grow at some rate. While this will maintain the revenue level, it will not maintain market share.

Figure 28-11 shows revenue and market share predictions for both 2% and 5% churn, assuming that the overall market is growing at a rate of 2% per year. This demonstrates the hard challenges of churn for large players that

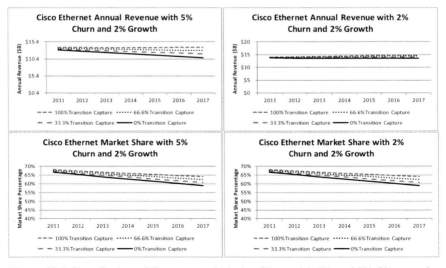

Figure 28-5 Cisco Projected Revenue and Market Share with 5% and 2% Churn and 2% Market Growth

are losing their monopoly position. With 5% churn and 2% market growth, Cisco needs to capture 100% of the transitions from its competitors to maintain flat revenue. With a 2% Churn rate, all of the transition capture scenarios yield some positive revenue growth. In all scenarios there is a loss of market share. As Indicated before, the spreadsheets that generate these models are available on the web site for reference.

Combating Churn

It is clear through the analysis above and the discussions of the cellular and CaaS industries, that churn is something that is critical to manage and invest in minimizing. Investments fall into three buckets from a churn perspective:

Investments to reduce churn in high churn probability installed base customers.

Investments to maintain satisfaction in low churn probability installed base customers.

Investments to capture transitions from competitors.

It is important to plan the marketing and sales activities with a clear view on how investment will be split among these three categories. A focus only on the first two will result in installed base erosion as shown earlier. Common marketing and sales wisdom is that it costs more, sometimes much more, to capture a new customer than to retain an existing customer. In keeping with the theme of the book, there is not enough room to detail marketing and sales plan for each of the three categories, but here are some basic thoughts.

Reducing churn in high churn probability installed base customers.
This is of the highest importance. The challenge is having a clear methodology to identify high probability churn customers before they go down the path to an alternative. In the cellular industry, because churn is such a major issue, they have built programs that use calling data, length of contract, device age, calls to the call center, and even social group data to predict probability of specific customer churn. For any business, taking the time to understand the KPI (Key Performance Indicators) of dissatisfaction and transition are critical. Through interviews with customers that have

left, develop a list of factors that were attributed to the change. Develop from that list, precursors of each KPI and understand how to evaluate which customers exhibit these precursors. For example, in the cellular industry a device change is a potential transition. Device change can be caused by the end of a contract and a desire for a new device, but battery life can cause a customer to get a new device even if they are happy with the one they have (and want to avoid the hassle of changing devices). For these users, they are quite comfortable with their device, but after a couple of years use, the battery fails. As batteries are hard and expensive to replace (unless they are bought from China on eBay), the user may decide to change the device, resulting in some percentage transitioning to a new cellar carrier. This action has two costs: first the cost of a new subsidized device if the customer is retained or the loss of the customer if he/she leaves. If a cellular provider offered a new battery, even without any plan extension strings, at 22 months, some percentage of the churn could be reduced.

Similarly, in a major purchase world, the end of the depreciation cycle on a major investment often means a new investment will be coming. Capturing depreciation data from customers when initial sales happen can lead to actions to minimize an RFP and a competitive bid position. Having offers that are made prior to the cycle conclusion and thus thwarting a RFP can result in reduced churn.

Maintaining satisfaction in low churn probability installed base customers.

This area is the most simple to deal with. You have to make sure your customers do not go to churn through dissatisfaction. For every company, understanding the level of satisfaction and loyalty (probability to recommend is a good indicator) is a major task. It is important to really listen to your customers. As in many things, perception is reality. Even if you have done everything right, if your customer does not believe you value them, the probability of an early churn or a churn if the customer moves to the higher probability is likely.

Capturing transitions from competitors.

Depending on your market, this may become the most significant part of the activity, or may be almost ignored. In the CaaS market, the 25% annual churn results in a requirement to have a constant sales and marketing activity to replace churn. As the analysis showed, even in low transition markets the rate of transition capture can have a major impact on revenue, and installed base and market share. One major challenge is in the sales organization. If you have read Chapter 19: Time Based Sale Management, one key element is the lost sales cycles for disqualifying and unsuccessful sales engagements. Therefore, salespeople who have major installed base revenue to manage may not be motivated for transition selling. The concept of segmenting your sales force between the installed base and gatherers/hunters where the focus is different can be an effective way of meeting this challenge. Another critical point is to understand the market precursors for a transition. These may be RFPs, but can be other items.

A small Value Added Reseller I know in the Data Networking and Voice Systems business uses a specific technique to get early data. Each of their salespeople joins all of the commercial real estate professional groups in their territory. These are typically a group of real estate brokers that represent property owners and potential commercial lessees. They often have a regular breakfast meeting. The salespeople from this company would join those groups and then offer a small incentive ($100) for a broker to pass on information when a company was signing a lease for a new space. This allowed the salesperson to begin selling prior to any activity on the customer side. As most customers do not begin the actual plans for the build-out of a space until the lease is signed, this enables the salesperson to be the first-In and potentially make the deal. This company attributed all of its growth revenue to this strategy alone.

Retain, Replace, Grow

In the real world of churn, each company must have a clear plan for each of these elements. They need to be integrated into a cohesive plan that starts with the strategy and ends with the structure of the sales force and the marketing programs. Clear allocation of resources needs to be defined, or the results will not meet the needs of the company.

Chapter 29 Sell Your Weakness

In building a marketing plan, often one of the first steps is building a SWOT analysis. An analysis of your Strengths, Weaknesses, Opportunities and Threats is a basic tenant of marketing. Often the next step is to focus on how to position the strengths to win in the market.

The premise of this chapter is that you need to position your weaknesses, in many cases even more than your strengths. This is because of a very simple reality- your strengths will take care of themselves. However your competitors will attack your weaknesses. By leading with a weakness, reconstituted as a strength, you will immediately put yourself in a better position. How does this work?

Let's postulate that you are building a new tablet to compete with Apple. What would a SWOT for your new product look like with reference to the iPad?

Strengths	Weakness
• Low Price • Replaceable Battery • External Memory add	• Lower screen resolution • Slower Processor • Google App Store • Low internal memory • Limited Battery Life
Opportunities	Threats
• Education • Non-gaming/television • Focused Applications	• Apple pricing reductions

As you can see from this SWOT, the competitive product is essentially a slimmed down, lower performance/resolution product that competes on price. However, the advantages to the price competitive position are obvious. The key question in the customer's mind is not whether this is a less expensive product, but whether it is of sufficient capability as referenced to the iPad. So the key point is to define the comparison points to where the product has strengths..by not describing them but letting the potential buyer define them. So we would leave off the price comparison and the advantages of the replaceable battery and expandable memory as benefits per se and focus on how they are benefits for the weaknesses.

With that in mind, here are some weakness-based positioning statements:

New optimized resolution screen matches use in advanced applications. This new screen is designed to optimize the

presentation of advanced applications that use advanced graphics and text.

Enables applications from the open Google apps store representing over 60% of deployed devices. The Google apps store is the fastest growing source of applications in the world today.

Expandable memory enables user defined memory cost. This eliminates having to guess at the purchase time which results in less than 50% memory use on average. With this feature you can optimize your memory and expand whenever you want. The memory expansion uses readily available memory which is 50% less than at point of purchase pricing.

Replaceable battery enables extended battery life, significantly more than devices with fixed batteries. Up to 12 hours with 3 batteries.

Hopefully after reading these, you may see this is a competitive device, however, there is a point to each of these statements and whether it will stick:

The point with this statement on screen resolution is that the basic statement will be read by many people without noticing the qualifiers. This is especially true as the qualifiers are in the second sentence. The key point is that an optimized display is now associated with your product and that may be enough that an actual resolution comparison does not happen. This can be extended by side by side pictures of applications where screen resolution is relatively unimportant.

This weakness (access to the Google apps store) is reduced by using facts that are either irrelevant or are based on a statistical point that may not indicate actual reality. The fact that 60% of devices use the store has no impact on what is in the store and "fastest growing" can be a representation of growth as a number or growth as a percentage. As we have chosen percentage, an increase from 1 application to 3 is much greater than from 1 million to 1.2 million.

By focusing on the memory expansion as relative to use, and equating it with on-demand, the value of internal memory is reduced.

Even though the provided battery has only 50% of the expected life of the iPad battery in a similar use, the fact that this device has changeable batteries allows the claim that it actually has extended life. If you bought 2 stand-by batteries, the actual available life between required charges is now 150% of the iPad. As the "Up to 12 hours is in the second sentence, many will not see the 3 battery disclaimer and there is no message that you only get one battery with your purchase.

The point of all of these claims is that under intense examination the claim may be found to be less flattering than on first view, but all have the same two characteristics:

On a first reading or being told they sound reasonable, the majority of buyers will click the box and move on.

If the claim is challenged, there is a reasonable logic for why the claim was made.

Obviously, in addition to these claims, some of the strength claims may be made as well, but the impact of making these claims is strong. Generally, the first thing you say about your product is the one people feel that you are most proud of. If that is one of the weakness statements, the general result is to mentally accept it, without extensive analysis. Imagine for a moment you have had the 4 claims and now go look at the competition. The first thing you realize is that the competitive product is twice the price, but it advertises the following:

New Retinal Display with better resolution that your TV.

Applications from iTunes, the largest app store on the market

Pick your memory based on your need: 16G, 32G, 64G

Full 8 hours of battery life

Did you actually read those and think:

The iPad has great resolution, but it is not optimized, which is better for my apps.

iTunes may be the biggest now, but it is not growing in apps or users like Google.

I have to decide on memory now, what if I am wrong?

The iPad is only 8 hours, the other tablet is 12 hours.

If your responses to any or hopefully all of these matched those above, we have taken a weakness and either turned it into a strength or at a minimum neutralized or reduced it.

Take the time to look at many successful companies and products and you will find that they do not shirk away from positioning their weaknesses. In fact, one Dow 30 technology company regularly positions their products as better in any category that they actually are not leading. I found it very illuminating when a product manager would come in and say, "...but our management is so much better than theirs, but they are claiming theirs is the best in the industry. I can prove ours is better. How can they say they are better than us?" The point was that the opportunity to prove that only came occasionally. For the vast majority of buyers, the claim would stand.

As with other chapters in this book, the concepts of selling your weakness can be reinforced by the PT Barnum line: "You can fool some of the people all the time...."

Chapter 30 Never Apologize

Before I start, there are times you need to apologize in business. If you made a commitment and were not able to keep it, you need to apologize, if you did not deliver something you promised, you need to apologize. However the point of this chapter is never to apologize for your products or company unless you failed the customer.

'Never apologize' means to treat everything you do as if it was EXACTLY how you planned, even if you would do it differently if you could change it. The point is never to apologize for anything that the customer does not know you did wrong. Never assume the customer knows that you would have done it differently.

An example of this is the following:

When building your new widget, your team decided to incorporate 6 levels of misdirection. Eighteen months later, when you introduce your product, your competitor XXXX has just introduced their product with 10 levels of misdirection. A customer says, "We like your product, but XXXX has 10 levels of misdirection". What should you answer be?

We are going to have 12 levels of misdirection in our next product.

We tried to do more, but our hardware is limited at this point

We told the engineers that 6 was not enough, but they did not believe us

We analyzed the number of levels in our design process and concluded that 6 was the optimal number as the complexity of managing 10 levels increases the unreliability of the system by 50%. We firmly believe that 6 levels is the best design.

As the buyer, which answer gives you confidence in buying this product versus one from XXXX? The point is that the fourth answer is not an apology. It clearly states you are proud of your product, but more importantly says that the fact that you only have 6 levels was not an oversight, but was a clear plan. Never mind that you may go to 12 levels in your next product, for this product you have to sell what you have:

therefore, you cannot apologize. All of the other answers are apologies and validate that buying XXXX with their 10 levels is the better decision.

The clear point t is to always act as if what has come to pass is exactly what you planned, unless that is not possible at all. If you start any conversation by admitting that what you have today, which is an outcome of your planning and judgment of the past is wrong, then any future plans or judgment and any recommendations will immediately come under suspicion.

As you begin to think this way, you can combine never apologizing with selling your weaknesses. The point is to bring up a weakness that could be understood and position it as a planned activity right from the beginning. As in the previous chapter, the PT Barnum logic applies.

A good example of this happened in the early 2000s when Ethernet/IP phones were coming into the market. One manufacturer had put a 1/4 PC size screen on the phone and could put web-like graphics on the device. The company I was with at the time did not have the capability to do this quickly. I knew that this would come up in many customer meetings, so I would always talk to it before the customer had a chance to raise the issue. I would say, "I know that there has been discussion about putting so called "micro-browsers" on phones. We looked at this and believe that it really has no value except in a few isolated instances, such as for getting credit card information in a retail point of sale location. For the average user who has a PC or other large screen, paying to have a small browser has no value. For these reasons, we prefer to focus on enabling our text displays for those specific applications and this reduces overall costs by 20% or more."

The point was that for most of the buyers, all of whom had a PC sitting on their desk, this was sufficient to take the question off the table. One good example of how this changes the discussion was in a large university where the lower level buyer really liked this micro-browser feature. When I made the comments in front of his boss, he argued that having a micro-browser on the phone in the dorm rooms would let the students use it to order pizzas and the university would get a commission on every sale. I responded that that was potentially an issue as the students would not pay more for using the phone as they all already had computers to do the ordering. In addition, putting an expensive phone into a dorm room would

Philip Edholm

be subject to damage or theft. The boss immediately agreed and essentially took the entire concept off the table. When the RFP came out, there was no requirement for this capability, which would have been there if we had not discussed it.

Another example might be a technician user interface where the competition has built a new interface using graphics and you have an older text style interface. Your position should be to indicate that you are focused on the text style interface as it optimizes the experience base of their trained technicians and does not introduce the errors of a newer less tested interface.

In all of these cases, it is appropriate to acknowledge the competitive path, but not as a realistic option today. For example, you might say, "while we fundamentally believe that 6 levels is the right number today, we will continue to analyze the options. As our powerful management capabilities increase, if we are able to expand this and it benefits the customers and does not decrease reliability, we will consider expanding our levels." The point is to tie your change from the current "plan" to something that is happening now or in the future, not to a decision in the past.

I know that this chapter, and to some extent the previous comment might seem a bit of marketing flim-flam. The point is that you always have a product or service that has some strengths and some weaknesses. It is very rare to have an offer that is better than the competition in every aspect (including price). The key message is to clearly think through your positioning, remembering that the customer will give positive weight to anything you emphasize and negative weight when you apologize. Of course, your sales team needs to understand this positioning as well.

Finally, many years ago I came across an ad that came in one of those mailers with 40 or 50 postcard size ads. The ad was for a VHF/UHF antenna that had the UHF part with a molded plastic piece that was designed to look like a satellite antenna. In fact, it was just a normal set of what are called "rabbit ears" (for VHF) and a loop around the plastic "dish" (for UHF). So it was a simple off-the-air television antenna, no more, no less. However, the ad text was brilliant (reproduced here from memory as I lost the card, but I remember it clearly), "*Not technological razzle dazzle, but pure design brilliance made the TV Dish a marketing breakthrough. You do not pay for satellite as you are not getting satellite signals. You do not pay for cable because it does not use cable. The TV Dish grabs signals right out of the air, just like rabbit ears.*" The point of this is that if you read it with the reference of someone who does not understand the differences between satellite, cable, UHF or VHF: the result is that it sounds really good..... What's more, re-read it and you will find it is 100% honest. The product is not a technical marvel, and it is a marketing breakthrough. You don't pay for what it does not do and it is just like rabbit ears because it is rabbit ears. Think of this as the ultimate

in never apologize. It takes a product that is essentially no different than something you would disregard, and by making the UHF loop look like a satellite dish, it now is not about apologizing over the rabbit ears, but positioning all of the weaknesses as strengths. I am sure that whoever did this ad made lots of money, selling a product that would have sold for $10 for $20, by the addition of a little plastic and a great message. Just to be clear, I would never endorse nor generate this level of ad myself, but, it makes clear that how you position and say something makes a huge difference. Maybe that shows I am not really a marketer, but to quote one wag, "How can you tell when a marketing guy is lying? His lips are moving!"

Chapter 31 First In - Last In

In every sales situation, someone is first in the door with the customer with a novel sales proposition, someone is last and there may be other sellers in between. For the marketing team, as part of the role of building the tools for the sales process, having a clear view of what are the key First-In, Last-In and even in-between sales propositions is critical. While these propositions may be common across competitors, often they will vary somewhat with competitors as well. By having a clear strategy for your sales teams that emphasizes understanding and responding to First In - Last In causes them to be much more aware of the competition and how they are positioning.

First-In

When you are First-In you have the advantage of setting the stage for the discussion. As the customer has not heard from your competitors yet, you can define some or most of the basis of the discussion. Because of this, having a clear view of which topics you believe are most important to discuss based on giving you advantage will be required.

One of the key dangers in being First-In is that you are talking to someone that has no opinions yet. Another is that you can fall into the trap of being the educator, instead of selling. So it is very important to identify the key points that you have to make in your First-In position. The points fall into three categories:

Optimizing your weaknesses - As was discussed in the "Sell Your Weakness" chapter, you need to define the discussion ground for your weaknesses. You know that your competitors will bring them up in their meeting, so you must be clear in both defining and positioning your weaknesses. If you do a good job of this then when your competitor brings the point up as a strength, the buyer will discount their message. Think back to the 6 levels of misdirection in the previous chapter. If you had that discussion with the prospect first, when the competitor raises their 10 levels, it is already been discussed and the customer may really question if they need that complexity.

Emphasize your strengths - While we have to sell our weaknesses, as the First In, you must also cover your strengths in the event your competitor is positioning their weaknesses as strengths. When positioning your strengths, you need to be sure to define the analysis mechanism s that it is not negated in the competition's positioning. For example, in the world of networks, throughput in packets per second of a device is often defined based on the size of packets. As there are many more small packets in a given stream than large and the processing is the same, a stream of all small packets is much harder to deal with than a stream of all large packets. If you know your competitor is going to position 100% throughput, but is postulating this only being with all large packets, your positioning of your superior performance needs to be something like, "we deliver 100% throughput, not only with the all large packet scenario used by some of our competitors, but in the real-world scenario of a 50/50 mix of packets, which results in a workload that is 3 times the large packet test."

Leave a few landmines - as the First In, you have the opportunity to define and leave a few "landmines". A landmine is something that will directly refute a claim your competition will make as fact or raise an issue they are uncomfortable with. The point is that this is not limited to features or performance, but could be anything you know they will say or not want to discuss. The point is to put together an argument that will cause the buyer to treat that claim with suspicion and ultimately to discredit your competition. If you are selling cars and you know that your competitor is going to say something about how they do well on some third party analyst XXX report, having a comment in your section like "we do not participate in the XXX report, because it requires vendors to pay the survey firm for the review and you are essentially buying your rating." If in fact there is a charge to participate, when your competitor says that they are great because they were chosen by XXX as a "Superior Car", the customer is thinking that it has no meaning because it was bought. This can become even more uncomfortable if the buyer asks, "so, did you pay for that?" Obviously the answer of yes is going to be an issue and if the competitor now tries to say the review is unbiased it sounds hollow and defensive.

The First In position can be a powerful advantage if you have the foresight and knowledge to use it. However, it can also be a serious disadvantage as you will not be able to always respond to the competitor's positioning if they come after you.

Last-In

The Last In position has a serious disadvantage and a significant positive. Your competitors have had an opportunity to position their strengths, weaknesses and even may have left a few "landmines" The first thing to realize about this is that you have to understand what the competitor is doing. Getting good public information about what your competitor is positioning is important. Note that this is often going to come through post-mortems with your sales teams. As a marketing leader, having regular debriefs with sales teams is critical. First you get information, but also, you will build an expectation that they need to listen and document what came up.

Once you have this view, you can prepare a reactive strategy that will not appear to the customer to be reactive. The point is to address the issues that are in the buyer's mind, without letting the competitive positioning drive the discussion.

To better understand this, let's assume we are Last In to the First In discussed previously and we have a good idea of how that First In advantage will be used.

Weaknesses - Don't ignore your weaknesses and hope your competitors did not bring them up- they did. You will need to address these head on, but understanding how the competition positioned the value. As discussed in the previous chapter, I knew the competition was going to bring up the phone browser, to ignore it would have turned it into a question and immediately put me on the defensive, "Do you have a browser for you phone?" There is really no way to answer this except with no and then you are defending. If your weakness is a clear technical negative, then use the technique of good enough, "you don't need more resolution in a handheld unless you are watching movies or television and obviously that is not what your employees are using this for at work". This is part of the optimized screen part of the presentation.

Strengths - If you competitor is good, they will have positioned their weaknesses vis-a-vis you as some form of strength. The challenge here is that you have to redefine the landscape to your value, "Of course screen resolution is important as most of your users will be doing training videos that need high resolution to see the information detail presented."

Landmines - You know the landmines are there, so you have one of two choices, ignore the point and do not use it, or actively defuse it. If your claim is that you need 10 levels of misdirection, then you need to start, not by saying that your product has 10 levels, but by describing the requirements that necessitate 10 levels. You would start by saying something like, "Misdirection is a powerful tool in managing the systems of today. What is critical to realize is what drives requirements for misdirection. In many organizations. there are three levels of employees (executives, managers, and general), three key departments (sales, development and finance/services), and three time zones. As the key value of misdirection is the capability to isolate and secure these, we find that at least 9 levels of misdirection is the normal requirement. In designing our product, we included 10 to be sure we enabled one level of a unique exception or for management. While some say you can get by with less, we feel this is critical and we have built our management system to simplify the management of this powerful function. "

The final point on Last In is to remember that your goal is to change the perception, but not enough to cause the First In competitor to be called back. You want to assure that your final positioning is what goes into the decision process: you want to be the prosecutor (I always found it interesting that in US courts the criminal prosecutor is the last to speak to the jury before the judge moves the trial to the jury).

In Between

In the event there are more than two competitors and you find yourself in the middle, you have a larger challenge. The earlier competitor(s) will have set the First In positions generally about your offer and any specifics to their offer. You will have to take into account any that were in before you and then think about those that will come later.

Philip Edholm

As personal preference, I would always prefer first or last to the middle, and if given the option, I will generally take first as I believe the capability to position your weaknesses well and leave landmines is a big advantage. Also, if you are first in a larger group, the probability of being able to get a return meeting is higher.

Chapter 32 So What? - Understanding a Benefit

Describing a benefit of a product or service is a basic element of marketing. The challenge is that, many times, the benefit is described in such a way that the end value to the purchaser is not clear and concise. Often features are positioned as benefits without defining the true value. For example, if I were to say that a benefit of my product is that it is easy to use, your reaction would probably be one of interest, but there is little qualification or quantification of the benefit. On the other hand, if I said that my product reduces training costs be an average of $500 per employee, you would immediately understand the value.

One clear way of getting to a benefit is to ask the question "So what?", when a benefit or feature is described. In this way, a feature or an intermediate "benefit" can be translated into the ultimate benefit and value. When there is no answer to the nth "So what?", you have reached the point of the true benefit.

For example:

Vendor: "My product has an intuitive user interface."

Potential Customer: "So what?"

Vendor: "It is easy to use."

Potential Customer: "So what?"

Vendor: "Users can train and support themselves."

Potential Customer: "So what?"

Vendor: "You have less training and support"

Potential Customer: "So what?"

Vendor: "On average it costs $500 less for training and half as many support calls"

Potential Customer: "OK, I understand the training part, but so what on the support?"

Vendor: "You can have fewer support people."

Potential Customer: "So what?"

Vendor: "You save 30% of the on your support group and save $500 per employee for training."

At the end, both of the impact areas of the intuitive user interface were translated to a cost reduction benefit.

Types of Benefits

If the process described above is followed, benefits will fall into a small set of categories. When selling to a private enterprise, the benefits fall into three categories: reducing cost, increasing revenue, and meeting a regulatory requirement. Any "benefit" that does not fit into these categories is probably not a real benefit. For example, a benefit that it makes you or your employees feel good is not a benefit to spend money on.

The benefit categories are obvious. Cost reduction benefits reduce the overall cost of doing business today at current volumes and pricing. In the P&L they apply to the Cost of Sales and the R&D and SG&A costs typically (though they may be applied to debt as a separate category). Revenue increases are things that impact the revenue the company generates, either by increasing volume, pricing, or some other factor. Regulatory is simply capabilities that must be purchased as a regulatory requirement of doing business in the locale where the business is located.

Both cost reduction and revenue increase can be illustrated in an actual benefit model. This is important, as what often is positioned as a benefit will not fit into these models directly. For example, a statement about virtualization that "it allows you to deploy multiple apps on a server" is true, but has not addressed the end benefit. As the end benefit is going to be a reduction in the cost of operating the IT infrastructure, adding a characteristic of the economic impact to the benefit is critical "virtualization allows you to deploy multiple apps on a server, reducing by half the average wasted server cycles and typically reducing the cost of a data center by 30-40%".

In a similar way revenue benefits can be expressed in similar terms. A product that expands the addressable market by 30% should result in a 30% increase in revenue at the current rate of capture. Expressing the benefit as a percentage increase in revenue is much more powerful than leaving it at "easier for customers to use". The fact that lack of ease of use is a reason why many are not buying today drives this benefit and value.

The regulatory benefit may be as simple as a requirement of doing business or may be much more complicated. A requirement to have a fire extinguisher will prompt the purchase of a fire extinguisher, but only to the level it meets the requirement.

In other industry segments, the benefit statements might be quite different.

In a non-profit, there is no "revenue" benefit. In this case, cost savings benefits can be associated to "delivering more services". The reason is simple: if a benefit enables more services, it is typically only doing it by reducing the cost of delivering services, therefore allowing more services to be delivered within the non-profit budget. However, a fund-raising tool that increases contributions is different, so there will be benefits associated with contributions and fund raising.

In government, there are regulatory and cost benefits, but there is also the value of the services delivered to the constituents of the entity. For example, while web applications may have cost benefits by automating transactions, it may also increase satisfaction as it allows applications to be done quickly and without a trip to an office. So in government the revenue factor is replaced by constituent satisfaction. To be clear, this is a valuable factor, especially to politicians trying to get re-elected, if they can claim credit for a popular value.

Benefit Variability

If your product delivers an annual benefit with a value of $100 and costs $200, you will be well positioned against someone who has a $50 annual benefit value and costs $200 or someone who costs $300 and has a $100 annual benefit value. In both cases, your product has a lower Return on Investment (ROI) than the competitor. Your return is 2 years, while both of the others are over 3 years. The challenge comes when your competitor is positioned as a $100 cost and a $75 annual benefit value, resulting in a 16 month payback. By defining your benefits in terms of the actual estimated value, it is easy to see how you need to position. As payback and benefits are part of a decision, they are important, but not everything. Be careful not to be caught in the middle as described in Chapter 17 "Death in the Middle", as this can be a real trap in benefit positioning.

Chapter 33 Outrageous Elevator Pitches

An elevator pitch is the 20-30 second sound bite that describes something. It is intended to only do one thing: get the person with whom you are talking to request more information. The point is to describe, in a few words, a capability/feature/benefit/value so that the receiver has no choice but to ask the next question.

With this in mind, an elevator pitch must be at the edge of your achievable reality. For example, which of these two sound bites is more enticing:

"Our product delivers 20% cost reduction on average."

"Our product delivers up to 60% cost reduction in actual customers."

Obviously the later is more enticing, though both are potentially true for the same offer. If your average cost reduction is 20%, but one customer claimed to have a 60% cost reduction, then the latter is equally true. The listener will hear the 60%, probably not noticing that you said "up to".

In the elevator pitch you do not want to exaggerate or misrepresent, but you want to choose your facts for biggest impact. The result is that you begin to define yourself by the limits of the envelop you are covering. If for example your product is 76% faster that your competition, you can claim it is "almost twice as fast". Not only does this sound better, but it is shorter.

To build an elevator pitch, list the up to 5 key points about your product or solution. It is not required to have 5 points: that should be the maximum.

To illustrate the process, we will use for ZYZGR, a small company that provides parts to medical device manufacturers as an example.

The first point should be a point of reference to clearly articulate the space that the offer is in. It needs to use words that can be understood by someone who is not an expert in your business. For example, saying *"ZYZGR builds ronax capacitors for portable devices"* is fairly meaningless, but saying *"ZYZGR delivers components for handheld medical devices"* would be more clear.

The second point should be a statement of value. It may be more than one, but should define how the product relates to your customers and what the benefit it delivers. It also can define your position. For example:

" ZYZGR delivers components for handheld medical devices that are used by 9 of the top 10 vendor platforms. Our products enable our customers to develop their products up to 20% more quickly."

Finally, if possible relate to your competition in an unnamed way. This makes it clear how you are differentiated in your space. This enables a solid close on the pitch:

" ZYZGR delivers components for handheld medical devices that are used by 9 of the top 10 vendor platforms. Our products enable our customers to develop their products up to 20% more quickly with up to 50% reduction compared to alternatives."

This pitch makes ZYZGR sound like much more than it might be. The fact that ZYZGR devices have been tested may mean they have been used. Both the 20% claim of time to market and the 50% claim for cost were best case scenarios. But there is nothing that is not true. This pitch would be effective at getting a next question from any medical device manufacturer that it was given to. It also form the basis for a quick follow-up about the opportunities associated with the described benefits.

The elevator pitch is only outrageous in that it is intended to elicit a response and lead to the next step in the conversation. It needs to maximize your position, while minimizing any confusion on your position. Think of the elevator pitch as a movie trailer for your business. How can you make what you do understandable and desirable in 30 seconds?

Another way to get good at the elevator pitch is to do one for yourself, as an individual, in your current work role, or in some other role. As you do this, you will develop the clarity of seeing the key elements to include in your personal elevator pitch.

Chapter 34 Partnering is Dating, Sex, and Marriage

In business, there is much mentioned of partnering as a way to build and manage a business. The challenge is that partnering is much like dating, sex, and then the marriage that follows. If we are not clear up front about why we are doing the partnership, it is doomed to failure. I put this section under marketing as that seemed the best place for it, though partnering is a whole company activity.

The Dating Period

In the beginning, two entities consider partnering for many reasons: they have compatible offers, they meet at customer locations, customers have told them to work together, or one sees the other as a valuable assist to their business. Very rarely does a partnership in the business world start with a matchmaker, with the exception of customers through VARs. This means that often neither of the partners starts with a clear understanding of what the value of a partnership might be for themselves, and what the other partner wants or needs out of the relationship. In the initial period, one of three things can happen: one partner is selling the other on the relationship, both are selling each other on the relationship, or there is a clear dialog about how each will benefit.

Partnering as Sex

If the goal of the discussion is to have a partnership and the discussion stays at the level of "let me tell you why you want this", the partnering exercise often has a goal of the partnership alone. Whether one or both of the partners sees the relationship purely in terms of the value to them and is "selling" the other partner to get them to agree, the value is defined in the partnership, not the outcomes it will produce. In many cases, the outcomes are left to assumptions that are not codified by the other partner.

A small company sees a partnership with a large company as a way to accelerate their revenue and expand their customer engagement. The larger company sees the partnership with the smaller company as removing an objection without investing in building a narrow component. In the partnership discussion the small company is focused on getting the partnership and positioning why they are the best at this component. The larger company is focused on getting the relationship and positions its large installed base.

However, the partnering discussion never really addresses the needs of each after the partnership is consummated. The small company is not clear on its position, that it needs the large company to sell products without extensive support as its volume is challenged by the size of staff. The larger company is not clear about the fact that it sees this product only being used in a small percentage of its customers and will only be sold it when absolutely required: in addition, it will not compensate its salespeople as the product has very low margins and their compensation is margin based.

The result is a great feeling of satisfaction when the agreement is reached and the partnership is announced. The market generally reacts positively, as the natural attraction between the partners is seen. However, as the months move on the partnership is seen by one or both parties as being less than satisfactory. The small company does not see the anticipated revenue increase, or the large company does not see the small company as being responsive. The problem is that the partners did not adequately vet their views of the partnership up front.

Partnering as Marriage

The key to building a long term partnership is that each partner is able to clearly articulate and understand the needs and outcomes of the both partners in the relationship. This is not saying what you THINK they will gain, but actually having them tell you what they need.

In this way, the partnership is defined clearly as to what each partner brings into the relationship and what each is going to receive. Typically simple partnerships such as a channel resale relationship are easy to understand in this way, but as partnerships move to less clearly defined relationships, having a clear win-win value is essential. This is what is lost when partnering becomes a selling exercise with the goal being the partnership itself.

To make partnering work, there has to be a clear representation of what each intends to get out of the partnership and what conflicts or other issues may arise. Just agreeing to partner is not enough: there must be a clear short- and medium-term value for each partner. In the channel partner relationship, the values are clear. The manufacturer gets representation and sales of its products, the channel partner gets a product to sell, along with the margin and service revenues that go with that.

When we consider relationships that are more complex, defining the values at the beginning is harder, recognizing that they will not change over time is equally hard. This is because there is generally some overlap between the parties. The technology business is an area where this has been painfully obvious over the last 10 years. At the end of the last millennium, the IT industry was relatively well defined and structured. In most cases the overall solution had a set of layers, each derived from a major category, often delivered by a dominant player in that category. Starting with the network (Cisco), the server (HP, Dell, IBM, Sun), the software infrastructure (Microsoft, Oracle), the apps (SAP, PeopleSoft,), and finally business consulting (IBM, EDS, Perrot): the market was well structured. Relationships existed between the players at the layers, some exclusive, some less so. However, Tech/IT industry stock value is not driven by dividends, it is driven by growth. Therefore, all of the companies were under intense pressure to grow, and were equally concerned about their "partners" growing. A comment by a very senior HP executive in 2007 clarified this for me. At the time, HP was about $100B in revenue. He commented that expectations in the equity markets was that HP would grow at 5% per year, which was equivalent to adding a $5B Fortune 500 company every year.

In the end the pressure to grow, when the overall market was growing at less than 5% caused fundamental shifts. Oracle, for example, moved up into the applications space, competing with the application vendors who built their applications on the Oracle database. Oracle then acquired Sun, moving into the hardware and platform arena, competing with HP, IBM , and the other server and storage vendors. Cisco moved up from the network to the server space, competing with IBM and HP in their core businesses, causing HP to invest heavily in data networking. HP acquired EDS to move up to compete with IBM in the services level. The result is that the IT industry has moved back to more of a vertically integrated solutions business as it has matured. That is where it started in the 1960s, and now it appears to be moving back. The result is that the partnerships that were created have become transitory and are no longer applicable.

Planning for Divorce

While some partnerships last a long time, essentially without change, a critical part of the strategic planning process is to plan for change. It is imperative that each partnership that has a material impact on a business be evaluated on an annual basis. This evaluation should consist of three parts: 1. analyzing the outcomes of the last year in the relationship, 2. reviewing the next year's goals and directions, and 3.a scenario review of the next 3-5 years of the relationship.

When the partnership is established and annually thereafter, a joint plan and goals for each year should be generated. These should clearly define what the value is to each party and how that value translates into specific business benefits for each partner, in real financial terms. At the end of every year, the previous year's plan should be analyzed and the actual results compared to the plan. By doing this across multiple partnerships, it is possible to see if there are specific trends, either limited to a given relationship, overall in a type of partner, or broader market impacting impact. If there is a variance to the goals, either positive, negative or just different, the actual outcomes need to be understood.

With a clear view of how the previous year went, a plan with specific goals should be defined for the upcoming year. This needs to include the values, the actions expected of both parties and the anticipated outcomes for both parties. This may be a negotiated and open discussion with the partner or may be more closed. Regardless of how it is done, it should be clear to each party what the expectations of the other party are, not just in actions, but in outcomes. I have seen multiple times, when a partner was actually told what the outcome expectations were of the other partner, but there ensued a discussion as the other partner realized that the expectations were not grounded in the reality from their point of view.

Finally, a scenario analysis of the next 3-5 years should be undertaken centered on changes that might happen in the relationship. Define at least 5 events that would have a major impact on the relationship and that need to be considered. These may be acquisitions, space changes and adjacency expansion, new relationships on either side or any other event that would change the partnership. Each of these should be briefly analyzed for impact and actions that would need to happen. For each event, consider what precursors or indicators there could be that the event was going to happen so you could be aware of them.

In 2004, Nortel had a strong partnership with Airespace, a manufacturer of WiFi equipment. The relationship was a strong OEM relationship, enhanced by significant integration between the companies. Even though the WiFi component could be a substantial part of the revenue for a customer, Nortel did not have an internal plan to replace Airespace. In late 2004, multiple events came up that should have been seen as precursors to a potential acquisition. IBM, who was the largest customer of Cisco and bought over $1B from them annually decided to commit to Airespace as their preferred WiFi solution, and began to introduce the Nortel data portfolio with Airespace. Also, Microsoft, a major Cisco networking customer, decided to deploy an Airespace WiFi solution for their campus. This was followed by a couple of other major deals. In about October of 2004, I talked to both the GM who owned the business and the President of the group, expressing a concern that this was not a technology issue, but was becoming a threat to Cisco at a core business level. I was assured that there were no concerns: the Airespace management team was not interested in an acquisition. By the holiday break, Cisco had made an offer to acquire the company, and despite attempts to put together a consortium to thwart the offer, Cisco prevailed in acquiring the company for $450M, about 15 times the $30M revenue of the company at the time. This caused great upheaval as there was no planning for this event.

Partnering Life-Cycle

Partnering is a life cycle that has a beginning, many middles and, in most cases has an end. Planning for the cycle, both initially and repeatedly through the relationship is required for success. This planning should be clear on the expected outcomes by both parties, clear alignments of areas of control and expertise, defined goals and plans, and scenario planning for events that could dramatically change the partnership. Partnerships are both required and can be very productive. However they are never easy. Some of the companies that have the worst reputations as partners have that reputation because they are honest about their goals in the partnership. For example, Microsoft is very clear on their goals, even if they are in conflict with a potential partner. Often this clarity points to the early demise of the partnership : this is not necessarily bad. If the partnership is

Philip Edholm

tactical for one party, it will have a short life cycle and it is better for the other party to understand that going into the relationship. Make sure that you are not planning a marriage when your partner is just dating.

Technology

The technology section is relatively brief, reflecting the complexity of the area and the fact that many technology areas are so very market/industry specific. However, as a technologist, there are a few topics that I feel are good for the non-technologist to understand, and even may help the technologist as well.

Chapter 35 The Three Phases of Technology

The value of technology is a transient thing. Just as value changes over time as discussed in the chapter on The Value Add Economy, technology and its relative value changes over time. Based on past technology absorption cycles, technology seems to go through three phases: the Tactical use

Figure 35-1 Three Phases of Technology Absorption

phase, the Strategic phase, and finally the Utility phase. While some areas of technology may re-cycle with a secondary or even tertiary wave of new value, many times the transition to the utility point is a final change to the cycle and represents a long term plateau for the technology.

The Tactical Phase

When a new technology is introduced to the market, the first uses of that technology are often a tactical application of the technology to the existing structure of solutions or processes. In the machine shop of 1800, tools were powered typically using a water wheel that turned a central overhead shaft. Off that central shaft, belts would power individual pieces of equipment. From 1800

Figure 35-2 Machine Shop circa 1900 (Henry Ford Museum)

through the early 1900s, this mechanism of power distribution in the machine shop did not change. What changed was the power source. In the early 1800s, the water wheel was replaced by a steam engine. This was a tactical application of a new technology and enabled a change in the hours of operation for the machine shop. The machine shop was no longer dependent on the amount of water that could be stored or seasonal rainfall. In the early 1900s, the steam engines began to be replaced by large electric motors, but the power distribution system remained unchanged. The point is that this tactical phase can be defined by a lack of changes in the overall system limitations. The tools are still locked into the physical machine shop and cannot be located more than a few feet from a power shaft. Relocation and changes are complex and the operator danger of exposed belts is still in the environment. Figure 35-2 (Lowe, 2006) shows a machine shop from this period.

The Strategic Phase

After some period of time, and often due to additional technology elements

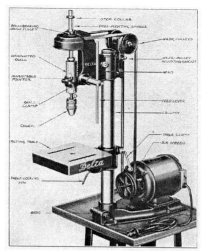

Figure 35-3 Moving the Motor to the Tool (Marshon, 2010)

coming to bear, a technology moves into a Strategic Phase. In the Strategic Phase the technology changes the overall system in ways that now create significant, often overwhelming, strategic advantage for those that adopt it first. In the Strategic Phase the technology changes the overall process in ways that have profound impacts. In the machine shop, the advent of cost effective smaller motors meant that the motor could now be co-located with the machine tool. So instead of the drill press being powered for the overhead shaft with a belt, it now had a small motor and was powered with a wired electrical

distribution as shown in Figure 35-3 (Marshon, 2010). In the machine shop this had a number of advantages. The elimination of the shafts and belts meant that the shop was easier to change and much safer. The elimination of a complex belt and pulley system reduced maintenance costs dramatically. The collocation of power meant that the only power used was for tools that were active as well. Finally the cost of adding a new tool was now based on that tool and not an expansion of a central plant. However, this was not the real strategic transformation. That came with the realization that the new locally powered tools could be moved out of

Figure 35-4 US Army Truck Machine Shop - circa 1943 (Corps, 1943)

the machine shop and taken to the job site. Figure 35-4 (Corps, 1943) is a machine shop built into a truck to be used for vehicle repair by the US Army in WWII. As time progressed, tool motors and the tools became smaller, resulting in hand held tools.

During this time, the radical change was that the tools moved out of the machine shop, which meant that instead of having to bring all the work to the shop, the tools could be brought to the work. This was a profound strategic shift and the adoption of these new capabilities and how they were used changed the competitive landscape in many ways.

The Utility Phase

At some point the transformations of the Strategic Phase come to a point where the changes are no longer so significant that they actually create strategic advantage. At this point, everyone has adopted the technology and it's use has become common. For example, can you generate strategic business advantage with electric office lighting? The obvious answer is *"no"* because all of the competitors in any given industry have electric lighting. If one business was the only business with electric office lighting, it would be a great strategic advantage, especially in northern climes with shorter light days in the winter. However, as we all use office lighting in essentially the same way, there is no advantage. Similarly, the power tool has moved to a point where

Figure 35-5 Portable Power Drill - circa 1950s (Henry, 2013)

there is no strategic advantage. Many of us have a "machine shop" in our garage (drill, power saw, sander, saber saw, router, etc.), so there is no real advantage. Further refinements, while generating new capabilities often do not create a new set of transitions. For example, the advent of battery-powered tools created a very minor new wave, through enabling tools to be used where there was no local power. For many technologies, the transition to the Utility Phase represents a final stage where the technology will continue to provide value, but will do so in essentially a utility way, where the value is fixed and the analysis is based on cost, not variable value. When buying a drill, the analysis of the buying decision has little to do with the actual drilling capability, but is based purely on cost and a few minor differentiations such as corded versus battery and other feature/brand decisions.

Value creation

As a technology moves through the phases, the value that is created changes. Obviously for the adopters, the impact is measured in their business success, either through increasing revenue or reducing cost. The revenue increase can be either by gaining share in an existing market or growing overall market size or wallet share in adjacencies.

For the vendors of the technology, value is also created in the transitions. While in some ways this is similar to the Crossing the Chasm (Moore, 1991)models and the resultant gorillas, chimpanzees and monkeys, it is really fundamentally different. In the chasm world, Moore is looking at a single technology and its phases. In crossing the chasm he defines how that technology moves from the early adopters to the applications-specific adopters that then generate the tornado of adoption, leading eventually to broad acceptance. He argues that this process generally creates value is a specific way, with one or two gorillas, with large or majority market share, a small number of chimpanzees with relative smaller share, and finally a group of monkeys with very little share. He demonstrates that the value created by the technology accrues very unequally to the gorillas and virtually not at all to the monkeys.

The difference in the Phase model is that each phase introduces a new generation of potential gorillas. This may not obviate the previous generation, but may expand the space in such a way that new competitors at different junctures are created. In the machine shop example, this is clear

271

both in the transition from the tactical to strategic and from the strategic to utility phases. The first transition did not change the tool industry greatly, though the advent of powered shop floor tools did change that industry. Obviously the electric motor manufacturers were a completely different group than the fixed steam engine manufacturers. The strategic transition and the strategic to utility both generated new entrants and value. Many of the existing tool manufacturers made the transition from belt to electric power, but new entrants changed the market. Similarly, the transition from fixed to portable tools introduced new players. Throughout this process, those who recognized the changes succeeded.

As a business person, understanding the transitions in your industry enables you to see how to manage your value creation.

Re-Cycle Impact

The Re-Cycle is when a technology that is in utility moves back because of a new advance. This is different than a whole new technology and may be related only to a specific optimization. As was mentioned earlier, the introduction of battery-powered hand tools was a re-cycle in the utility "machine shop" technology that had reached a utility phase in the late 50s, early 60s with modern hand tools. The introduction of battery power moved the industry back to a new strategic position as these tools could be used without having to be connected to the power distribution network. For the user of the tools, this was a significant advantage. For the vendors, it was an opportunity to reposition and even enter new markets. Entering a mature market without a Re-Cycle is a challenging heads up competition, but doing so in a re-cycle is much easier.

Re-Cycles have three major differences to a primary cycle. Generally they do not return all the way to the tactical phase, though there may be some short-term elements that are there; the strategic phase is generally much shorter than a primary cycle; and the opportunity for value creation or disruption on both the user and vendor sides are much lower. However, in most industries, the Re-Cycle is the only disruptor that can be seen and defined.

Analyzing a Technology

For each new technology that comes into the market, understanding how that technology will be adopted is the critical challenge. Further understanding when a technology will cause a Re-Cycle is also important. The challenge is that while hindsight can clearly show us when the phases and transitions have occurred, it is much harder to see where you are at particular time and in a particular industry. The danger is that a user or vendor who does not understand the transition and the next phase runs the risk of making decisions that are based on the previous value. The user who does not see the transition to strategic can have a major market position erosion, but missing the transition from strategic to utility runs the risk of overspending on something that no longer delivers strategic differentiation.

In 2004 Nicholas Carr wrote an article in the Harvard Business Review "IT Doesn't Matter" in which he argued that the IT industry was moving from the strategic phase to the utility phase. While his forecast has not been completely validated, a number of the points he made have come true. In the IT industry, the overall industry is clearly becoming more of a utility, as is evidenced by the movement to cloud computing models. However, there continue to be Re-Cycles of the industry that are creating new transitions, though they are much smaller in value impact than the major transitions of the past.

I am going to attempt to provide a few examples, though, with the exception of the Information Technology area, these are limited to my knowledge base of an industry. The intent is to enable the reader to think about your area and industry and understand whether you are in a major transition or what the Re-Cycles are. Finally, as with most analysis, this was done in early 2012, and reflects technology and industry positions at that time.

A few examples of this are:

Information Systems

Computer information systems used in business have gone through all three of these phases since widespread adoption began in the late 50s. As computers were brought into business in the 60s through 80s, they generally were used to automate existing processes. For example, a paper-based payroll system was moved to a computer, so checks were generated automatically instead of being typed by hand. The inventory management system replaced a hand ledger based system. This use of technology to essentially automate existing business processes continued until the late 1980s. As that decade came to a close, information technology began to change the way the business process functioned. Wal-Mart implemented a system in the late 80s which impacted its top 200 suppliers. Instead of Wal-Mart placing orders and taking ownership of the products from these suppliers when the product was shipped, Wal-Mart implemented a system using a new capability called EDI (Electronic Data Interchange) and changed the process. In the new system, the 200 vendors owned the inventory in the Wal-Mart warehouses and were only paid when the products were shipped from there to a Wal-Mart store. In addition, Wal-Mart would send inventory levels to the vendors using EDI and they were expected to manage the inventory. So the vendors now owned the responsibility for inventory levels and the costs for expedited shipping if they misjudged the volume.

This change continued through the 90s and into the 2000s in the retail industry. An industry that was based on buying inventory and selling it in 1985, changed to managing shelf space by 2005. In most grocery stores in the US today, a significant part of the shelf inventory is directly managed and stocked by the supplying vendor and payment for the item from the retailer to the vendor does not occur until the item moves through the check-out process. In fact, stores such as Costco have a goal of not owning any inventory from outside vendors in the store.

In industry after industry, the use of information technology to fundamentally change the process of the business can be seen. The advent of the web browser and the easy interaction of an individual with a server representing a business accelerated the transformation. eBay changed the process of selling and buying items that used to be done through the classified ads, in a very strategic way. When you advertised in the classifieds, you ad would reach a circulation of thousands. So if your paper reached 200,000 people, and 0.01% were interested in what you were selling at that point in time, there would be 20 potential buyers. If you listed on eBay and there were 100M eBay users, the same 0.01% would yield 10,000 potential buyers. Similarly, if you were a buyer, the options from sellers increases exponentially. What is interesting is that Craigslist is really not strategic like eBay as it is still local, it is a tactical change from classifieds to on-line.

Similarly, if we look at banking, we find the percentage of transaction that are done with a human has dropped by orders of magnitude. In manufacturing the integration of just-in-time (JIT)processes with effective automation has reduced the inventory and stock levels.

Looking forward, there are some potential Re-Cycles, but not another major overall transition coming.

Cloud computing- the movement of computing from the customer premise to a cloud service will have a short term strategic value for some businesses in that services that were only available to larger companies will now be available to a wider range. This may have significant impact in some markets.

Social networking- the advent of social systems, combined with video is a potential major strategic advantage for businesses that are distributed and have a partitioned structure that could benefit from cross-pollination.

Information/Interaction convergence- bringing together the information process with real-time human interaction has the potential of driving both personal productivity gain as well as much better Time To Conclusion for many business processes that have events that are dependent on humans to accelerate. There are no doubt others, but this is an adequate list for illustration.

Auto Industry

Obviously the automobile industry moved to a utility phase many years ago, but there are some major Re-Cycles that are happening now. Over the last 5 years the concept of kinetic energy retention, as implemented in hybrid cars has been a Re-Cycle that has changed the industry. Toyota achieved over 90% market share in hybrid cars by early 2012. This had a demonstrable impact on Toyota, who shipped a total of 124,540 units in the US in January of 2012, of which 16,065 were hybrids, so 12% of Toyota revenue is due to this Re-Cycle. Of the total 914K cars shipped that month (Marty Padgett, 2012), Toyota has a 13.6% market share. If Toyota had not built the Prius, the 16,065 hybrids sold probably would not have gone to Toyota, but would have been split as other sales with all of the other vendors. If this was true, only 2,560 of those 16,065 hybrid car purchases would have been other Toyota models. The total Toyota sales would have dropped to 111,000, and their share would have dropped to 12.1% or a loss of 1.5 points of market share. The gap between Toyota and the fourth place (GM and Ford were larger in overall sales) Chrysler would have changed from 3.5 share points to about 2 share points. So the hybrid Re-Cycle was key to Toyota building its 2012 position. However, the electric hybrid Re-Cycle is quickly moving to a utility phase as most manufacturers adopt it and the differentiation decreases. The key is whether Toyota can maintain the share gain the hybrid gave them.

The next round of automotive Re-Cycles probably will occur in two areas, alternative fuels and in-car technology integration. In the alternative fuel arena, the need for an alternative fuel system that can deliver longer range than plug-in electrics and have the fueling availability of gasoline is a major Re-Cycle. Obviously companies like Fiskar and Tesla are betting this is an opportunity to change the market with that Re-Cycle.

The in-car technology Re-Cycle is less clear whether it will create true strategic advantage. Systems such as Sync by Ford and Microsoft generally use voice to access existing systems. The advent of storage, sensors and adaptive systems will enable cars to do significant new things; the question is whether this creates a real strategic value and will enable the vendors to change their positions.

Biotech and Pharma
While I am not an expert in this area, it would appear to me that there may be a major transition coming. It would appear that the majority of the medical breakthroughs of the past 30 years are used to treat the symptoms of disease, age, and lifestyle. While there is no doubt that the recent focus on lifestyle, exercise, and diet are aimed at extending life, the general medical system seems to be in the mold of a tactical application of new technologies to treat conditions. It would appear that the understanding of what causes these conditions can translate into a new area of condition

avoidance, enhanced by technology. For example. plaque build-up in arteries causes heart issue and strokes. If we had a medical technology that would eliminate plaque deposits with minimal side effects and regardless of diet and genetics, it would be a strategic advantage to those who took it. If you could eliminate the percentage probability of a heart attack or other malady caused by this by having a preventative treatment, it would be a strategic value.

The real opportunity is to not treat individual ailments, but to treat all of the potential ailments with technology that prevents the specific ailment from emerging. Much as with vaccinations, the change is that medicine moves from tactical treatment of a condition to strategic prevention. The major change is that while 5M people may develop heart disease over a period, all of the population will need the preventative treatment. But the real strategic value is that by volume structuring the cost of prevention may be much less than the cost of treatment.

Energy

The energy industry is in some ways similar to the machine shop of the 1900s. We have built an overall system on the premise of centralized power generation and massive distribution infrastructure. However, it is interesting to examine if there is a technology change that is coming that will change that dynamic in a strategic way.

Solar power generation has been applied in two ways, as an alternative central solution and as a local power generation. As a central power solution, it does not have great advantage today over fuel-based alternatives, though that may change with fuel pricing. However, the central generation does not change the need for a complex and maximum demand based distribution system.

The new technology is not solar alone, but combining local power generation with local power storage. This combination creates a significant strategic transition. By moving the power generation to the edge and using some form of efficient energy storage, the distribution system can be dramatically curtailed. The central generation would be limited to providing topping off to the local storage when demand exceeds supply.

The result is a much more efficient and effective system. If the storage system can equal the transmission system in effectiveness, then the system will be more efficient at lower cost. Before assuming this is not possible, think what someone in 1900 would have said about a battery powered hand-held drill...not to mention the iPhone you are using as a compass.

Conclusions

As part of the strategy of any business, a clear view on the technology phases of the industry(s) you are participating in is critical. Take the time to define where you are and whether there is the potential of major or Re-Cycle transitions in your space. Identify scenarios that could impact your business and think through the potential opportunities these can create for changing your position. Also be clear on the advantage for you and your vendor or customers, depending on where you are in the use chain. Being aware of the Three Phases of Technology Absorption will assure that you are not surprised by changes and hopefully will enable you to surprise your competitors.

Chapter 36 The Development Equation

In every company I have been in, there has been a perennial challenge with managing the delivery of Research and Development projects. As the project progressed, the outcomes became variable, some projects would run over in budget, some in delivery, while others would miss in their content or the final quality.

What became clear was there were two very different factors at play: 1. the accuracy of the manager and his team in estimating the program based on the requirements and the timing, and 2. the required actions for quality delivery, and changes that occurred during the program.

The initial estimate is where the most time gets focused. Getting a clear view of the requirements and the resources to meet the deliverable timing becomes a critical step in the program launch. However, after this step the program enters the development phase and that is when the real challenges begin.

For example, a program is launched with a 12 month schedule to deliver a set of capabilities and functionality, either in hardware or software or a combination. All of a sudden major issues arise with 3 months left. The content is short or the schedule is long. Or the product delivers and the result is plagued with quality issues. The question is always, "What happened?"

The reality is that in almost every program was altered at some point and the team did not analyze the fact that it was now unbalanced and the result is

$$\text{Time to Delivery} = \frac{\text{Features} + \text{Quality}}{\text{Resources}}$$

Figure 36-1 The Development Equation

always a bad outcome. The Development Equation is a way to think of this as a simple tool that has to be balanced for any project. The equation has the four elements that must be both defined: 1. the time to deliver the outcome, 2. the features/capabilities of the result, 3. the quality to be built into the result, and 4. the resources available. The equation shown in

Figure 36-1 is the way these align.

Time to Delivery

This is the allocated time from the initial start of the program to the final result. It includes any pre-design or other work not complete at the time of program start. It also may include any detailed specifications or architecture work. Architecture here refers to the general design. It can mean how the software or hardware is structured, or in a more basic sense the architecture of the packaging. It clearly includes any final testing and release structure time.

Features

This is the defined content of the program. It may be hardware or software, or even a consulting program result like a report. It is inclusive of all requirements, including documentation and design activities.

Quality

This is the plan to deliver quality in the result. The quality element may include time during the definition and design process for Design for Quality programs as well as defined testing both at intermediate stages and of the final outcome. It this result is a product to be used in a larger system, the quality element may include systems testing or be part of a software release testing process.

Resources

What are the defined resources that are committed to delivering the program. These are the resources that can be used for the Time to Delivery or a defined portion of achieve the required results. The resource number is not a headcount number, but rather a man month or man year number based on the estimated requirements to meet the features and quality requirements in the available Time to Delivery. In addition to the quantity of resources the quality also needs to be taken into account. Both skill and experience level will have a major impact on productivity.

Balancing the Equation with Risk at the Beginning

At the beginning when the program is estimated, there are a set of assumptions that are made based on the knowledge base at that point in time. Generally a requirements document is generated that details the required feature outcomes of the program at some initial level of specificity. This is combined with the required quality time and resources to generate the project plan. The project plan is generally based on time duration for certain activities that are not resource parallel sensitive and others where the resource pool drives increased or decreased schedule. These are typically mapped against the requirements for Time to Delivery in an iterative process. The challenge is that often many, if not all of these factors are, to a great extent, defined separately and then the resulting equation either does not balance, or is balanced through risk. For example, the required delivery for the product is 12 months. Based on the company plan for quality, the test program takes 2 months at the end of development, so the development time is 10 months. Based on the feature requirements, the development team has defined that they can do the project in 10 months with 10 resources working on it for the entire time. The quality team is included for their two months in the resource plan. However, management is under pressure and cannot allocate 10 resources, so the team is only given 9 staff. The result is that the equation is now unbalanced. This actually exacerbated by the fact that most people overestimate their capability and skill, so most estimates are at least 20% low, so our actual formula at the outset should look more like Figure 36-2. As you can see, the extra factor is added to features and the resources are decreased. The result is that the program that is now defined with 9 staff is actually 25% less than the probable requirement, so the time to Delivery will be 25% longer.

$$\text{Time to Delivery} = \frac{(\text{Features } + 20\%) + \text{Quality}}{\text{Resources } - 10\%}$$

Figure 36-2 Result of Unanticipated Features

The program team has been challenged to "step up" and make the delivery. Being good corporate citizens, they agree to the all of the factors in the original equation, hoping that at some point a miracle will occur. But, as we all know, the miracle does not occur and the actual time required is equal to the original estimate. As management refuses to allow either the delivery date or the feature content to change, there is only one way to balance the equation., the resultant Quality MUST be reduced. As the development team has 9 people to do 100 man months of work, the actual time to deliver the program is 11 months, so the product goes to the test team with only a month to do the necessary testing. The test team squeezes the test cycles by half and, as a result, only finds 70-80% of the issues and the released product is not of great quality.

Or alternatively, management agrees that having a valid test cycle is critical and will not change that and the actual time required is 10% over the estimate, resulting in 100 man months of work, which results in 12.2 months to complete the R&D, which results in a 14.2 month Time to Delivery, which is then represented as a 2.2 month slip or a 22% miss against the original schedule. No one on the team gets a reward as the goal is less than a 20 % slip, which sounds reasonable.

At the beginning of a program, a realistic view is very important. Do a realistic view and then do your analysis with a 20% (or if you are adventurous, a 10%) cushion. Be very careful not to allow this initial squeeze to cause failure. If you are in the management role, do not let yourself define an equation that is not realistic and balanced.

Ch..ch..ch..changes

Now we have kicked off our program, we feel good because we have included a 10% cushion and the program is a go. Generally the team now moves forward and focuses on the activity to deliver, but very quickly things can begin to impact the outcome. As the team moves through the detailed requirements, new requirements come from customers or the marketplace that are perceived as both being mandatory and do not allow the elimination of other features and content. As the design team refines their design they realize that something they had planned to do in one way will need to change requiring more resources. And finally, one of the team members needs to spend 2 months resolving quality issues on a previous relapse. Meanwhile, the team leadership and management continue to position that the outcome is still the same. However, we now have moved closer and closer to unbalancing our equation again. In Figure 36-3, we now have added in the changes. The original estimate of feature content was to allow a 10% cushion, but now the changes in requirements and design complexity has moved that to an actual 20% increase and the loss of 2 months decreases the resources pool by 2.2%.

As the program goes on, the resources are further reduced due to external influences, and the content is still required, The commitment for Time to Delivery is seen as fixed and a firm commitment, so once again the result is a reduction in time for test and quality.

Original Plan

$$\text{Time to Delivery} = \frac{(\text{Features} + 10\%) + \text{Quality}}{\text{Resources}}$$

Current Plan

$$\text{Original Time to Delivery} \approx \frac{(\text{Features} + 20\%) + \text{Quality}}{\text{Resources} - 2.2\%}$$

Outcome

$$\text{Original Time to Delivery} \approx \frac{(\text{Features} + 20\%) + \boxed{\text{Quality}}}{\text{Resources} - 2.2\%}$$

Figure 36-3 Changes and Impact

As in the initial planning, a continuous process or a specific process at certain points in a program to review the equation assumptions in a realistic fashion is required. Feature creep is a common process in development or other programs, and is an important reason to have some cushion at the beginning. The organization is not served well by any of the outcomes of not managing this correctly. Slipping the schedule results in loss of customer confidence and has potentially major impacts on revenue and position in the market. If schedule, feature content, and resources are fixed, then the only area to balance the equation is in reduced quality as shown on the "Outcome" line. Reducing quality will have a major negative impact on customer confidence and follow-on purchases, will increase support costs, and will signal customers to never adopt first release products as they are assumed to have mediocre quality. Finally, building a "hero" mentality in the company where teams take on heroically delivering against all odds will work once or maybe twice, but over time will result in low morale and employee defections.

Philip Edholm

Conclusion

This chapter is all about being realistic. While we may all want to believe in miracles or hero results, they infrequently happen. In most cases, a baby takes 9 months and the project will take as long as is required to deliver the Features and the Quality desired. Changing these will have an impact and, in the end, the outcome will not be desirable. In one company I was in, there was a redesign of a product to reduce costs by using newer parts. Part of that redesign was a change from a proprietary vendor operating system to Linux, an open OS. The value of this change was to be able to use newer tools and eliminate the cost of the proprietary OS vendor. The team faced a difficult decision, the schedule was tight and the resources limited and rewriting all of the software to the Linux system would take too long. So they opted for a shim software that sat on top of Linux and made it look like the old OS to the software. While these type of implementations are common, they are acknowledged to be risky and unreliable, but it was the only answer to get the project done in the time frame demanded by management. After the product was released, a number of issues came up in customer sites, many issues occurred at random at unique times of high load or use. The result was three fold: major customer dissatisfaction and revenue loss, replacing many of the units with older higher cost units that did not have the problem, and a major engineering program to rewrite the software directly on Linux. The result of this decision was a negative profit impact in the millions of dollars, significantly exceeding the cost of actually doing the program right in the first place (a few more months of engineering). Finally all of the direct project managers were fired, but not the leaders who demanded the flawed schedule.

I will leave you with a Dilbert strip, that to me, is the best example of how we delude ourselves... and then fail. Scott Adams gets to the crux of the problem. While some leaders, like Steve Jobs seemed to be able to create environments where the Development Equation would not apply or could be ignored, for most of us that are regular humans, it will apply.

© Scott Adams, Inc./Dist. by UFS, Inc.

Figure 36-4 Dilbert - Planning for Optimism

Chapter 37 Architecture Principles

I decided to include one chapter on a topic that I think is very important in any company that is building products that are part of systems and even for companies that are building point products. There are a couple of key principles that I believe apply across virtually any architecture of a system. While each system will have a myriad of components and decisions, I will later describe two general architectural principles that I have found help guide me in making and analyzing my architectural decisions.

Architectural Principles are less rules than they are common sense. In any architectural endeavor there are three elements: 1. standards, 2. optimization and 3. principles.

For example, if you hire an architect to design a house for you he will use a set of building standards in the design. These include standards for electrical and plumbing, but also for other areas. For example, if a room is specified as having an 8 foot ceiling, this standard carries forward into the building materials. The sheetrock for the wall covering is 8 feet long and the 2x4 studs for the walls are precut at a little more than 92 inches to accommodate 3 rows of 2x4s used in wall construction (one on the bottom and two on the top). In this way the builder need not cut either the studs or the sheetrock, minimizing labor and waste.

The architect's primary role is the optimization of the design to the location, your family's needs and your preferences. The number of bedrooms in the house is driven by your number of children (and maybe resale value). Whether to have a formal living room and family room or a single great room is a decision. How the structure sits on the lot and relates to the surrounding area is important as is the style of the house.

Principles are more basic. They guide us, but are not standards in the same way. For example, when we build a house, the dining room is generally adjacent to the kitchen. This is so it is easy to get food to the table. A design to put the dining room on the opposite side of the house from the kitchen is clearly seen as violating that principle. Similarly, in modern homes, each bedroom has a single door from a hallway. A design where each bedroom had a door into the adjacent bedroom would be seen as poor. It is clear that having to walk through three bedrooms to get to the fourth has significant issues. What is interesting is that these principles evolve over time. The great palaces like Versailles had the kitchen in the basement and a series of rooms would have doors to each other. However the lifestyles of the residents and the number of servants was very different. These rules are generally obvious, even an amateur can understand when a principle is being violated , even when the argument to violate a principle sounds good. For example, if your architect said this to you, "One of the new design principles that I am building into my houses is optimizing the input and output functions by collocating them. This reduces time and effort" what would you reaction be? While this sounds good, the result would be putting the toilet in the kitchen for optimization. Obviously, while there may be some logic for this, the result would be unacceptable.

For purposes of this chapter I am going to discuss two architectural principles for companies that deliver systems, components or products. The first is how to allocate functions in a distributed layered system, and the second is how to deliver high availability.

Distributed Architectural Principle

This section is about how to manage the complexity and intelligence in a distributed system. A distributed system is one where there are layers and each layer has a different level of function. Typically such a system has a mesh and tree layout. Figure 37-1 shows a conceptual model of a distributed system.

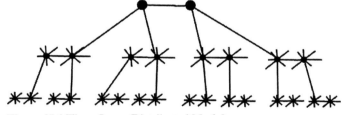

Figure 37-1 Three Layer Distributed Model

Examples of distributed systems are:

The road system with highways at the core and distributing through cities to suburban streets
The power distribution system
The phone system
The Internet

A shipping distribution system

For simplicity and because it generally is true in practice, we will consider that a distribution system has three levels; an edge, a core, and a middle. In Figure 37-1, the core is on the top, the edge on the bottom, and the middle in the middle. Figure 37-2 shows the same concept, but drawn as concentric circles. This may be easier to visualize for some systems.

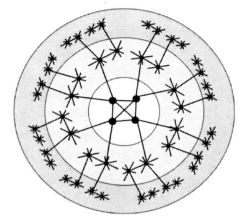

Figure 37-2 Circular representation of Three Layer Model

The layers of the model can be attributed with different values. In all of these models, there are many more points at the edge than in the core. Figure 37-3 illustrates another way of looking at these 3 levels. On the left

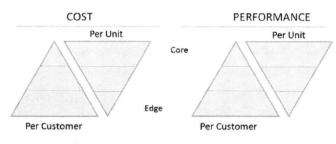

Figure 37-3 Layers with Cost and Performance

is a comparison of cost, from a device and a user perspective. The point is that while the cost of things in the core are very expensive, the average cost per user is dominated by the cost of the things at the edge. Similarly, if we look at performance or capacity or bandwidth or some other measure of capability, a similar rule applies as shown on the right.

Relative Cost

To illustrate the way cost is attributed to layers in the model, we will examine a couple of examples. Take a road system for example. In California there are 2,311 miles of interstate highways. That is the core, with mileage as a measure of the size. At the next level there are other highways and inter-city routes. Based on available data, this is about 30 times the interstate highway system, the total of freeways and highways in California is about 75,000 miles. California has about 2.3M miles of total paved roads with about 700K miles in urban settings and 1.6M in rural settings. Finally, California has about 12 million homes (all types). Of these about 6 million are single family dwellings. If we assume that of the paved roads, at least 70% are in conjunction with homes (country roads to homes, short roads, suburban streets, etc), then we have 75,000 miles of highways, 700K miles of city streets and 1.6M miles of residential roads. In addition to the residential roads, each residence has a driveway, so there are 9 million driveways.

	Road Cost			Driveway Cost			Total ($B)	$/Home (000s)
	Miles (000s)	$M/Mile	Total ($B)	Number (M)	Cost each (000s)	Total ($B)		
Freeways/Highways	75	$ 8	$ 600				$ 600	$ 6.67
City/Urban	700	$ 2	$ 1,400				$ 1,400	$ 15.56
Residential/Rural	1,600	$ 1	$ 1,920	9	20	180	$ 2,100	$ 23.33

Figure 37-4 Comparative Cost for the California Road Systems at Three Levels of Distributed Architecture

If we use this data we can calculate the cost of each level of the road model. Costs for construction vary greatly, but typically the highway will be somewhere around $8M per mile, the average for urban and rural streets is about $2M per mile and the rural road/residential street is about $1.2M per mile. If the average driveway is 20x100 feet if we include the garage and added pads and the cost is $10 per square foot, the average driveway/parking costs about $20,000 dollars per unit. So we now can calculate our total cost for each layer. If we then divide this number by the total number of end residences of 9 million we can calculate the cost attributable to each level per home in California.

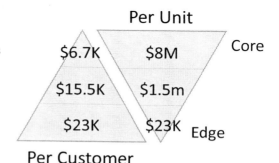

Figure 37-5 Costs of California Road System Per Home

Figure 37-4 shows this data for the California road system.

If we take this data and apply it to the cost pyramids from Figure 37-3, we have a cost pyramid that is shown in Figure 37-5.

Another great example of a distributed system is the cost of Information Technology. While the core data centers have high cost, much of the per user cost is associated with things that are defined as a cost for each user (the PC, application software, support, etc.). IT is similar to the road system, things in the core are very expensive, but the majority of the cost is defined at the edge.

Relative Performance

Similar to the cost analysis, performance follows the same type of distribution, While edge PCs individually do not have the power of the core servers, if you add them all up they have incredible capacity, but we do not use it most of the time. The opportunity is to optimize use by moving the capability to a shared level where it can be used at a much greater percentage. In the phone system the number of end points far exceeds to capacity of the core, but the core network links have much more capacity than the edge. The freeway is built to handle 10s of thousand of cars per day, the driveway only handles one or 2.

Complexity and Intelligence

If the three layer model as shown in Figure 37-6 represents the two sides of cost and performance, then how does this impact architecture and design. If we want to optimize cost only, we would drive all of the intelligence and complexity up to the top where it could be amortized over the largest group of users. This is shown on the left in Figure 37-6. Similarly, if we want to optimize performance and capacity, we would drive complexity and intelligence out to the edge where it can be replicated in volume.

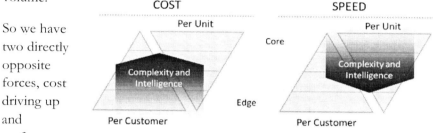

So we have two directly opposite forces, cost driving up and performance driving

Figure 37-6 Contrasting Drivers of Complexity

down. In the end, the only way to optimize both is to put complexity and intelligence in the middle. Figure 37-7 shows what this means for a distributed system.

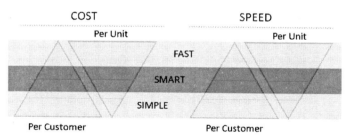

Figure 37-7 Three Layers and Resultant Complexity Model

As is illustrated, the complexity and intelligence moves to the middle layer with a simple layer below and a fast layer above. If we examine some systems, we will find that virtually all systems are of this structure. I say virtually, because I have never found one that does not fit this model, but never say never. Systems get to this point by design or by serendipity. Take the phone system, it has cheap phones and wiring at the edge, a switching fabric in the middle and high-speed trunks in the core. Or look at the newer Internet architectures. They deploy Ethernet for simplicity and performance at the edge, have a

291

router layer in the middle, and use MPLS tagging to make the core fast (and much less intelligent). MPLS tagging uses a simple tag to represent a path through the core, minimizing the billions of potential options down to a small number. These paths can then be shared by many streams of user information.

Similarly the road system has it's layers. In the residential neighborhood, the driveways do not have Stop signs or traffic lights, and even many of the intersections do not have these. As we move to the urban core we have a complex and intelligent system for moving vehicles, including turn lanes, sensors, aligned lights, etc. Finally we come to fast; the freeway system with very defined on-ramps and off-ramps as well as defined paths and movement.

In all of these cases, the design of the system reflects the three layers; Simple, Smart, Fast. However, sometimes there are examples of systems and designs going to this point not through intelligent design, but rather evolution. Take the IT infrastructure in the enterprise as shown in Figure 37-8. In 1990 almost all of the business application s and rules and all of the complexity were in the core in mainframes and minicomputers. By 1995-7 the state of the art was using a technology called "Thick Clients", where all of the business rules moved

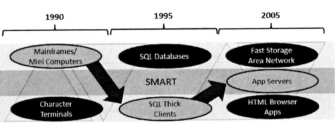

Figure 37-8 IT Migration from Central to Middle Complexity

into an application running in the desktop and the back end was just a SQL database server and all of the business rules and logic were run in the application on the client The promise was faster deployment and new graphic capabilities using the poser of the PC. However, it quickly became clear that the cost of maintaining these systems was much higher. At the same time the browser emerged as a viable desktop, and now we have the model shown at the right, a simple browser at the desk or mobile devices, application intelligence in the middle and a Storage Area Network with speed and distributed data at the top. Essentially, after 10-15 years we moved from a system that was artificially oriented to the top because of early technology, through a systems artificially driven to the bottom by new technology to the ideal architecture of a three layer model.

Applying the Distributed Philosophy

The key to using this model is really understanding where the edge and the core are, realizing that one edge may be adjacent to or even be the next level core. A good application example of this was the advent of WiFi access points (AP) (the antenna on the ceiling or under the desk) in the enterprise networks around 200?. Many were advocating that all of the intelligence of the wireless system should be in the access point, and the traffic coming from the access point would just be like any other. However, it was obvious that moving the intelligence up from the access point into the network was the right thing to do. This made the access points simpler, moved the complexity of mobility and AP to AP handoffs up to a central node, and took advantage of the difference in bandwidth between the terrestrial network capacity and the wireless (see Chapter 40; Edholm's Law of Bandwidth for a more complete explanation) . Over the last 10 years, the wireless control function has moved into the mid-level switches, reflecting exactly this architecture.

Any distributed system can be mapped and through this process you can decide if the architectural decision you are making are optimal or required further though. Again, while never say never, violating these principles needs careful attention.

Delivering Availability

As our computing and communications systems have become an integral part of our lives, the concept of availability or up-time has become an expected reality. In the phone system, the expected availability was five-9s, or 99.999% of the time available. This means that a telephone should only be unavailable 5 minutes per year on average. As the phone was seen as a lifeline and emergency system, the expectations set were high. Customers have come to expect four or five nines in many of the systems we use, from cable TV to the Internet, to our cars and the new drive by wire systems (where availability needs to be even higher).

In the end there are only two ways to make something have high availability; you either make it very reliable or you introduce redundancy. In Figure 37-9, the coffee cup represents reliability. When you pick up a ceramic coffee cup your expectation of reliability is high because it is simple and therefore failure probabilities are low. Similarly, by reducing complexity we can dramatically increase reliability and therefore availability in a device or a system. When they first came out , microwave ovens had a simple twist dial to set the microwave time. Contrast that simplicity and reliability with the newer microprocessor driven microwaves with 50 buttons

Figure 37-9 Two Mechanisms of Availability: Simplicity and Redundancy (Johnson, 2008) (Unknown, 2012)

and programs. In many ways the nostalgia for the "good old days" is a reflection of simplicity and reliability.

The problem with relying on simplicity and reliability alone is that the systems are so simple that they cannot provide the capabilities we need. To do that, things must become more complex, and then the only way to achieve availability with complexity is through redundancy. If we have two systems that each has an availability of three-9s (99.9%), then the resulting system will have six-9s of reliability. The first system is there 99.9% of the time and then the redundant one takes over and also has 99.9%. This means that there is 99.9% during the .01% of failure, resulting in six-9s of availability (.0001% failure or 99.9999% availability).

So what is the problem? The problem is that what was described above is an active-passive or hot stand-by form of redundancy. In this mechanism, we have two units doing the work that one would do if we were not so worried about availability. This means that our second unit, which only is used for about .1% of the time costs the same as the first unit. While this can be thought of as doubling the cost, another way to think about it is that that second unit only operates 1/1000 of the time, so the real cost is 1000 times what we paid for it. Regardless of how it is considered, it is an expensive option. Figure 37-10 contrasts the active-passive with an alternative called active-active. In the active-active, both units are always operating, but when one fails the work is re-allocated to the most important tasks with the resources still available. The easiest way I find to think about this is to consider your personal automobiles. It is highly unlikely that you have a spare car in the garage that is only used if your primary car fails. The Corvette you bought for your 45th birthday does not count. Though you only drive it occasionally, it fulfills an entirely different need than availability. You may use a

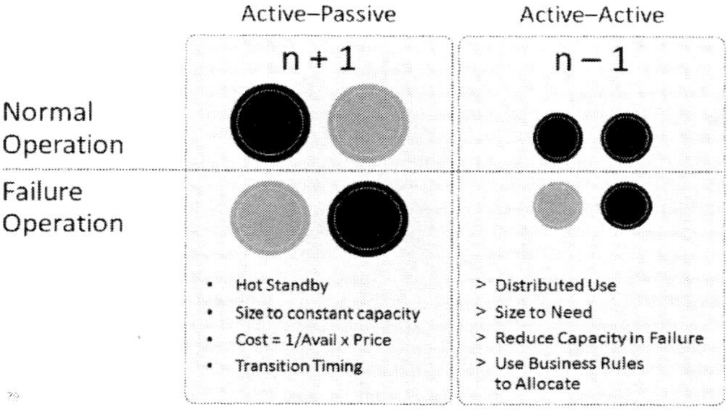

Figure 37-10 Active-Active versus Active-Passive

rental (a form of partially reserved spare capacity), but more likely, you and your spouse both have cars. In the event that one of your cars has to go into the shop, you have to use some form of business rules to allocate the remaining car. In my household this means that my wife gets the car. This is an example of active-active.

In addition to utilization of the resource, there are other reasons that active-active is superior. The process of planning for transition to the hot standby is generally well understood, though there are often issues when it happens. However, the transition back to the primary from the secondary is generally never well considered.

Another form of active-passive is simultaneous operation. In the Space Shuttle, there were certain systems in which there were four separate systems doing the same calculations and the results were compared to see if they would agree. While this has both a high guarantee of availability of the result and inherent reliability, it is a very expensive solution.

If it can be achieved, active-active is a significantly better mechanism for redundancy. It can be used in an N+1 configuration, where N is the minimum for operation and during normal capacity there is additional capacity of +1; in this case, the load is balanced across multiple systems and functions. Active-passive is N-1, where the capacity available is always some number less than what was purchased. In the Space Shuttle, we would have potentially paired systems for error checking and a set of units that were doing other less critical tasks and could be rapidly switched in if one or both of the primary units failed.

An example of how to apply active-active is shown in Figure 37-11. This is for the links from the data network switch in the wiring closet connecting to end users up to the core switches in a campus data network. Obviously making the core switches redundant increases reliability and availability, while doing the same at the wiring closet is hard as there is only one connection to each user. On the left, the active-passive standard of "Spanning Tree" was designed to turn off one of the uplinks so there would not be loops in the data path. The impact of this was to reduce the core capacity by 50% in normal operation. On the right are two implementations of active-active. The

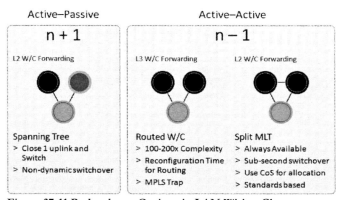

Figure 37-11 Redundancy Options in LAN Wiring Closets

first changes the wiring closet Ethernet switch from simple Layer 2 Ethernet forwarding to complete Layer 3 IP routing. This results in a significant, even order of magnitude, increase in complexity of the wiring closet device that is non-redundant. In this case, the core is now 100% utilized, but the overall availability is actually reduced due to the dramatic increase in complexity. Finally the far right shows a technology called SMLT (Split Multi-Link Trunking), where the traffic is allocated using standard load sharing between the two uplinks and the core switches are both active. This technology enabled rapid switchover at failure and active-

active utilization.

Architecting for Right

These two examples are fairly generic in the technology world, but they illustrate the importance of applying sound architectural principles. In your industry, market, technology and products, what are the architectural guiding principles that need to be considered for success? If you can clearly define those, you will be on a path to succeed, not to build a toilet in the middle of your kitchen.

Chapter 38 OEM Pitfalls

There are two very different OEM relationships: 1. Those through which the OEM provider only sells their product through a vendor that adds significant value to the OEM product, and 2. those through which the OEM product is available essentially unchanged to the end customers in some other way. In either case the vendor (the company in the middle between the OEM and the end customer) is taking the OEM product and delivering it to their customer.

In the first category, which I will refer to as a Component OEM, the OEM vendor is selling something to the vendor that is incorporated into the vendor's product and is generally not visible to the end customer. A good example of this is the processor in a PC. While Intel has built a program around Intel Inside, the average user would not have any idea absent of a sticker about what processor is in a PC. Even more, the OEM provider of the memory in the PC is totally hidden to the end purchaser. The component OEM is a very important part of the overall ecosystem in virtually all products. There are very few products today that are produced in a vertical integrated fashion; most incorporate a significant percentage of the content as OEM components. In an automobile for example there are innumerable OEM components. Most will be common between manufacturers. For example, tires, brake systems, ignition systems, radios, fuel injections systems and many others are examples of OEM components that are sold to auto manufacturers and are used without significant change. Others are differentiated being components manufactured to the car manufacturer's design.

The second category is one in which a vendor OEMs a product and sells it as its own product without significant modification or incorporation into their product offer. In this Solution Element OEM, the product is generally visible as an identifiable part of the vendor's product or solution. Generally it is also available directly to the customer in some other way. For example, it may also be sold directly by the OEM or through alternative channels. In this case the value of buying the OEM Solution element from the vendor is that the vendor is incorporating it into their system, but it is not integrated. Often this type of OEM includes what is called "white labeling" or "rebranding" where the vendor puts their name on the product so it appears that it is their product. However, this often is very transparent as the end customer quickly realizes that the OEM Solution Element is from the OEM vendor. Often the vendor does not really try to hide their relationship as the chosen OEM vendor is a leader in the category. Generally the Solution Element OEM could be purchased separately and the rest of the vendor solution would be able to be used, albeit without complete functionality. For this reason tires, even though they are available directly are not OEM Solution Elements in a car purchase. Also, generally the OEM Solution Element has some level of specified value to the end buyer. Generally when buying a new car, the buyer spends little if any time on the OEM manufacturer of the tires, it is assumed they are a "good" part of the car, just as the buyer would not ask who manufactured the brake system.

Let's first look at the Component OEM case, and then the Solution Element OEM scenario.

The OEM Component Decision

The OEM component decision or make/buy decision can really be thought of as a pure financial decision. There are two parts to the decision: 1. what is the cost impact and 2. what is the revenue impact. In the end, the right point to analyze both of these is at the gross profit line. While gross profit percentage is effective for analyzing cost, focusing on gross profit $ will cover both impacts. The reason that a focus on margin is not enough is that there are costs associated with the "make" decision that are below the margin line, in R&D for example.

Cost-Based Analysis

The first analysis is from the overall cost perspective. Assuming that the internal versus OEM decision has no impact on the functionality of the product, then it is purely a cost decision. In reality this comes down to a volume question: is the volume of the vendor's use of this component sufficient that the vendor can design, test, and manufacture the component for less cost than to buy it from the OEM provider? Obviously the impact of this analysis is in both the Cost of Sales and in the cost of R&D, and potentially some SG&A. In the margin, unit cost of the component at the anticipated volume will generate a potential difference in manufactured cost and therefore of Gross Margin. The second element is the cost of design, testing, and support of having the design in house. In this cost element there are really three separate cost elements that need to be understood: 1. the initial cost of getting to an acceptable level of capability and performance in the component, 2. the cost of support for maintaining that level of capability, and 3. the costs of any enhancements or expansions that are anticipated. If the plan is based on a 5 year use of an internally designed component versus an OEM, the analysis cannot just include the initial design, it must include ongoing investments for enhancements.

To illustrate this analysis, the following simple model demonstrates the principles. ACME is planning to manufacture a new widget in 6 months at an anticipated volume of 10 million units per year, the average widget selling for $1,000. Within each widget there is a modulator. Based on the functions of the modulator, ACME engineers have decided that a component from an OEM is sufficient. The ACME engineers have decided that they can build an equivalent component in-house and believe their cost will be less than OEM. In negotiations with the OEM, ACME has received guaranteed pricing for 5 years with included price reductions for each year. The initial price for the OEM modulator is $2 with 10% reductions each year. The internal team has estimated that they can build modulators for $1. To do this they need a team of 8 engineers for 6 months and then a support team of 4 engineers for the rest of the 5 years. The average engineer will cost $200,000 per year including all overhead, burden, and management. Which is the right choice for ACME? If we did a simple model, we can save $.50 per unit, with a volume of 10 million units, that is a savings of $5M. However, this is not sufficient as it does not take into account either the forward pricing reductions or the cost of internal design. To do that we need to build a simple model based on a set of assumptions. It is paramount that we remove potential variables out of the model so the impact of the make/buy decision is isolated. While you may have more complicated models, this introduction of the make/buy variables will be the same. While these may not be realistic, they are used to make the model and this specific analysis easy to understand:

The shipments start 6 months into the first year at full volume, so the volume is 100K units in the first year and 200K in the next 4 years.

The price stays at $1,000 per unit for the entire time.

The cost of all of the other components in the widget are $498 and this does not change over the 5 year period

The OEM modulator starts at $2.00 and decreases by 5% every year. This decrease is on the year boundary.

The internally produced modulator will cost $1.00 initially, and also decreases at 5% per year.

The model includes base R&D and SG&A at 15% and 25% of the revenue line. This makes these components of the model irrelevant to the comparison.

In the first year the added engineering team will have 8 headcount for 6 months at a cost of $800K (8 * $200K *.5) and $400K for the next 6 months (4*200K*.5) for a total engineering charge of $1.2M

In the subsequent years, the added engineering will be 4 headcount for each year at a cost of $800K (4*200K). Figure 38-1 is the P&L model for this business using the OEM component. On the per unit cost line, the cost of the modulator starts at $2 in the first year and drops to $1.63 in year 5. The Additional Engineering line in the R&D costs is left blank as there is no internal design to build, support and test a modulator. The key indicator is the large $90.19 on the bottom right. That is the total gross profit over the 5 year period that the business would generate if the OEM modulator is used.

OEM Component P&L						
	Year 1	Year 2	Year 3	Year 4	Year 5	5 Year totals
Units Sold	100,000	200,000	200,000	200,000	200,000	900,000
Revenue per Unit	$ 1,000	$ 1,000	$ 1,000	$ 1,000	$ 1,000	
Revenue ($M)	$ 100.00	$ 200.00	$ 200.00	$ 200.00	$ 200.00	$ 900.00
All Other Costs per Unit	498	498	498	498	498	
Modulator Cost	$ 2.00	$ 1.90	$ 1.81	$ 1.71	$ 1.63	
Cost per unit	500.00	499.90	499.81	499.71	499.63	
Total Cost of Sales ($M)	50	99.98	99.961	99.94295	99.9258	450
Gross Margin ($M)	$ 50.00	$ 100.02	$ 100.04	$ 100.06	$ 100.07	$ 450.19
Gross Margin %	*50.00%*	*50.01%*	*50.02%*	*50.03%*	*50.04%*	*50.02%*
Base R&D ($M)	$ 15.00	$ 30.00	$ 30.00	$ 30.00	$ 30.00	135
Base R&D %	*15%*	*15%*	*15%*	*15%*	*15%*	*15%*
Additional Engineering	$ -	$ -	$ -	$ -	$ -	-
Total R&D ($M)	$ 15.00	$ 30.00	$ 30.00	$ 30.00	$ 30.00	135
Total R&D %	*15%*	*15%*	*15%*	*15%*	*15%*	*15%*
SG&A ($M)	$ 25.00	$ 50.00	$ 50.00	$ 50.00	$ 50.00	225
SG&A %	*25%*	*25%*	*25%*	*25%*	*25%*	*25%*
Gross Profit ($M)	$ 10.00	$ 20.02	$ 20.04	$ 20.06	$ 20.07	$ 90.19
Gross Profit %	*10.00%*	*10.01%*	*10.02%*	*10.03%*	*10.04%*	*10.02%*

Figure 38-1 OEM Component P&L Example

Figure 38-2 is the same model with the internally designed and built modulator. The modulator cost starts at $1.00 and drops to $.81. The added engineering costs are now included at $1.2M for the first year and $800K for the next four years. All of the other factors are the same, so the result of a gross profit of $86.6M is comparable to the $90.19 from the OEM decision model. This analysis shows that if ACME decides to build the internal component, it will reduce the 5 year profit in the business by $3.6M or a reduction in profitability of 4%. So, if this is the actual cost, then this is a bad decision.

Internal Component P&L						
	Year 1	Year 2	Year 3	Year 4	Year 5	5 Year totals
Units Sold	100,000	200,000	200,000	200,000	200,000	900,000
Revenue per Unit	$ 1,000	$ 1,000	$ 1,000	$ 1,000	$ 1,000	
Revenue ($M)	$ 100.00	$ 200.00	$ 200.00	$ 200.00	$ 200.00	$ 900.00
All Other Costs per Unit	498	498	498	498	498	
Modulator Cost	$ 1.00	$ 0.95	$ 0.90	$ 0.86	$ 0.81	
Cost per unit	499.00	498.95	498.90	498.86	498.81	
Total Cost of Sales ($M)	49.9	99.79	99.7805	99.77148	99.7629	449
Gross Margin ($M)	$ 50.10	$ 100.21	$ 100.22	$ 100.23	$ 100.24	$ 451.00
Gross Margin %	50.10%	50.11%	50.11%	50.11%	50.12%	50.11%
Base R&D ($M)	$ 15.00	$ 30.00	$ 30.00	$ 30.00	$ 30.00	135
Base R&D %	15%	15%	15%	15%	15%	15%
Additional Engineering	$ 1.20	$ 0.80	$ 0.80	$ 0.80	$ 0.80	4
Total R&D ($M)	$ 16.20	$ 30.80	$ 30.80	$ 30.80	$ 30.80	139
Total R&D %	16%	15%	15%	15%	15%	15%
SG&A ($M)	$ 25.00	$ 50.00	$ 50.00	$ 50.00	$ 50.00	225
SG&A %	25%	25%	25%	25%	25%	25%
Gross Profit ($M)	$ 8.90	$ 19.41	$ 19.42	$ 19.43	$ 19.44	$ 86.60
Gross Profit %	8.90%	9.71%	9.71%	9.71%	9.72%	9.62%

Figure 38-2 Internal Design P&L Example

However, the ACCME engineering team has re-looked at the challenge and has decided that they can do better. After extensive review, they have decided that they can reduce the cost to just $0.50 for their widget design and reduce the engineering to 2 for the development stage and 1 for the rest of the time. Figure 38-3 shows this revised plan. Based on this new view of the plan, the ACME team has shown that the internally designed component would generate an increase in profit of $110,000. If you were the manager of the ACME product team, which decision would you choose; OEM or internal? Based on the risk, the OEM decision is the right one. The cut to the bone internal project plan is very risky, and especially when compared to the potential that OEM will either add functionality of drive further cost reductions. In this case the OEM decision is still the right one.

Internal Component P&L - Revised						
	Year 1	Year 2	Year 3	Year 4	Year 5	5 Year totals
Units Sold	100,000	200,000	200,000	200,000	200,000	900,000
Revenue per Unit	$ 1,000	$ 1,000	$ 1,000	$ 1,000	$ 1,000	
Revenue ($M)	**$ 100.00**	**$ 200.00**	**$ 200.00**	**$ 200.00**	**$ 200.00**	**$ 900.00**
All Other Costs per Unit	498	498	498	498	498	
Modulator Cost	$ 0.50	$ 0.48	$ 0.45	$ 0.43	$ 0.41	
Cost per unit	498.50	498.48	498.45	498.43	498.41	
Total Cost of Sales ($M)	**49.85**	**99.695**	**99.69025**	**99.68574**	**99.68145**	**449**
Gross Margin ($M)	**$ 50.15**	**$ 100.31**	**$ 100.31**	**$ 100.31**	**$ 100.32**	**$ 451.40**
Gross Margin %	*50.15%*	*50.15%*	*50.15%*	*50.16%*	*50.16%*	*50.16%*
Base R&D ($M)	$ 15.00	$ 30.00	$ 30.00	$ 30.00	$ 30.00	135
Base R&D %	*15%*	*15%*	*15%*	*15%*	*15%*	*15%*
Additional Engineering	$ 0.30	$ 0.20	$ 0.20	$ 0.20	$ 0.20	1
Total R&D ($M)	**$ 15.30**	**$ 30.20**	**$ 30.20**	**$ 30.20**	**$ 30.20**	**136**
Total R&D %	*15%*	*15%*	*15%*	*15%*	*15%*	*15%*
SG&A ($M)	**$ 25.00**	**$ 50.00**	**$ 50.00**	**$ 50.00**	**$ 50.00**	**225**
SG&A %	*25%*	*25%*	*25%*	*25%*	*25%*	*25%*
Gross Profit ($M)	**$ 9.85**	**$ 20.11**	**$ 20.11**	**$ 20.11**	**$ 20.12**	**$90.30**
Gross Profit %	*9.85%*	*10.05%*	*10.05%*	*10.06%*	*10.06%*	*10.03%*

Figure 38-3 Revised Internal Design P&L Example

However, the OEM decision is not always right. The following example is from Omnicore, who is a major player in their market. The part is the Corepart, which represents 60% of the cost of the product. The OEM has quoted a price of $300 for their Corepart, the Omnicore team has experience in building similar parts and can build the part for a cost of $200 with 20 engineers for 6 months and 10 engineers for the next 4.5 years for support. The two models shown in Figure 38-4 shows the analysis for Omnicore (all other variables including the 5% cost reduction have been kept the same to make it easy to see the differences).

Obviously this is a great make decision as the Omnicore team has a realistic estimate of their cost and it increases profitability by almost $70M.

Revenue Impacting Decision

In the above analysis, the make/buy cost-based decision is for a component that has equal value whether OEM'd or manufactured internally. Another class of make/buy decision is when the internal component will enable differentiated value in the product and result in revenue impact. While this

OEM Component P&L						
	Year 1	Year 2	Year 3	Year 4	Year 5	5 Year totals
Units Sold	100,000	200,000	200,000	200,000	200,000	900,000
Revenue per Unit	$ 1,000	$ 1,000	$ 1,000	$ 1,000	$ 1,000	
Revenue ($M)	$ 100.00	$ 200.00	$ 200.00	$ 200.00	$ 200.00	$ 900.00
All Other Costs per Unit	200	200	200	200	200	
Modulator Cost	$ 300.00	$ 285.00	$ 270.75	$ 257.21	$ 244.35	
Cost per unit	500.00	485.00	470.75	457.21	444.35	
Total Cost of Sales ($M)	50	97	94.15	91.4425	88.87038	421
Gross Margin ($M)	$ 50.00	$ 103.00	$ 105.85	$ 108.56	$ 111.13	$ 478.54
Gross Margin %	50.00%	51.50%	52.93%	54.28%	55.56%	53.17%
Base R&D ($M)	$ 15.00	$ 30.00	$ 30.00	$ 30.00	$ 30.00	135
Base R&D %	15%	15%	15%	15%	15%	15%
Additional Engineering	$ -	$ -	$ -	$ -	$ -	-
Total R&D ($M)	$ 15.00	$ 30.00	$ 30.00	$ 30.00	$ 30.00	135
Total R&D %	15%	15%	15%	15%	15%	15%
SG&A ($M)	$ 25.00	$ 50.00	$ 50.00	$ 50.00	$ 50.00	225
SG&A %	25%	25%	25%	25%	25%	25%
Gross Profit ($M)	$ 10.00	$ 23.00	$ 25.85	$ 28.56	$ 31.13	$ 118.54
Gross Profit %	10.00%	11.50%	12.93%	14.28%	15.56%	13.17%

Internal Component P&L						
	Year 1	Year 2	Year 3	Year 4	Year 5	5 Year totals
Units Sold	100,000	200,000	200,000	200,000	200,000	900,000
Revenue per Unit	$ 1,000	$ 1,000	$ 1,000	$ 1,000	$ 1,000	
Revenue ($M)	$ 100.00	$ 200.00	$ 200.00	$ 200.00	$ 200.00	$ 900.00
All Other Costs per Unit	200	200	200	200	200	
Modulator Cost	$ 200.00	$ 190.00	$ 180.50	$ 171.48	$ 162.90	
Cost per unit	400.00	390.00	380.50	371.48	362.90	
Total Cost of Sales ($M)	40	78	76.1	74.295	72.58025	341
Gross Margin ($M)	$ 60.00	$ 122.00	$ 123.90	$ 125.71	$ 127.42	$ 559.02
Gross Margin %	60.00%	61.00%	61.95%	62.85%	63.71%	62.11%
Base R&D ($M)	$ 15.00	$ 30.00	$ 30.00	$ 30.00	$ 30.00	135
Base R&D %	15%	15%	15%	15%	15%	15%
Additional Engineering	$ -	$ -	$ -	$ -	$ -	-
Total R&D ($M)	$ 15.00	$ 30.00	$ 30.00	$ 30.00	$ 30.00	135
Total R&D %	15%	15%	15%	15%	15%	15%
SG&A ($M)	$ 25.00	$ 50.00	$ 50.00	$ 50.00	$ 50.00	225
SG&A %	25%	25%	25%	25%	25%	25%
Gross Profit ($M)	$ 20.00	$ 42.00	$ 43.90	$ 45.71	$ 47.42	$ 199.02
Gross Profit %	20.00%	21.00%	21.95%	22.85%	23.71%	22.11%

Figure 38-4 Internal Build Decision Example

value could be negative (of lower capability) relative to the OEM, resulting in lower price or volume, for this analysis, we will assume that the internal part has a positive impact. To simplify the analysis, we will use the ACME case from the previous section, using the first two analysis assumptions ($2 to $1 cost, 8 to 4 engineers). However, we will now add on two positive impacts on our market share:

> The internal component will add an additional feature and capability that will enable ACME to increase price by 10%. This functionality will also increase sales volume by 20% over the 5 years.

Figure 38-5 shows this comparative model. The OEM model is the same as in the previous analysis, but the internally manufactured scenario now reflects both the revenue and volume increases.

This new analysis shows that ACME will increase the overall profitability by $65M by using the internal component that enables differentiation. Regardless of whether there is a cost impact or a price/volume impact, the make/buy decision is one that can be analyzed and a data based quantitative decision can be made. It is critical to be realistic and not accept the NIH (Not Invented Here) mentality. Ask the key questions:

> *Will building this myself add real value to my product that people will pay more for?*

> *Will building this myself increase the percentage of wins?*

> *Is my plan to build this realistic and does it anticipate changes and uncertainties?*

Unless the internal design answers yes to one or all of these and generates significant return versus the risk, the OEM decision is the right one.

The Solution Element OEM Decision

In this thought process, I will start with the answer and then build out why it is true. The Solution Element OEM only work to solve two problems:

> *If you are planning your own replacement product or element and this is just a way to get into the market or*

> *If it is a small part of the overall offer with strategic importance or value.*

OEM Component P&L						
	Year 1	Year 2	Year 3	Year 4	Year 5	5 Year totals
Units Sold	100,000	200,000	200,000	200,000	200,000	900,000
Revenue per Unit	$ 1,000	$ 1,000	$ 1,000	$ 1,000	$ 1,000	
Revenue ($M)	$ 100.00	$ 200.00	$ 200.00	$ 200.00	$ 200.00	$ 900.00
All Other Costs per Unit	498	498	498	498	498	
Modulator Cost	$ 2.00	$ 1.90	$ 1.81	$ 1.71	$ 1.63	
Cost per unit	500.00	499.90	499.81	499.71	499.63	
Total Cost of Sales ($M)	50	99.98	99.961	99.94295	99.9258	450
Gross Margin ($M)	$ 50.00	$ 100.02	$ 100.04	$ 100.06	$ 100.07	$ 450.19
Gross Margin %	50.00%	50.01%	50.02%	50.03%	50.04%	50.02%
Base R&D ($M)	$ 15.00	$ 30.00	$ 30.00	$ 30.00	$ 30.00	135
Base R&D %	15%	15%	15%	15%	15%	15%
Additional Engineering	$ -	$ -	$ -	$ -	$ -	-
Total R&D ($M)	$ 15.00	$ 30.00	$ 30.00	$ 30.00	$ 30.00	135
Total R&D %	15%	15%	15%	15%	15%	15%
SG&A ($M)	$ 25.00	$ 50.00	$ 50.00	$ 50.00	$ 50.00	225
SG&A %	25%	25%	25%	25%	25%	25%
Gross Profit ($M)	$ 10.00	$ 20.02	$ 20.04	$ 20.06	$ 20.07	$ 90.19
Gross Profit %	10.00%	10.01%	10.02%	10.03%	10.04%	10.02%

Internal Component P&L						
	Year 1	Year 2	Year 3	Year 4	Year 5	5 Year totals
Units Sold	110,000	220,000	220,000	220,000	220,000	990,000
Revenue per Unit	1,100	1,100	1,100	1,100	1,100	
Revenue ($M)	121	242	242	242	242	1,089
All Other Costs per Unit	498	498	498	498	498	
Modulator Cost	$ 1.00	$ 0.95	$ 0.90	$ 0.86	$ 0.81	
Cost per unit	499.00	498.95	498.90	498.86	498.81	
Total Cost of Sales ($M)	54.89	109.769	109.7586	109.7486	109.7392	494
Gross Margin ($M)	$ 66.11	$ 132.23	$ 132.24	$ 132.25	$ 132.26	$ 595.09
Gross Margin %	54.64%	54.64%	54.65%	54.65%	54.65%	54.65%
Base R&D ($M)	$ 18.15	$ 36.30	$ 36.30	$ 36.30	$ 36.30	163
Base R&D %	15%	15%	15%	15%	15%	15%
Additional Engineering	$ 1.20	$ 0.80	$ 0.80	$ 0.80	$ 0.80	4
Total R&D ($M)	$ 19.35	$ 37.10	$ 37.10	$ 37.10	$ 37.10	168
Total R&D %	16%	15%	15%	15%	15%	15%
SG&A ($M)	$ 30.25	$ 60.50	$ 60.50	$ 60.50	$ 60.50	272
SG&A %	25%	25%	25%	25%	25%	25%
Gross Profit ($M)	$ 16.51	$ 34.63	$ 34.64	$ 34.65	$ 34.66	$ 155.09
Gross Profit %	13.64%	14.31%	14.31%	14.32%	14.32%	14.24%

Figure 38-5 Differentiated Value Example

The first of these is obvious. If you have decided to enter the market and use an OEM to get an early entry and clearly understand how you are going to manage the transition, this is a great use of the OEM. While it may be challenging to find an OEM partner that will agree to this, it will work. While I reserve moral or ethical judgment of anyone that leads a partner to believe this a long term relationship when it is just short term, it is a definite path even without their agreement, though their response when you bypass them will be very negative. As a company, your reputation as a partner will be dependent on your clarity at the beginning of such a relationship.

In the second case, when looking at an OEM Solution Element as a large opportunity, often there is an extensive analysis and a great business plan. I have seen this process repeated over and over through my career. The company does not have a product in an adjacent space and there is lots of money being made there. So the company decides to OEM a product because it is a great way to make money

Wrong!

In Solution Element OEMs, there is a simple rule that always applies:

> *Unless the Solution Element is a small part of your overall offer and needs the rest of the offer for value the OEM plan will fail. The percentage is generally less than 5%, though 2% is even better.*

The reason for this is that whenever a Solution Element OEM is a large part of the overall offer or has value that is distinct from the overall offer, the end customer has alternative ways to buy it, and this alternative ALWAYS poach th plan. As I said, I have seen this multiple times in multiple companies with multiple products and the outcomes were ALWEAYS the same; after about 2-3 years of trying , the OEM deal was abandoned.

In all cases one or more of the following were the reasons the deals fell apart. To illustrate this, let's create a scenario. Bigco sells their "Solution A" to a large number of Fortune 50 companies. Meanwhile a new "Solution B" has come into the market. While it does not replace Solution A, it is bought by the same buyers and is perceived as being a "hot market". Bigco missed the opportunity to invest in Solution B, and their salespeople do not have anything to sell. Hotco is one of the three players in Solution B and their offer is pretty good. Bigco decides to OEM the Hotco offer. However, this is not exclusive and Hotco sells their products directly to the end customers and through channels, some of whom are also Bigco channel partners.

Greed

So now Bigco introduces Hotco's Solution B product. However, the Hotco direct salespeople are not compensated for Bigco revenue, so they actively sell against the Bigco product. The channels find they can get the Hotco version for lower cost than the Bigco version, so they sell that. The customers realize they can buy either product as they are the same (though branded differently), so they competitively bid for both, causing pricing conflicts.

In the late 80s I was in a networking company. Due to cost challenges, we had not invested in building a wiring closet chassis platform. The industry was moving away from using co-axial cables to twisted pair wiring and to implement this you needed a box to sit in the wiring closet to connect all of the twisted pair wires. This type of product had become popular and many of our customers were asking for it. In an effort to have a solution and not lose the customers and the revenue (we also sold other components that would be sold with the wiring closet chassis), we built an OEM relationship with one of the three manufacturers that had chassis products. In one of the first big deals we spent many months selling a large configuration to a Boston-based customer (they had our other products already and were happy). At the last minute the OEM chassis vendor offered the customer their product at a 10% additional discount and the customer decided to go direct. The regional VP of sales called the Sales VP for the OEM to complain, saying, "you stabbed me in the back". The response was amazingly candid, "No I didn't, I stabbed you in the heart and watched you die, you didn't expect me to leave that much money on the table did you?". The point was that this VP and the OEM would have received 20% less revenue (and much less profit) if they had done the deal through us. Needless to say, this relationship did not last.

Margin

In many ways greed is based on the challenges of margin in this type of deal. If the OEM product has a list price of $100 and a street price of $80 then the margin analysis is simple. If Hotco sells its products to its channel partners for a 35% discount off of list, the channels are buying the product at $65 and selling it for $80 for a gross margins of $15 or 18.75%. If the OEM price to Bigco is a 60% discount from list, then Bigco buys the product at $40 from Hotco. If Bigco has a cost increase of 10% to manage the delivery of the product, the actual Cost of Sales for Bigco is $44. If Bigco sells direct to their end customer at the street price, the gross margin is $36 or 45%. The challenge is that, if Bigco has built their business model on a 60% gross margin and 15% of gross profit, now the revenue from the Hotco has no profit if it is allocated the costs as done for other products. If it is not allocated all of the R&D cost percentages, then the revenue is not as valuable as other revenue.

This is exacerbated if the product goes through the channel. As the channel expects to buy the product for $65, the resulting margin for Bigco is $15 or just 23% on their Hotco sales. The challenge is that often the early assumption is that Bigco can charge more because it is Bigco. Unless the customers or channel have an overwhelming reason, either in capability or reduced overall cost through discounts, there will be a natural tendency to buy for less. This is especially true of the channels. What often happens is that the Bigco team decides that they need to get at least 40% gross margin on their Hotco revenues, so they have set their channel price at $73.33 ($44/60%). Unless there is some strong reason otherwise, the channel will buy the Hotco product and tell their customers they are the same product. For channels that do not buy from Hotco and are competing with the Hotco channels they are now caught in a serious crunch. They can either price to get a reasonable margin at $88 ($73+$15) and lose the bid on price, or price to the Hotco street price of $ 80 and live on reduced margin of $7 ($80-$73). After one or two of these deals, the channel will no doubt contact Hotco directly to become a Hotco partner (see Greed).

Reduced Product Set
While Bigco does OEM some of the products that Hotco has, the Bigco team decided to only OEM about 50% of the Hotco products, as there is cost of actually bringing a product into Bigco. The ones they did not get are lower volume, so they were seen as less of a requirement. The result of this is simple. Any customer that decides they want those capabilities will

naturally buy everything from Hotco or their channels. If the primary reason to go to Bigco was that Bigco offered a complete solution, the need to buy the Hotco product changes that and then all of the business goes to Hotco path.

Time to Release

Part of the value that Bigco brings is the integration of the Hotco products into the overall Bigco offer. This requires Bigco to do some engineering for branding to each Hotco release, to change the documentation, to add it to the Bigco ordering system and to make sure the Bigco support team is fully up to speed. The result is that it takes Bigco 6 months from when they get the first Beta version of the Hotco product to have it available to their customers and channels. However, Hotco gets the product out 2 months after the Beta release, which means the Hotco branded product are always 4 months earlier into the market. This includes new products, but also includes upgrades and even support releases. The result is that any customers that have chosen the Bigco path are behind.

The "Not Invented Here" (NIH) factor

The internal engineering team at Bigco, while they have not been authorized nor have budget for a program, believe they could build a much better product than Hotco. The result of this is that Bigco talks about its future offer in Solution B that it wants to build. The result is twofold: 1. Bigco cannot decide to acquire Hotco, which could change the game and 2. The Bigco customer perceives that Bigco is not really committed to a long term relationship with Hotco, leading them to believe that they are better off buying directly from Hotco or even looking at Hotco competitors.

The Competitive Acquisition

In many ways this is the ultimate indictment of the strategic OEM without an internal plan. If the OEM relationship becomes somewhat successful, the result is that the company that the OEM product is purchased from now becomes successful. This opens the door to that company being purchased by a competitor. Such a purchase would have three potential impacts: 1.it has a positive revenue and technology value to the competitor, complete with insights into how it integrates to your product or technology, 2. it includes a list of customers using the product that are your customers and now will probably need to look to your competitor for support, and 3.

it has a negative impact on you as you must replace the OEM that is lost. A look at the Cisco acquisitions through the years shows times when they spent much more to acquire a company than it was worth as the acquired company had a major OEM relationship with a competitor (Airespace, Jabber). This is the final pitfall of a large-scale OEM that actually succeeds in building volume. A more detailed discussion of the Airespace acquisition is in Chapter 34.

The Outcome
The result of all of these factors, which often come up together or sequentially is that ALL major OEM relationships of this type are doomed to failure. There are probably others, but there are no paths to success.

I joined a large telecommunications company that had started a path for an OEM relationship with a video system vendor that was the third ranked market share player. Their products were reasonable, and it was a plan to provide some minimal integration into the core products, but generally the video system sale was separate. The logic was that our company had deep relationships with the customers and channels and we could drive large revenue. The original business plan was to do $100M in revenue over 2 years (in a market with $4B in total revenue). This was seen as an easy goal. In this case many of the issues above surfaced: it was a small subset of the overall product line; the OEM integration time was a 6 month delay; the general salespeople of the OEM company were not compensated on our revenue; and the margins were not sufficient to support the P&L. The result was that after 2 years the revenues were less than $10M and the overall profit plan had become a loss.

When Does it Work
If the OEM Solution Element is something you must include in your offer to sell the rest of the offer and the cost of building it yourself is high, then an OEM relationship makes sense. If it is a small percentage, then you really don't care if it is bought from you or not, so the value of buying it from you becomes ease for your channels and customers. The point is that the small but strategic piece is an acceptable answer. If you cannot sell your solution without this element and your customers do not want to buy it separately, then having an OEM to sell it makes sense.

However, in the end, this is not about making huge revenue, it is about selling the rest of the offer. If it becomes a major part of your offer and a large source of new revenue, then the risks detailed above begin to apply.

Conclusions

The conclusion for this section is simple.

Analyze Component OEM relationships and the make/buy decision clearly and with data. Do not let a desire for an internal path introduce extreme risk into the program. Analyze:

Cost comparisons on both the component cost and the cost of engineering and support

Revenue increase on both price and volume and the potential increased costs

For the Solution Element OEM, follow the three rules:

DO use Solution Element OEMs when they are a small part of your overall offer and include strategic value you do not want to invest in and

DO use Solution Element OEMs to enter markets early and

AVOID any other Solution Element OEM relationship as it will inevitably fail.

Chapter 39 Why Will We Win?

Every development organization has certain areas where they realize the best values to win. If we paraphrase PT Barnum, "You can excel in everything some of the time and excel in some things all of the time, but you cannot excel at everything all of the time". As a development team, it is not reasonable to assume that you will be the best in every facet of the development task. The challenge is to pick which areas will define your uniqueness and where you want to excel.

You may decide to be first to market, and accept less functionality or lower quality to achieve that goals. You may decide to throw all of your efforts behind a single product and do everything perfectly, while your competitors are launching two or three products with different optimizations. You may decide to focus on a set of unique features, even though this means that you will be second in the market, or you may define a rock-solid quality as being of paramount importance.

Regardless of what you choose, you have to make a choice. Just like in Chapter 36 "The Development Equation", if you do not make an active choice, it will be made for you by some factors you do not understand. A focus on Time to Market may drive a significant drop in quality. I joined a company in the middle of a major "innovation" drive. The mantra was that the company was increasing the number of new product releases from 25 to 60. This was positioned as demonstrating the companies revived vigor in innovation and leadership. A year later the company had horrendous quality problems. Virtually all of the products from the year before were demonstrating major issues in the customer deployments. The decision to focus on a broad and ramped up set of new products and releases had caused the organization to bypass and reduce a number of processes and practices that generated the quality the company had been known for. All of a sudden the mantra changed from innovation to quality. The result was that the number of innovative things had now dropped below the level previous to the innovation drive.

This is the worst kind of management of a development organization. When we change the focus of excellence very rapidly, the organization is very challenged to accept and deliver the change. To minimize this churn, each organization needs to have a clear view of what all of the factors are in your industry/technology/market. Some generic categories that may be included are:

Time to Market

Breadth of products

Innovation in number of products

Feature quantity

Feature innovation

Performance

Price/Cost

User Experience

Support Experience

Service Experience

Customizability

Standards Support

Size

Power

Efficiency

ASIC design

Software architecture

......

Use this list and/or your own to create what you see as the potential areas in which you can excel. Then tie those back clearly to the value to the

customers and their ability to receive and pay for that value. Does breadth
of product really increase revenue, or are more options only spreading the
revenue across many different products? This can become a discussion
with the Marketing, Sales, and Strategy team about how to support the
differentiators.

As part of this process, define a clear path from any market differentiators
to the excellence factors in your development organization. Be clear on
which factors you are going to have as the focus and which are not. As you
develop this plan, be very clear on how this positions you versus where you
perceive you competitors to be focused. This is a great place to use the "So
What" analysis. Take one of those key values and ask the "So What"
question until you get to the real customer value. Remember that the value
you are focused on needs to be couched in those you are not.

> *We are focused on Product Breadth Versus Quality*
>
> *"So What"*
>
> *It allows us to address a very broad fractured market with many customers.*
>
> *"So What"*
>
> *We are increasing our revenue by increasing the number of customers, but not focused on repeat business*
>
> *"So What"*
>
> *We need to churn new customers rapidly due to follow-on-sales loses due to quality problems*

I am not arguing whether this is a good or bad strategy, but the concept is
reasonably easy.

An alternative would be a focus on quality at the expense of number of
products. The conclusion from that might be that the Product
Management team needs to clearly focus on only those products and
markets where volume can be achieved with smaller percentage of all of the
product options. A focus on segments where re-buys and up-sells are

critical would emphasize the quality in ongoing revenue.

When you have your excellence areas defined, make sure that they are reflected in the rest of the organization. From your marketing, to how you sell, to your support, these all need to be aligned to assure that the values built into the product are properly exposed and leveraged in the market.

Think about a few companies that have different levels of reputation for their products. Apple has a great reputation for quality, ease of use, and innovation. However, their products are not always the first to market (witness MP3 players, RIM, and other), and the Apple portfolio is small when compared with an HP or Dell in terms of the number of platforms. They also limit the variability (and the complexity). The iPad is a single product with 3 variations in memory and 3 variations in network (WiFi Only, WiFi/3G AT&T, and WiFi/#G Version). In the end, the vast majority of the components are common. Apple has resisted having a hard keyboard model, or other options or complexity. Also, while their date goals are never published, the Apple release is driven as much by getting the product right as meeting a date. This is reflective of a development strategy in which excellence in packaging and user experience will win against early market entries, broad product offering and specialized options.

A company like Sony is focused on innovation and new products. It includes large breadth, but does not have the same level of quality nor focus. Sony has many more products and changes them very often. They are much less focused on the experience, and much more on volume and scale.

The discussion around what makes you win is crucial and needs to happen not only in the R&D team, but also to the rest of the company. The decisions you make, whether well thought out or arrived at through random serendipity must be reflected in your overall marketing, sales, customer, and segmentation strategies.

Chapter 40 Edholm's Law of Bandwidth

I put this chapter in for two reasons: first because I think the observations in the Law of Bandwidth continue to be valuable, but more importantly to illustrate the concept of observation and thought. I have included the text of the article in IEEE Spectrum (Cherry, 2004) at the end of this chapter. This article labeled this as Edholm's Law.

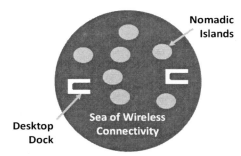

Figure 40-1 Three Types of Available Bandwidth

The thought process that led to the creation of the Law of Bandwidth started in about 2002. At that time the structure of data networks was becoming clear. There were going to be three kinds of network connectivity: 1. cellular wireless was going to provide service that was available in many if not all locations, 2. nomadic hot spots would be available in some locations, and 3. desktop wired connectivity would be available in a few locations. Figure 40-1 is a depiction of this model, with the sea depicted with islands and docks in it. In 2004, the technologies were defined; the "sea" was a GPRS and UMTS moving to 3G at less than 1 Mbps, the "nomadic islands" were 802.11WiFi at about 5-10 Mbps or cable/DSL home networks, and the "desktop dock" was a 10 Mbps switched LAN moving to 100 Mbps.

The initial view was that this presented a challenge for the delivery of information to the end points. As the end points were large (read PCs) and the files were getting large (video, etc.), there became an interesting challenge: if the device was able to use all three networks, its use of the networks would need to be different as the capabilities and costs were very different. This led to the thought that content filtering and management could be used to manage the delivery of content, based on specific network connectivity. This led to a consideration of an advanced technology development in this area. The assumption, as shown in Figure 40-2 was that the variety of types of information could be cached (i.e. stored) and then delivered based on importance, size, and available network bandwidth. So, if there was a large video file to be downloaded, it would not be transmitted over the low bandwidth, high cost cellular data network, but

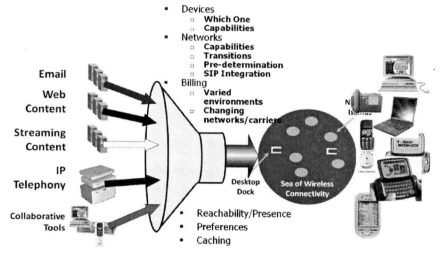

Figure 40-2 Bandwidth Defined Content Delivery

over a nomadic or desktop connection. If you went to a Starbucks to get your morning coffee and spent 7 minutes there, the adaptive cache could send specific information during that time at the higher bandwidth of the nomadic WiFi network, maximizing delivery, while minimizing cost.

In looking at this concept, the question of how changes in available bandwidth on each of the networks would impact the solutions, both from an engineering and value perspectives. This led to a model of how bandwidth was changing over time. Figure 40-3 shows an updated view of

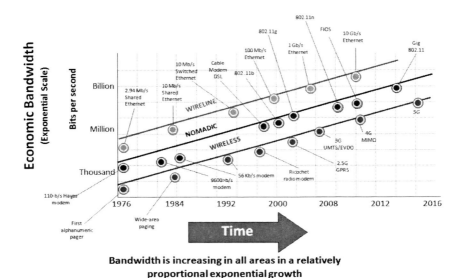

Bandwidth is increasing in all areas in a relatively proportional exponential growth

Figure 40-3 The Law of Bandwidth Lines with Examples of technology Points

this from 2010 (compare to the IEE article graph from 2004). This view includes some of the technologies that are in the market and some that are anticipated and their delivered bandwidth to a user. This is not the transport bandwidth as in wireless and WiFI networks the bandwidth is shared, and in campus LANs the architecture delivers less bandwidth at the edge than the speed of the last link. The observation that, if the technologies were normalized, there would be three parallel lines of available bandwidth and that the ratio would be 1:10:100 for wireless : nomadic : wired. The next observation harkened back to the content delivery concept. The realization that bandwidth is directly correlated to the user interface of a specific application transformed a simple observation of bandwidth into one of how change will happen. Figure 40-4 adds the concept of applications needing specific bandwidth. For example, no human can type faster than around 300 bits per second. 300 bps = 37.5 8-bit characters per second x 60 = 2250 characters per minute - if the average word is 5 characters and a space, then 2250 characters per minute / 61 = 321 Words per minute. Per Guinness, the world record for the fastest typist in the world types at 150 words per minute, with a top speed of 170 words per minute. She recorded 37, 500 key strokes in 50 minutes, or 750 key strokes per minute, or 12.5 characters per second x 8 = 100 bps. In receiving information, it is common that normal 70% comprehension reading is about 250 characters per minute and speed reading can increase this to around 500. This means that the receiving speed for humans for text is somewhere between 2K and 4K of bandwidth. So the bandwidth requirement for text is about 4Kbps.

Similarly, if we look at human voice, the telephony standard is 64 Kbps, which can be easily compressed to about 16 Kbps. Web pages vary, but a web page optimized for a small device like a smartphone is about 100Kbps on average, while a larger screen may be 200 Kbps or more. While web pages are relatively low because here is time for the human to decide what to do next between pages, video is a stream of frames, resulting in higher bandwidth. Typically a video is from 3-400Kbps up to 10 Mbps, depending on resolution and compression mechanisms.

Ultimately this results in a series of user interface bands that are fixed at a vertical bandwidth based on the human capability. On Figure 40-4 these are shown as the horizontal bands. As time progresses and bandwidth on

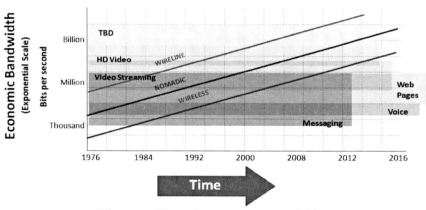

When a specific requirement becomes available
economically on a transport technology, adoption
explodes from specialization to general use

Figure 40-4 The Law of Bandwidth with Application Bands

each type of network increases, each network progressively gets to a point where it can support a specific type of traffic at a cost effective level. The result is that types of user actions that were only available on a high speed wired desktop network move to the nomadic and then eventually to the wireless. Based on the model, this transition is about a 7 year cycle, as shown in Figure 40-5.

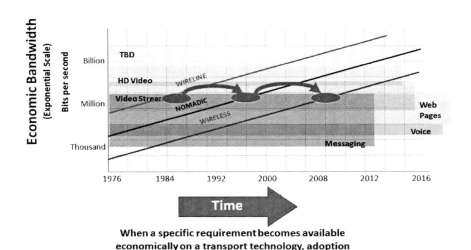

When a specific requirement becomes available
economically on a transport technology, adoption
explodes from specialization to general use

Figure 40-5 Relative Time Lag of Three Bandwidth Types

Finally, TBD (To Be Determined) on the band above the high-definition
video refers to requirements beyond our current limitations of two
dimensional or 3D displays. This is because the current display technology
and the human eye are the limits on the ability to receive information. The human eye has about 6-7 million cones (pixels) of resolution in the diameter of the core non-peripheral vision. This is where you see detail. Though the human eye is capable of receiving light through almost a 200 degree arc, the acute vision is limited to about 15 degrees.

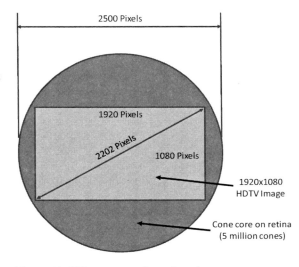

Figure 40-6 Human Eye Cone Density

Of the about 7 million cones in the core visual field (Cones are for resolution, rods are for movement - there are about 100M rods in the peripheral field), a HDTV image captures the circular field of about 5 million as shown in Figure 40-6. As the cones are more dense in that 15 degree core, this is probably closer to 5 million cones.

If the image had twice as much resolution, and if you sat at a distance where the screen matched the back of your eye, you could not see the additional resolution. The Society of Motion Picture and television Engineers recommends an angle of no less than 30 degrees and no more than 60 to watch a screen based video. The THX standard recommends a 40 degree angle for 16x9 pictures. The point of this is that at this distance the pixels on the screen are optimized to the cone density in the eye.

If the average mechanism for the future is watching images in a fixed size display at a fixed distance, then this is the image size. If that image can be delivered as a streamed image, then there is no need for more bandwidth. An HDTV image can be delivered with virtually no artifacts at 10Mbps (even less with aggressive compression). If we assume that this can become 3D/stereo with a second image at the same rate, then the bandwidth requirement is 20 Mbps. If the peripheral vision is not about resolution, but motion, then we can fill the side fields of a three screen monitor with similar bandwidth for both as in Figure 40-7. These screens are typically not used for work, but as annunciation spaces. If they are used for work, then when the user moves to that screen (as represented by a mouse or other active detection), the bandwidth is concentrated there as the other screens

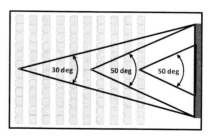

Public Theater

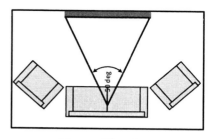

Home Theater

Figure 40-7 Home versus Theater Viewing Distance

will not be changing. So our total bandwidth for a 3D maximum resolutions system with side peripheral is about 40 Mbps. While the recent discussion of 4K video (versus the 2K horizontal pixels of HDTV at 1980) has had a lot of discussion, the primary requirement is where customers are seated closer than the 50 degree angle and therefore are only able to see a small part of the screen as shown in Figure 40-8. This is a comparison of the movie theater to the home theater , where the seating position can be set at a proper distance.

All of this discussion leads back to the Law of Bandwidth as the maximum required bandwidth to deliver a high quality, full resolution, and absorbing video image is less than 40 Mbps. If it is a single display and not 3D, it is less than 10 Mbps. This leads to the ceiling on bandwidth requirements as shown in Figure 40-8. So, until we get a new human I/O interface such as a neural plug (the Matrix movie brain plug), for fixed distance viewing, the

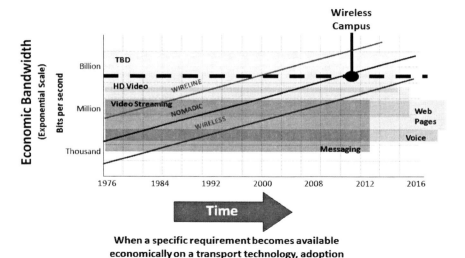

When a specific requirement becomes available
economically on a transport technology, adoption
explodes from specialization to general use

Figure 40-8 Evolution to Nomadic Data over Fixed Connectivity

bandwidth is fixed. As the capabilities of networks increase this can be met by the nomadic network and then by the wireless. In fact, between 2012 and 2014 the migration of office traffic from wired nets to wireless will be significant. This is especially true as many new devices such as the iPad are not designed to use a wired connection. If the Law of Bandwidth holds, the 5G wireless networks of 2017 and their bandwidth increase should make the wireless network similar.   Based on past advances, the 5G wireless should exceed the 4G by 8-12 times. The question then is how this impacts the market when we have universal bandwidth that can deliver any video or application as a video anywhere.

In 2008 I spoke at a Hospitality conference in Austin, Texas. After going through these points, a member of the audience asked, "does this mean that in 10 years our customers will be watching videos from the cellular network...and we will lose that revenue too?" The point he was making was that the wireless network has almost completely eliminated the revenue that hotels get from their customers for phone calls as these are now done on cellular phones. If video moves the same way, the revenue for in-room entertainment also goes away. for a hotel operator that saw in-room entertainment as a major revenue producer, this change is unsettling. In reality, the advent of free WiFi and streaming has already begun this transition.

Observation

The Law of Bandwidth, Moore's Laws and many others, are just observations of set of data that can be defined in a way that makes it possible to extrapolate a future. There is no magic, and this process can be used in your own pursuits. Lay out a set of facts, and then try graphing them to define relationships. Out of this, you may begin to see a pattern. With practice, you will begin to see correlations in many parts of your life. For example, there appears to be a Law of Inverse Temperature: the colder a place is in the winter, the warmer it is kept indoors; conversely, the hotter a place is in the summer, the cooler it is kept indoors. If you go to Minneapolis in January the buildings are all 76 degrees inside, while the AC keeps the rooms in Miami at 72 when it is 90 degrees and 100% humidity outside. Being from California, I find that our houses are colder in the winter and warmer in the summer. I believe that there is an underlying driver to this, which is optimizing body temperature for short term exposure to the outside. If you are in a 76-78 degree building in Minneapolis, you are warmer for the 5 minutes it takes you to get to your car or another building than if you were only warmed to 68 degrees. Similarly, the cool interiors prepare you for the intense heat and humidity in the summer in Miami.

By developing your powers of observation, you will rapidly begin to see patterns in the world around you, both at work and at home. This is a critical part of building up the capability to define the future and strategies as well. As a final note, do not try to apply this to politicians; I have found no rule that can adequately define the chaos of politics.

IEEE Spectrum Article By Steven Cherry / July 2004:

This was the original article published in the 2004 IEEE Spectrum
magazine (Cherry, 2004) documenting the Law of Bandwidth. The lines on
the graph differ slightly as they were drawn at transmission speed, no
average user bandwidth.

Some telecommunications technologies, like cellular telephony, can be used
as you move around freely. Others, like Wi-Fi, can be used while moving
from place to place but aren't fully mobile. A third category can be used
only with equipment tied to a specific location, as Ethernet is to your
office's desktop computer. For lack of better terms, we'll call these three
categories wireless, nomadic, and wireline.

It seems intuitive that the least mobile systems have the highest data rates.
And it's obvious that all three get faster over time: we now routinely achieve
cellular data rates that match those of the best dial-up modem speeds of the
early 1990s.

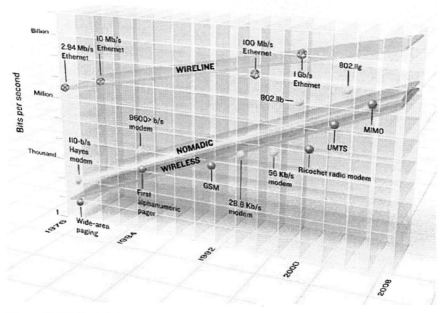

Figure 40-9 Edholm's Law of Bandwidth, IEEE Spectrum Magazine, July 2004

But there's even more to say about data rates. At a recent conference

Philip Edholm

devoted to Internet telephony, John H. Yoakum of Nortel Networks, in
Brampton, Ont., Canada, presented a new law that he attributed to a
colleague, Phil Edholm, Nortel's chief technology officer and vice president
of network architecture.

According to Edholm's Law, the three telecommunications categories
march almost in lock step: their data rates increase on similar exponential
curves, the slower rates trailing the faster ones by a predictable time lag. As
the chart shows, if you plot data rates logarithmically against time, you can
fit three straight lines to the results: the three maintain more or less the same
relationship. (Interestingly, though, extrapolating forward indicates a
convergence between the rates of nomadic and wireless technologies
around 2030. Perhaps that's not too surprising, since both rely on the same
core technology, radio.)

For example, five years ago, wireless ran at about 5 to 10 kilobits per
second, the nomadic bandwidth dial-up ran at 30 to 56 kb/s, and the typical
office local-area network (LAN) ran at about 10 megabits per second.
Today, wireless technology delivers 100 kb/s through cellular networks, and
nomadic bandwidth for a home wireless LAN with DSL or cable
broadband access is about 1 to 2 Mb/s. The typical wireline LAN is way up
there at 100 Mb/s.

If we project forward, Edholm's Law says that in about five years 3G
(third-generation) wireless will routinely deliver 1 Mb/s, Wi-Fi will bring
nomadic access to 10 Mb/s, and office desktops will connect at a standard
of 1 gigabit per second.

As The Data Rates of these transport modes increase, applications can
successfully migrate from wireline to nomadic to wireless. Take streaming
music, which wasn't practical on a home desktop machine until about 1998.
We could stream music wirelessly to a laptop in a coffee shop by 2003 and
should be able to do the same thing to a cellphone by about 2008.

At a recent conference in New York City, Hossein Eslambolchi, president
of AT and T Labs, in Bedminster, N.J., made an observation similar to
Edholm's. In fact, he asserted that telecommunications data rates aren't
rising just in a Moore's Law-like way: they're rising at exactly the Moore's
Law rate: doubling every 18 months. If the state of home access in 1980

was a 1200-bit-per-second narrowband modem, we would expect a thousandfold increase in 21 years. Sure enough, Eslambolchi says, 2001 was the year we started to see consumer adoption of broadband faster than 1 Mb/s.

One consequence is clear: whenever the bandwidth demand of an application native to one transport category meets the rising edge of another category, there is a perfect opportunity for an adoption explosion by a new and larger pool of potential users.

Another consequence, Edholm notes, is that we may someday see the end of wireline. Its continued use depends on a consumer need for ever-higher data rates, and he believes that there may come a time when no more is needed. But applications such as HDTV, high-quality videoconferencing, and three-dimensional displays all have the potential of continuing to require more and more bandwidth. And beyond these, holographic imaging, virtual reality, immersive reality for telemedicine distance learning, and other high-bandwidth applications will probably continue to keep the demand for wireline connectivity strong.

At some point, though, we'll reach some fundamental human limit: the human eyeball can process only so many pixels per second, for example. When wireless can hit those limits, we can abandon our wirelines, and all telecommunications will be completely untethered and mobile.

Chapter 41 Don't Develop for You

This seems like a really simple and obvious truth, but over many years, I have seen it ignored, trampled, desecrated and dropped. When you develop anything, remember it is not for you, it is for your customers. While there are some people who have a natural flair for style, and some who have a feel for how things should work, it is rare that someone gets it exactly right. If you are left-handed and design for your hand, what will be the impact on the right-handed user if it is difficult to use. As 87% of the potential customer base is right-handed, a left-handed optimization would be poor. While this is obvious, the reality is that design and development based on your needs and criteria has a very high probability of missing the mark.

This is not to say that occasionally a Steve Jobs comes along who has an intrinsic sense of what is right. However, that was driven by both a unique view as well as continual path to eliminate complexity and make things simple and wonderful.

So if you cannot develop for you, who do you develop for? Your customers obviously. And often your customers' background, knowledge and capability are dramatically different that yours. So the only way to get it right is to make sure you start by designing for them. Do not assume that if you can use it, someone else can. If you are a PhD in Physics, your capability to remember what a button does may be very different than someone trained as a psychologist. A good example of this is the iPhone. When I got my first iPhone, I was really upset that there were many functions that required use of the touch-screen, when a button was a much more obvious choice. A good example of this is the camera function. In order to "shoot" the picture, you have to touch a point on the touch screen. I expressed to one of my team how it would have been so much better if Apple had just put one additional button on the outside of the case that was application sensitive. It could be the shutter in the camera, the mute on the phone, and send for an email. After thinking about it for a minute, his response was profound, "You could figure that out, but could your wife? Would she understand that the same button did 20 functions or would she be frustrated by not remembering what it would do. While I believe my wife could remember, the point was valid. I naturally assume and understand context as the driver of the function, but that is not universal. For someone who learns the use of a button and then it changes, the result could be very frustrating.

Time and time again in the design and development process these questions are raised. You and your team always need to ask the same questions, "Will it delight the customers". This means you should not try to oversell the thing you are developing, but rather get an honest and clear opinion of it. Asking the simple question, "was it less complicated than you expected?" is an obvious way of kicking off that discussion.

Philip Edholm

The Business of You

This final section of the book is an attempt to put down some insights that will help you in evaluating your current job, your career and the options you have looking forward. Generally these chapters are shorter, as the concepts are easier to explain.

The focus of this section is to help you think through what is your measure of success and how you plan to achieve it. It is not intended to be a roadmap, but a set of guideposts you can use in building you own road.

Chapter 42 My Work Satisfiers – What are Yours?

This thought process came out of a discussion of interview questions to ask a candidate. The CEO of the company I was with said he always asked the question, "So what are your work satisfiers, what gets you up and going in the morning and raring to go and what are your dis-satisfiers that make you want to stay home and not go to the office?" For him, the key was whether the candidate talked about positive first or negative first. Anyone who started their answer by something like, "well what really pisses me off is people who....", would not have a chance at a job, even if the thing he mentioned was something that no one would like in their company. The CEO was looking only for "glass half full" people. So this question got me to thinking and I decided there were three key work satisfiers for me:

Having an impact

Having fun

Making money

For me, those are the three things I evaluate in any job or role. All of the other things fit in or come under these three in my mind. Let me explain each a little more clearly.

Having an Impact

To me, having an impact is that, when you leave or look back on something you were driving or a key part of, you can see things that would not have happened if you were not there. The impact can be small or large, it can be within the company or in the industry the company is in. Impact can be on the company, its products, its capabilities, but in the end, it should drive profitability and growth. Impact can also be on the industry by transformation. By creating a standard or even by innovating generally, an individual can have an impact on many others.

Having Fun

For some of you, this may seem a little blasphemous. How and why would I have fun at work? But the reality is that you spend about 35-40% of your time working, and if it is fun and enjoyable that time is much better.

Philip Edholm

Further, when you are having fun, your impact is much higher. When I say fun, I am not talking about playing around, I am talking about enjoying what you do and who you do it with. If your job is repairing something, the fun may be in making it work. The chemistry with your co-workers and your team is also critical. The day you wake up and realize you are paid for something you would do anyway is when you are having fun. Another key aspect of fun is learning, something that is always important in any role.

Make Money

Finally, making money is a key value of work. I have found that when you are having an impact and you are having fun, people will throw money at you to keep you as part of their organization. Generally successful people do not set out to do well financially, that comes with success in having an impact and having fun.

My De-motivators

As I said, the genesis for this was a question that had both a positive and a negative. If you ask me what is important in work, I will tell you the three points above. If you ask me what turns me off, I will avoid the question and focus on what gets me motivated. But the three positive points above can point to some negative areas: a closed organization where there is no dialog or potential for impact; a political environment where you cannot trust your co-workers and the fun is sucked out through distrust; and a company that is a follower in the market with no hope of being able to drive a change.

What are yours?

I do not expect you to just adopt what I use, but rather to come up with what makes sense to you. Remember that work is not just something you do, but defines who you are for a big part of your life. If you understand what gets you motivated and gets you to leap out of bed, then you can make sure that is what you are pursuing.

Clearly understand what motivates and demotivates you, but always focus on talking up the positive and eliminating the negative.

Chapter 43 3 Rules of Work

In the 90s, I was in a Blythe, a mid-size software company and the CEO had a saying about his view for work:

More is better than less,

Sooner is better than later, and

Don't work with jerks.

I find this to be a great adjunct to the satisfiers in the previous chapter as it is less about how to evaluate yourself and more how to evaluate the organization and how things are done.

More is Better than Less

Under some circumstance more is not better (the extra 30 pounds I am carrying), or sometimes "more is just more" (Line from the movie Sabrina (Pollack, 1995)). But generally, especially in business, more is, in fact, better than less. More revenue is generally better. More features is generally better. Even more cost reduction is better if you need to reduce cost (maybe I really need more dieting).

The thought process of always asking the question, "is there more that we can do/find/drive/sell/..?" helps crystallize the focus on results and outcomes. This is not to imply you should delude yourself, but rather to ask, "why are we not at the next level?" In Sytek, when we were owned by General Instrument, at every meeting the GI management team would challenge assumptions, "Why can't you charge more for that product? "Why can't we sell more of that?" "Can we reduce the cost of this?"

One factor that was often attributed to Steve Jobs was his unwillingness to accept less (Isaacson, 2011). While this was often expressed as a drive for simplicity, it really is a need for more. To make things simple requires huge effort. Steve Jobs refused to accept complexity, demanding the greater effort to simplify. In many ways, this was a hallmark of Apple through the Steve Jobs years. Steve jobs never settled, he always demanded more, both of himself and his teams.

Philip Edholm

Through this process, you are continually looking to see if you understood both the definition of more and whether it could be attained. This continual challenging of the assumptions or limitations leads to a natural drive for more.

Sooner is better than later

If I can get something sooner it is almost always an advantage. In the early phases of a market, a difference of a few months can mean significant shifts in market share for years to come. The entire business model of companies have been built on sooner is better; FedEx built its business by getting the package there the next day, much sooner than First Class mail.

This can also be applied to decisions, making a decision quickly and eliminating uncertainty will increase the probability of success significantly. As will getting the data for that decision quickly. The old adage: "Time is Money" certainly leads itself to this area.

Don't Work With Jerks

In the previous chapter, I said that having fun was a critical element of my satisfiers. When you work with people that are jerks, whether through their arrogance, their attitude, or any other reason, it is hard to have fun and often hard to have an impact. This is one thing that sucks fun out of a job.

While we cannot always choose who we work with, identifying the jerks and getting them out of an organization is really important. That person who succeeds, but does so at the expense of everyone else, can show positive results for some time, but will damage the rest of the team. This is one of the most difficult challenges of management. Often someone who appears to be individually delivering results is doing so at the expense of the overall organization and its ability to succeed. While this characteristic is often recognized in sports as the outstanding player who never helps the team succeed, it is often less recognized in business. As a manager, when you evaluate your employees, ask if these employees are making the team succeed or themselves alone. The best contributors make everyone else succeed while succeeding themselves.

Chapter 44 The Quadrant Where Magic Happens

In all probability at some point in your career, you will either be asked to leave a job or will decide to move on from a job that is no longer meeting either your career, income, or other needs. Generally, by the time this happens, the situation has become untenable and the outcome is obvious. On leaving, you may feel a huge relief. The reality is that we should each be analyzing our job and periodically evaluating our future in the role and company. With the average person changing jobs every 3-8 years, this is analysis is something that needs to be done fairly regularly.

Figure 44-1 is a concept of looking at what you are doing today on a traditional 2x2 graph. On the horizontal axis is the company. If your company is a great place to work, it would go on the right. This would be a

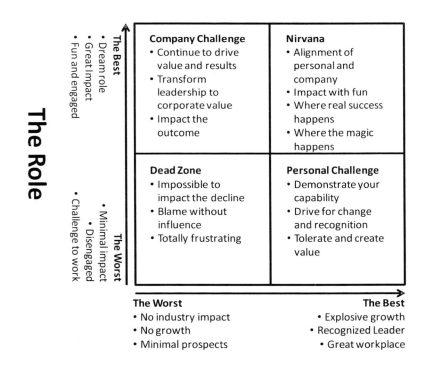

Figure 44-1 Company versus Role Matrix

company with great prospects, growth, excellent benefits, and a culture that is fun and rewarding. If your company is losing its position, treats the employees like s**t and promotes a back-stabbing high tension environment, it would be at the left.

The vertical axis is your role in the company from your ideal role at the top to the worst role imaginable at the bottom. If your role is satisfying you based on your satisfiers and is not de-motivating, then you are probably closer to the top. If you really don't want to be there or are continually frustrated, then your role would be towards the bottom.

The Magic Place

The upper right quadrant is where your role and the company align. You have a role that is meeting your needs and in which you are really contributing. This is combined with a company that is doing great and where you are proud to work and can't wait to get there to help the company succeed. This is where magic happens and careers are made. When you get that synergistic alignment, things happen that can change the world and your life. The day you wake up and say "Wow, I love doing what I am doing..and they pay me for this" and realize that your company is the only place you want to work, you are in the top right quadrant. You are making magic. Unfortunately, while we can all aspire to be in the upper right, the reality of work is that you will not be there all the time, though, after you have been there you will definitively want to get back.

Company Challenge or The Danger Zone

At some point, we almost all end up in a company where we are in a great role, but the company is on shaky ground. While it would be great to always work in an outstanding company, for a variety of reasons, this is not always true. A challenged company is one where the company, growth or culture is not where you believe it should be. A company that is in an industry that is in transformation and is caught in the past paradigm is a good example. Even in economic downturns, not all industries are impacted to the same degree. Unless the company can make a major transition, its opportunities will be limited.

However, even though the company is challenged, the role you are doing in the company is up to the top of the role axis. Your role may be one that is delivering great value or in an area you really enjoy. This is the upper left, you are enjoying your work, but the company is challenged. The Danger Zone is a high risk place to be as you will probably feel great, but may be in a very vulnerable position.

The question that you have to ask in this case is whether your hard work has a reasonable chance of impacting where the company goes. If the company continues to decline, then you may be riding that result down to keep from making a change. When you are in the upper left, you must continually evaluate your reasons for staying versus the company reasons that you may need to change. The worst thing you can do in the upper left is delude yourself into thinking that the company will get better just because you do not want to force yourself to make a change.

In the mid 2000s, I found myself in such a situation in a company that had been through a major market issue. It was a major telecom company that restructured from 95K employees to 35K over a 3 year period. The company had issues with financial reporting and the CEO and others were fired and then indicted for fraud. Through all of this I had a role that was , for me, my dream role. I had a small team that drove the overall technology strategy for one of the large business units. My team defined the product directions and evangelized our industry vision. Within the business unit, we were the go-to grouped for technology and business strategy. We built the 5 year strategy for this business and the business itself was growing and doing reasonably well. Meanwhile the company was continuing to churn as senior management was unable to drive an overall strategy to succeed. Finally, in 2009 the company went into bankruptcy and was broken up. I realized that I had ignored other opportunities that, in retrospect. I should have considered as I was so excited about my role. I let the role decide when I should have been paying more attention to the company.

This is not to say that you should not stay when you find yourself in the upper left, but if you are there, do a regular evaluation of whether the company is moving to the right. Do this at least every 6 months. If the company is public or you have access to the financial records, evaluate whether the company is growing relative to the competitors (is market share increasing or decreasing), is cash on hand growing, is debt increasing or decreasing? Each of these is a measure of whether the company is getting better financially. Then ask questions about the other aspects of the business: is the company vision and strategy more clear, are the customers more satisfied, are the employees happier, etc. The result should be to build a check-list of these and other factors that are important in your industry/market. By doing a clear, realistic evaluation, you can define if the company is moving to the right. If on successive analysis you conclude that it is not moving right and even may be moving left, then it is time to consider whether you need to look at alternatives.

Personal Challenge

In the lower right, you are in a great company, but your personal role is not what you want. You may be in a role that does not challenge you or does not appear to have a growth path for you. You may be in a group with an individual manager that is not good. Or you may be in the penalty box for some error or lack of success that happened.

In the upper left, your situation is quite different. In terms of the three satisfiers, you are having a personal impact and may be having fun, but the company is not doing the same. Another factor is money, often companies to the left are compensating their employees less than those on the right, either in salary, benefits, or bonuses. Often a company that is not succeeding blames the employees and does not reward them, even if they are the ones having an impact.

The question in the Personal Challenge is whether you can effectively change your position over a reasonable period of time. As with most things, what is effective and reasonable are for yourto decide. The first thing to realize is that most organizations go through some form of change on a regular basis, often every 12-18 months. So the situation you are in will probably change in that time period.

In the mid-80s I was in an organization where I had been in a upward path in a set of roles. There was an organization change and I got a new manager that saw my role very differently than I saw it, and with whom I had real challenges interacting. In a review he rebuffed my erudite communications style by telling me that I spoke in a way that was too hard for senior executives to understand, "Phil, by the time you are on your third sentence, all of us are trying to figure out what you said in the first two and we are not listening." I responded, "So I should use monosyllabic phrasing.", to which he responded "No, you need to use small words." Also, my lack of experience in sales was seen as a real negative in trying to drive the company forward. I was in a role where I was both unappreciated and limited in my future opportunities. However the company was growing rapidly, had just signed a major deal with one of the largest companies in the industry and was generally a great place to work. I decided that I wanted to stay and when an opportunity came up to move into sales, I moved. I was very successful in the sales role and about 20 months later replaced my original boss in the VP of Marketing role. Not only did the expertise I gained in this very different role help me throughout my career, it got me back on the right path in that company.

If you find yourself in the lower right, you need to have a plan. There are only three options: 1. work hard in your current role with a plan that that will get you moving up, 2. make a major role change in the organization to begin that path by distancing yourself from where you were, or 3. leave. The key is to have a plan. Define where you want to go in the organization and build a plan to get there. Find a mentor who will help you both define and analyze your plan and help with the steps to accomplish it. Once you have the plan, make regular assessments of both your progress and the outlook.

The Dead Zone

The lower left is the dead zone. This is where the company is on the bottom and you role is not good. While it may be possible for both your role and the company to move to the right and up at the same time it is really unlikely. If you find yourself in this position, it is probably time to look for other options. It may be better to move as a lateral to a company that is to the right than accept time in a dead zone company.

If you are in the dead zone you must do a realistic analysis of your personal and the company's outlooks. Use this to decide the urgency of planning your personal path forward.

I found myself in the Dead Zone in one role. The company was losing money and had high debt to cash and was not growing. The role I was in

Philip Edholm

did not enable me to have an impact and the frustration of the organization and the lack of clarity about how the company would succeed were a clear disincentive. A reorganization enabled an opportunity to leave, and I decided it was the right thing to do. In my career I have not left a role many times, but in this case the analysis clearly showed it was the right thing to do. This was emphasized by how much better I felt after I had decided.

Generally, if you are in the dead zone you need to start looking for a new role in a new company as soon as possible. Don't let time move to a conclusion where you are not in some level of control.

Chapter 45 Procrastination as an Optimizer of Performance

From an early age, we are all encouraged to get things done, The Nike, "Just Do It" slogan is a modern representation of what we have always been told, don't procrastinate, get things done quickly. We all know the sayings:

"The early bird gets the worm"

"Don't put off until tomorrow what you can do today"

"Early to bed and early to rise makes a man healthy, wealthy and wise"

"Be the eager beaver"

However, there is a cautionary children's tale that we should pay attention to: "The tortoise and the hare". In the tortoise and the hare, the hare starts the race strong, gets way ahead and then takes a nap while the much slower tortoise finishes the race first. I actually think this story should be modified a little to make clear what really happened.

Phil's Version of The Tortoise and the Hare

At 8 am, the Tortoise and the Hare are given a task by their the boss, the Rhinoceros, to "race" from their office at Point A to the Snail's office at Point C, passing through Point B. The task is to deliver a proposal to the Snail by the end of the day at 5 pm. The landscape of the area where the race is happening is shown in Figure 45-1. When the race starts, the Hare, eager beaver that he is, immediately rushes off and hurries down the path. Meanwhile the

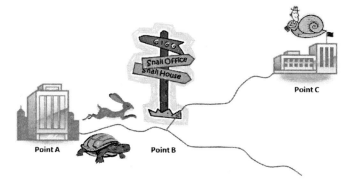

Figure 45-1 The Race Course

Tortoise, evaluates the activity, realizing that he can do it in the afternoon, after he completes some other activities It is now 11 am, the Hare has passed Pont B and is well on the way to Point C and completing the task well ahead of schedule. The Tortoise has completed three other tasks and is halfway to Point B. By 1 pm, the Hare is already at Point C, while the Tortoise is just approaching Point B after a good lunch. Just after 1, they each receive a text from the Rhinoceros that plans have changed. The Snail is actually at his house at Point D and they need to both deliver their plans there. The Tortoise merely turns right at Point B and heads for Point D. Meanwhile the Hare has to retrace all of his steps form Point C back to Point B and the go to Point D. In the end they both arrive before 5, but the Tortoise completed three additional projects. The Hare did not get the extra work done

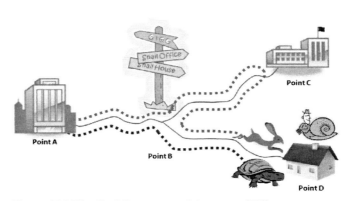

Figure 45-2 The final Outcome and Amount of Effort

because the goal changed and much of his early effort was wasted. Figure 45-2 shows the work as measured in distance travelled that each need to do to accomplish the same result.

The point of this "parable" is that doing something immediately is only the right decision if there is absolute certainty that the goal will not change. In the book "***Who Moved My Cheese? An Amazing Way to Deal with Change in Your Work and in Your Life***", by Spencer Johnson, he talks about how business changes and often you need to anticipate this change. While the book is more focused on how to plan for change, the underlying message is simple, things will change and in that context, effort expended on a goal that will change is often/generally wasted.

When approaching a project, a realistic view of what is required to complete it and a correlation of available resources should define the urgency. If there is no value in completing the task early, then scheduling it to start and proceed to completion is generally the right answer, as often something will change. This also assures there is time for clarification and definition. If the goal or path is not clear, then effort may be wasted because of that lack of clarity.

This is not intended to be a direction that everything should be ignored until it is an emergency. The best use of procrastination is to think of your activities as "Just in Time Delivery" and to manage you activities that way. Do not start a project before the time you need to complete it, but do not delay any further. But, when estimating the time for a project, you have to include interruptions that you cannot control.

At a personal level, I have found this strategy to be valuable in defining activities for a team and in managing and planning work. In many, if not a majority of, projects, there are changes that happen at some point such that, if the work had proceed full tilt from the start, would have meant that some significant part of the effort expended would have been wasted. An example was preparing a major strategic presentation. When the program started the central team sent out a large set of templates to be completed for the presentation. My team focused on putting together the underlying data, and not on completing the templates as those would be the last step in the process. There were repeated emails from the core team about where our templates were and one of the other teams spent all of their time completing the complex templates. A couple of weeks before the actual presentation, a management change in the core group led to a complete rewrite of the templates. For our team this was a minimal effort, but for the teams that had focus their work on filling out the previous templates it was a great disruption and caused major rework.

I will close with a new statement that I believe should rank with the earlier ones in this chapter:

"Don't do today that which you can do tomorrow, but focus on what has to be done today and will have the most impact."

Chapter 46 Learning versus Earning

When you start off in your career, your first job is often clearly a learning role. While you may have education or some other entry skills basis to enter the job market, in this first job you are learning many new things about working in a "real" environment. In fact, the ultimate learning role may be one where there is very little compensation: the intern position is a good example of this. The intern may not be paid a real wage, but only a small living stipend, or maybe nothing at all. In many professions, this non-paid apprenticeship is the only way to get over that initial learning phase.

At some point in your career, most of you will be hired for a job or role based on what you now know and the skills you have developed. In this role there may be little to no explicit focus on new learning, but rather on using your skills and knowledge in a high impact way.

Figure 46-1 shows a comparison of the type of role on the horizontal and the associated compensation for that role on the vertical. The illustrations in the box show that there is a band of compensation for any given role. The grey area in the middle is the band of realistic compensation

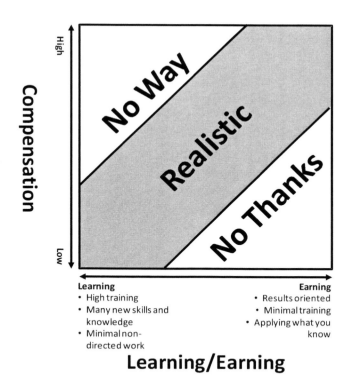

Figure 46-1 The Learning versus Earning Matrix

as a career moves from the beginning high learning phase to a later high earning phase. The white area at the top labeled "No Way" is the area where it is impossible to get the compensation level without having the knowledge and skills. No one will pay you this much to learn on the job (note that his is not true for politicians as we seem to expect that they can learn on the job). The white area at the bottom is where you would say "No Thanks" to a role where you are not compensated for your expertise and are not able to grow in new skills or knowledge either.

Within this model, a career can be thought of as a set of moves from the bottom left towards the top right. Note that I did not say the top right is a goal for everyone. Many will decide that they want to be in a role where they are continually learning and growing and will trade some level of compensation for that. A University Professor who could take their knowledge and translate it into significantly higher compensation in the public sector often is in academia because of the research and learning that only comes when associated with other, faculty and students in that environment.

Figure 46-2 shows a very simple model of a career. While this "career" only has five stages, most careers will have a new stage every 1-2 years. Let's call this Deb's

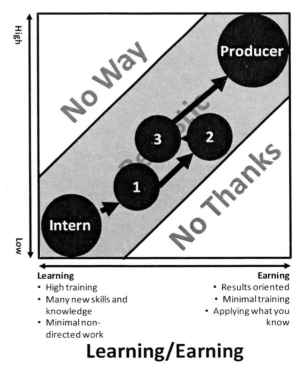

Figure 46-2 A Learning and Earning Career Path

career. Deb started as an intern. After acquiring a basic set of capabilities, Deb moved into Role 1 that had higher compensation, but was more focused on outcomes. After some time, she moved to Role 2. In Role 2 she is using the skills and knowledge from Role 1 and is now leading the delivery of what she was only supporting before. After some time, Deb realizes that in order to move to a higher level she needs a new set of skills and knowledge. To do this she takes a lateral move into Role 3, where for the same compensation she is in a new area and learning a much broader set of knowledge; for example, this might be a move from engineering to sales. This new knowledge, when combined with her previous skills and knowledge prepares her to move to the right, a role where there is little to no expectation of learning, but it is purely based on delivery. This role I have called a producer, as it is no longer learning, but focused purely on producing outcomes.

In every role in you r career, there will be a mix of learning and earning. It is important to understand, both from your view and your employer, What is that mix? Are you in this role because it is an opportunity to learn and grow? Does your employer see this as purely a earning role and expects only results? As you evaluate new roles within and outside your current organization, the learning versus earning tool is a good way to analyze the role. It may be a good idea to take a less compensated position if it leads to valuable learnings. On the other hand, if you have learned in a unique area, can you turn that into an earning role with high value.

In 1982 I faced a difficult decision. I had to make a choice between three jobs. I had been offered a job at IBM. It was a good job, doing robotic system design. It was a direct extension of what I had learned at General Motors and was a great fit for me. It was a big company in a role and field that were virtually identical to what I knew. I also had been offered a job at a large vehicle manufacturer that was less complex than the GM job I had before. It was obvious that this job had much less opportunity to learn new things, but the pay was 20% higher than the IBM job. The third opportunity was to go into a start-up networking company. This was an opportunity to take a small bit of knowledge and go into an entirely different direction. It was very different, a small company, new job type, a vendor versus a customer, and a new technology area. I eliminated the higher paying job that was similar, because I realized that it was a dead end.

The only career path was the job of the manager who was hiring me. Within 10 years that facility was completely gone. I actually accepted the IBM job, but then the VP from the start-up called me and talked about why his was such a wonderful opportunity. In the end, he explained to me that this was an opportunity to move into a new area with great learning and growth opportunities. In the end I took that job and called IBM and turned them down. Again, within about 15 years that entire IBM manufacturing operation had been shut down and moved to other locations, including Asia. The role I went into led to 9 years of different roles in a company that was growing and changing. The opportunity to learn in that role gave rise to a number of the topics in this book and challenged me to learn almost every day. Along the way we sold the company and I made enough money to guarantee my retirement and never have to worry. The decision to move to a learning role was the right one at the right time.

Later in my career I had two offers from companies that were moving to compete in the same market. This market was the convergence of telephony and networking, often called Voice over IP. My background was primarily in data. One of the companies was primarily a data company, while the other was primarily a voice/PBX company. The roles were similar and the compensation was the same. I decided to join the company that was coming from the Voice/PBX side as that was the area I knew nothing about. I felt my knowledge in networking would be valuable there, but more importantly, I could not learn what I did not know from people that only knew what I knew. At that company I led the development of VoIP and convergence, and 10 years later was given a Lifetime Achievement Award (from Frost and Sullivan, one of the most prestigious Analyst/Consulting companies in the world) for creating the VoIP market. The capability to grow and become a recognized expert and contributor was all based on the learning that I was able to achieve in the new role.

As you consider opportunities, map them for their earning/learning and compensation on a chart similar to the figures. Ask yourself a few questions about the job/role:

Is the learning I will get consistent with the path I am on?

If this is a learning role, is the learning worth the pay change in this role?

If this is an earning role, am I losing value without any new learning?

As you can tell from my comments and story, I have generally leaned towards roles where there was a significant opportunity for learning. While I also want to optimize my earnings, I am always careful to clearly understand what I will learn in a role. This is not to say that you should not be ready to exploit what you know, but always understand. When I joined the Voice/PBX company, they hired me because of my expertise in networking. I could have focused only on that area and would have never learned the rest of the convergence knowledge. Sometimes a role that is earning can be augmented with the right learning if you focus on how to make it happen.

Chapter 47 It's Always Your Decision

One of the wonderful things about business and a career in the business world is that you always get to say no if you want. No one can tell you to do something you do not want to do if you are willing to walk away. Whether you get up in the morning and go to work or go back to bed is your decision. Whether you stay in a job or move on is also your decision. So if it is always your decision, then what is the right decision? What do you base this decision on? Is it money , or the factors of impact and fun? What about ethics and your reputation?

One of the practical realities about business is that, if you do not break the law, there is little that anyone can do to you if you say no. In the first company where I was on the Executive Management team, we had monthly meetings with our "board". These meetings followed a basic format. The President would get up and report on the month, saying whether we met plan or not. Then the finance guy would get up and talk about the finances. As the executives we were reporting to (they owned 57% of our company) had a Harvard Business School finance person go through this financial reports for a week before this meeting, he would highlight the good and the bad in the inch thick report. He would highlight inventory issues, margin issues, deliverables, volumes, etc. Then the VP of Engineering and Operations would make his report. As it turned out, as the VP of Marketing, most of the levers of the business were under my control. My team managed the sales leads and the sales tools, so when sales had challenges, they generally were due to issues in those areas. We defined the product requirements, so if engineering had issues, it was with our requirements and schedule. We owned forecasting, so if there were inventory mismatches, it was also our responsibility. The result was that I often found myself being the focus of over 2 hours of a 4 hour meeting. After a particularly bad meeting where I had been taken to task repeatedly and had been beaten mercilessly, I got in the cab to the airport with one of the other VPs. I said that I just couldn't take it any longer, and that I was going to find a new job the next week. He responded with something that I have always remembered and often reflected on. "No matter how bad it gets, no matter how much they yell or scream or whatever they try to do, they *CANNOT* eat you."

For me that was an epiphany. They cannot eat you. They cannot eat you.

Philip Edholm

The worst anyone can do to you in business is to fire you. They cannot eat you. Once you realize that, every decision you make needs to be weighed against that clear fact; they cannot eat you.

My second job after graduating from University was as a facility project manager in a large manufacturing facility. I was one of 6 engineers in the Facilities group that managed the building construction and systems technology of the huge factory that built cars and trucks. I got into this role very suddenly as I was working as a foreman and was told that I was being promoted the next Monday. I immediately realized that I was replacing a long term veteran in the office, someone who was highly respected and was considered an institution. I rapidly found out that the reason I was there was that he had been fired for embezzling about $300K. He had become friendly, too friendly, with the contractors who did work for him at the facility. Having the contractors pay for his lunch every day led to one of them offering to recarpet his house if they won a deal. This led to other deals until finally he had specified a certain rack product that only one contractor could provide, resulting in a contract that was inflated by hundreds of thousands of dollars. In the end he was caught, and I came in and took on his job. On one hand, I had the lawyers investigating his dealing, while on the other, I had to deal with many of the same contractors to get my job done. Whether a contractor was clean or dirty was not known for most. While there were a few that had been proven to have been part of the fraud, the pall was over everyone. I realized very quickly how easy it is to slide down that slope where you assume that it really is not bad for your employer. Or for the customers or the other employees.

The result of this event, which happened very early in my career was a realization that, for me, every decision and position I would take should be couched in clear terms: what is best for the company and then what is best for the other stakeholders, including myself? If it is a public company, what is in the best interests of the shareholders is a clear imperative. While this is a basic question, I personally always look to longer term versus shorter term value. This is because, while a stock speculator may be interested in a short term spike in share price, for the long term investor and the other stakeholders, the long term viability and success of the company is paramount.

I have found that thinking this way removes the personal variables and makes decisions much easier. For me it makes decisions easy to sleep with.

Over the years, I have had occasions where there were opportunities to step outside my core tenets, often with either positive potential if I did something that was not clearly in line with the company or to have a negative impact by standing up against something that others were doing that was going to have a bad impact.

For example, in one role, I led a small team that built an OEM relationship with a new start-up company. We evaluated a number of options and picked the one that had the best value for our employer and our customers. The relationship was going very well and the small company was growing, in large part due to our relationship. After about a year, the start-up went into the process of doing an Initial Public Offering of their stock. As this process proceeded, I received a call from a broker of the listing brokerage indicating that I had been reserved a block of "friends and family" stock. This is stock that can be purchased at the IPO price, which is often only available to large investors and brokerage houses and banks. In a hot IPO, the price may double from the IPO price in the first day of trading. As I was offered shares at $12 per share, an increase from $12 to $18 (50%) in the first day was not unreasonable. I was offered 50K shares, so at a price increase of $6 per share, this could be a windfall of $300K in a single day. That was way over a year's salary at the time. My reaction was immediate and absolute. I told the broker I could not accept, though I appreciated the offer. I immediately called all my team members and told them that they needed to forgo this opportunity. The reason was simple: if I benefitted to such a degree from a decision I made for my employer, it would be immediately suspect. My decision now would be seen as not the best for the company, but the best for me. Even though there was no thought of this when the decision was made, the mere acceptance of personal gain would taint future decisions and recommendations.

Another example was in a company where I took on a new role and immediately became aware of a discrepancy in a major customer order. A large order had not come through from a customer and a sales manager had set up to have the product purchased by a third party to be delivered to the end customer in the next quarter. This enabled the company to take a revenue recognition in the earlier quarter. The third party was receiving separate compensation for this activity. The result was that the revenue from the previous quarter had been misstated. When I found out about this, I immediately went to the CEO of the company and told him that we needed to notify the board immediately. His reaction was to try to convince me to wait and get the product to the end customer. My reaction was simple, I did not know about this when it happened, but now that I did, I have responsibility to disclose it to the stakeholders. Even though it caused significant waves, the issue was raised and dealt with. As it turned out, the end customer ended up backing away from the deal and the revenue had to be reversed. By raising this immediately, I assured that it was not something that I was responsible for covering up.

In both of these cases, the impact was minimal; I lost a little potential income. While I upset some people, I kept my job and over time it was proved to be the right path. The alternative outcome is also a possibility as well- you may lose your job.

I was in a company that sold a software development product that had been derived out of the database market. This market had been built on a dual revenue model of charging both for the development seats and the deployment seats. This meant that a customer would pay about 20-30% of the total cost for a set of developer licenses that would allow developers to do the actual development of the package for the users. Then the customer would buy a set of deployment licenses for their users to actually use the application package the developers had created. This model was rapidly changing. Almost all of our competitors had moved to a deployment free license. In this model the developer seats were more expensive and there were multiple tiers, but the deployment was free. The challenge of moving to this model was that for one or two quarters after changing from deployment to development only pricing, there was a revenue disruption as the planned deployment revenue would go away faster than the growth in development licenses. For this reason the CEO of the company was resisting the change. As VP of Marketing, I saw the reality of what was happening in the market: our major competitor, who had moved to this model, was outselling us by 20 to one in the number of development seats and was growing twice as fast as we were. This meant that in a year, they would have 20 to 30 times as many developers using their product. As these developers moved they would use what they know and we would lose. In the Crossing the Chasm model, this is the Tornado, where market share and growth is paramount. However, the CEO was unwilling to go to the shareholders and explain the transition, so he resisted. It got to the point where every meeting we had became a heated discussion of this topic. In the end, he decided that the company was not big enough for him and me, and I was fired. As it turned out, the company was valued at $20 per share at the top for the time I was there and was a penny stock three years later. The company was never able to recover from that decision. The major competitor was acquired by one of the largest software companies in a huge acquisition. In the end I stuck to what was best, and it cost me my job.

It is always your decision. They cannot eat you, but they can fire you. But, in the end, it is you who has to live with your decisions and the consequences. The senior people in Enron made millions personally by manipulating the stock and creating personal wealth vehicles. I am sure they were able to convince themselves that it was not really bad for the company, just as I could have convinced myself that getting some stock at a favorable price was not really bad either.

In the end your decisions are about your ethics and credibility. The decisions you make will define who you are. Any decision or action that needs to be hidden is something that needs to be examined. It is perfectly acceptable to keep a decision private as having it be public would give your competitors advantage. However, a decision that would cause your stakeholders to question your ethics or credibility and is kept private for those reasons is a real issue. Be true to yourself, don't let yourself get sucked into something that you would not be proud of, and make good decisions.

Chapter 48 You are a Company of One

Back in 2000 the San Jose Mercury News asked three Silicon Valley luminaries (Larry Ellison, Scott McNealy and Andrew Grove) to write letters to the graduates of that year. As it was the millennium year, this was a monumental opportunity to address where the workplace, the country, technology and society were going. While both Larry and Scott talked about the great future, Andrew chose a different path. In his letter he told the graduates that they and only they would need to take responsibility for their careers as no one else would. He basically said that each of them was the president of their company of one. He emphasized that the days of a job being a role for life were over and that uncertainty and change were the future of the workplace.

Reading this letter at the beginning of a new age and reflecting on my career that has had a number of transformations made me realize that we are all companies of one. In the new world we define our own value and determine our own path. With the average person changing jobs every 5-7 years, a typical person will work for 5-8 different employers over their career. Or may start a company and have a wide variety of roles in that company. I realize that I have had 7 jobs and now one entrepreneur role over about 35 years, so my average seniority is a little over 4 years. Each time you make a job transition you are reselling the company of you, and you will be doing this over and over throughout your career.

Through this book there have been references to these concepts. In Chapter 5, the danger of not continually thinking about how your personal value add may be moving in the value pyramid will open the door to moving down in value. In Chapter 16, the concept of death in the middle can be thought of in relation to your career, caught between high-value and low income. In Chapter 46, the value of learning in building your career path was discussed, a critical component of any business. And in Chapter 45, your position, not only in the company, but through the company is part of the business of you.

If you begin to manage and plan for your career as you would a company, you realize that you exist in a market, with a given set of skills and knowledge. You can define how that market is changing, both from a value perspective and a skill perspective to define what is best for you. Realize that technology will change and the customers will change, and you need to continually adapt and change as well.

Make a clear plan on what skills and knowledge you have that are continual and which may be devalued by the transitions. Identify which skills and knowledge you need to meet your aspirations. Treat this process like a project. Plan when you need the skills and what is the plan to get there.

Think about your brand. How are you perceived both inside your current employer and in the industry. Do you have a plan to market yourself, starting in your group and moving out.

The keys in business that have been talked about in this book equally apply to the business of you: make sure you have a great product, make sure you market to your customers, and always think about what is next. Good luck with the business of you. I hope the time you have invested in this book will be rewarded with success in all of your endeavors.

Philip Edholm

Glossary of Acronyms and Definitions

I would like to thank Wikipedia for many of the definitions in this section. I found it unnecessary to change what was there for many of the terms.

API - Application Programmable Interface - An application programming interface is a specification intended to be used as an interface by software components to communicate with each other. An API may include specifications for routines, data structures, object classes, and variables. An API specification can take many forms, including an International Standard such as POSIX or vendor documentation such as the Microsoft Windows API, or the libraries of a programming language, e.g. Standard Template Library in C++ or Java API.

ASIC - Application-Specific Integrated Circuit - An application-specific integrated circuit (pronounced /ˈeɪsɪk/) is an integrated circuit (IC) customized for a particular use, rather than intended for general-purpose use. For example, a chip designed to run in a digital voice recorder is an ASIC. Application-specific standard products (ASSPs) are intermediate between ASICs and industry standard integrated circuits like the 7400 or the 4000 series.

BoLS = Bureau of Labor Statistics - Department in the US Department of Labor that produces statistics on US Labor rates.

bps - bits per second - A measure of how many binary bit transitions happen on a network connections per second. In telecommunications and computing, bit rate (sometimes written bitrate, data rate or as a variable R) is the number of bits that are conveyed or processed per unit of time.

CaaS - Communications as a Service - A definition of new offerings where telephony or advanced communications are delivered as a service from the computing cloud instead of with local servers.

CoG - Cost of Goods - Cost of Goods sold refer to the inventory costs of those goods a business has sold during a particular period. Costs are associated with particular goods using one of several formulas, including specific identification, first-in first-out (FIFO), or average cost. Costs include all costs of purchase, costs of conversion and other costs incurred in bringing the inventories to their present location and condition. Costs of goods made by the business include material, labor, and allocated overhead. The costs of those goods not yet sold are deferred as costs of inventory until the inventory is sold or written down in value.

CoS - Class of Service - A set of mechanisms to sort different network traffic types into classes and then modify the performance of the network to give different classes different priority and discard based on the class. Generally used to assure that certain classes such as real-time and preferred (such as a bank transaction) are granted preference in using network assets.

CRM- - Customer Relationship Management - Customer relationship management is a widely implemented model for managing a company's interactions with customers, clients, and sales prospects. It involves using technology to organize, automate, and synchronize business processes— principally sales activities, but also those for marketing, customer service, and technical support. The overall goals are to find, attract, and win new clients; nurture and retain those the company already has; entice former clients back into the fold; and reduce the costs of marketing and client service.[2] Customer relationship management describes a company-wide business strategy including customer-interface departments as well as other departments.[3] Measuring and valuing customer relationships is critical to implementing this strategy.

CRT - Cathode Ray Tube - The cathode ray tube is a vacuum tube containing an electron gun (a source of electrons) and a fluorescent screen used to view images. It has a means to accelerate and deflect the electron beam onto the fluorescent screen to create the images. The image may represent electrical waveforms (oscilloscope), pictures (television, computer monitor), radar targets and others. CRTs have also been used as memory devices, in which case the visible light emitted from the fluorescent material (if any) is not intended to have significant meaning to a visual observer (though the visible pattern on the tube face may cryptically represent the stored data).

CSO - Chief Strategy Officer - A chief strategy officer, or chief strategist, is an executive who is responsible for assisting the chief executive officer with creating, communicating, executing, and sustaining strategic initiatives within a company or agency.

CTO - Chief Technology Officer - A chief technology officer (or chief technical officer) is an executive-level position in a company or other entity whose occupant is focused on scientific and technological issues within an organization. The role became prominent with the ascent of the information technology (IT) industry, but has since become prevalent in technology-based industries of all types (e.g. biotechnology, energy, etc.). As a corporate officer position, the CTO typically reports directly to the chief executive officer (CEO) and is primarily concerned with long-term and "big picture" issues (while still having deep technical knowledge of the relevant field). Depending on company structure and hierarchy, there may also be positions such as director of R&D and vice president of engineering whom the CTO interacts with or oversees.

DoJ - Department of Justice (US) - The United States Department of Justice, also referred to as the Justice Department, is the United States federal executive department responsible for the enforcement of the law and administration of justice, equivalent to the justice or interior ministries of other countries.

DRP - Direct Repair Program - The direct repair program is an initiative, started by insurance carriers to have vehicle repairs done without having multiple estimates. It is based on defined and pre-approved rates for a variety of repairs and the ability of a certified shop to engage the customer to do the repairs without pre-approval from the insurance company.

DSL - Digital Subscriber Line - Digital subscriber line, originally digital subscriber loop) is a family of technologies that provide internet access by transmitting digital data over the wires of a local telephone network. In telecommunications marketing, the term DSL is widely understood to mean Asymmetric Digital Subscriber Line (ADSL), the most commonly installed DSL technology. DSL service is delivered simultaneously with wired telephone service on the same telephone line. This is possible because DSL uses higher frequency bands for data separated by filtering. On the customer premises, a DSL filter on each outlet removes the high frequency interference, to enable simultaneous use of the telephone and data.

EDI - Electronic Data Interchange - Electronic data interchange is the structured transmission of data between organizations by electronic means. It is used to transfer electronic documents or business data from one computer system to another computer system, i.e. from one trading partner to another trading partner without human intervention. It is more than mere e-mail; for instance, organizations might replace bills of lading and even cheques with appropriate EDI messages. It also refers specifically to a family of standard.

G&A - General and Administration - refers to the G&A components of SG&A, which includes; General: General operating expenses and taxes that are directly related to the general operation of the company, but don't relate to the other two categories. Administration: Executive salaries and general support and all associated taxes related to the overall administration of the company

GDP - Gross Domestic Product - Gross domestic product refers to the market value of all officially recognized final goods and services produced within a country in a given period. GDP per capita is often considered an indicator of a country's standard of living;[2][3] GDP per capita is not a measure of personal income. See Standard of living and GDP. Under economic theory, GDP per capita exactly equals the gross domestic income (GDI) per capita. See Gross domestic income.

GPRS - General Packet Radio Service - General packet radio service is a packet oriented mobile data service on the 2G and 3G cellular communication system's global system for mobile communications (GSM). GPRS was originally standardized by European Telecommunications Standards Institute (ETSI) in response to the earlier CDPD and i-mode packet-switched cellular technologies. It is now maintained by the 3rd Generation Partnership Project (3GPP).[

GTM - Go To Market - the term Go-To-Market strategy refers to the channels a company will use to connect with its customers/business and the organizational processes it develops (such as high tech product development) to guide customer interactions from initial contact through fulfillment. A firm's Go-To-Market strategy is the mechanism by which they propose to deliver their unique value proposition to their target market. That value proposition is based on the choices the business has made to focus on and invest in markets and solutions that they believe will respond positively to the increased attention.

HR - Human Resources - Human resource management (HRM, or simply HR) is the management of an organization's workforce, or human resources. The HR department is responsible for the attraction, selection, training, assessment, and rewarding of employees, while also overseeing organizational leadership and culture, and ensuring compliance with employment and labor laws. In circumstances where employees desire and are legally authorized to hold a collective bargaining agreement, HR will typically also serve as the company's primary liaison with the employees' representatives (usually a labor union).

HDTV - High Definition Television - High-definition television (HDTV) provides a resolution that is substantially higher than that of standard-definition television. Where Standard Definition (SD) is limited to about 400 active lines and about 600 pixel equivalents, High Definition (HD) is typically either 720 or 1080 lines and can be as many as 1920 pixel equivalent wide. In addition, where SD is "interlaced" (each frame has only every other line), in HD, "progressive" scanning has each line in every frame.

ICA - Innovative Communications Alliance - The Innovative Communications Alliance (ICA) was a telecommunications alliance between Microsoft and Nortel, created in July 2006, to co-develop, integrate, market, sell, and support unified communications products. The goal of the alliance was to make integrated hardware and software solutions that join together voice, video, and data communications without requiring gateways or middleware. Microsoft and Nortel shared developing technologies and patents for unified communications products. The ICA terminated in December of 2009 when Avaya acquired the Nortel enterprise assets.

IEEE - Institute of Electrical and Electronics Engineers - The Institute of Electrical and Electronics Engineers (read I-Triple-E) is a non-profit professional association headquartered in New York City that is dedicated to advancing technological innovation and excellence. It has more than 400,000 members in more than 160 countries, about 51.4% of whom reside in the United States.

IM - Instant Messaging - Instant messaging is a form of communication over the Internet, that offers an instantaneous transmission of text-based messages from sender to receiver. In push mode between two or more people using personal computers or other devices, along with shared clients, instant messaging basically offers real-time direct written language-based online chat. The user's text is conveyed over a network, such as the Internet. It may address point-to-point communications as well as multicast communications from one sender to many receivers. More advanced instant messaging allows enhanced modes of communication, such as live voice or video calling, video chat and inclusion of hyperlinks to media.

I/O - Input/Output - In computing, input/output, or I/O, refers to the communication between an information processing system (such as a computer), and the outside world, possibly a human, or another information processing system. Inputs are the signals or data received by the system, and outputs are the signals or data sent from it. The term can also be used as part of an action; to "perform I/O" is to perform an input or output operation. I/O devices are used by a person (or other system) to communicate with a computer. For instance, a keyboard or a mouse may be an input device for a computer, while monitors and printers are considered output devices for a computer. Devices for communication between computers, such as modems and network cards, typically serve for both input and output.

IP - Internet Protocol - The Internet Protocol (IP) is the principal communications protocol used for relaying datagrams (also known as network packets) across an internetwork using the Internet Protocol Suite. Responsible for routing packets across network boundaries, it is the primary protocol that establishes the Internet. IP is the primary protocol in the Internet Layer of the Internet Protocol Suite and has the task of delivering datagrams from the source host to the destination host solely based on the addresses. For this purpose, IP defines datagram structures that encapsulate the data to be delivered. It also defines addressing methods that are used to label the datagram source and destination. Historically, IP was the connectionless datagram service in the original Transmission Control Program introduced by Vint Cerf and Bob Kahn in 1974, the other being the connection-oriented Transmission Control Protocol (TCP). The Internet Protocol Suite is therefore often referred to as TCP/IP. The first major version of IP, Internet Protocol Version 4 (IPv4), is the dominant protocol of the internet. Its successor is Internet Protocol Version 6 (IPv6), which is increasing in use.

IPO - Initial Public Offering - An initial public offering or stock market launch, is the first sale of stock by a company to the public. It can be used by either small or large companies to raise expansion capital and become publicly traded enterprises. Many companies that undertake an IPO also request the assistance of an investment banking firm acting in the capacity of an underwriter to help them correctly assess the value of their shares, that is, the share price (IPO Initial Public Offerings, 2011).

ISV - Independent Software Vendor - An independent software vendor is a company specializing in making or selling software, designed for mass or niche markets. Such markets may be diverse, including software for real estate brokers, scheduling for healthcare personnel, barcode scanning, stock maintenance and even child care management software. Specialized products generally offer higher productivity to organizations than more generalized software such as basic spreadsheet or database packages. Most large software companies, including Microsoft, Google, Red Hat, Oracle, SAP, HP and IBM, have special programs for ISVs.

IT - Information Technology - Information Technology (IT) is the branch of engineering that deals with the use of computers and telecommunications to store, retrieve and transmit information. The acquisition, processing, storage and dissemination of vocal, pictorial, textual and numerical information by a microelectronics-based combination of computing and telecommunications are its main fields. The term in its modern sense first appeared in a 1958 article published in the Harvard Business Review, in which authors Leavitt and Whisler commented that "the new technology does not yet have a single established name. We shall call it information technology (IT)." Some of the modern and emerging fields of Information technology are next generation web technologies, bioinformatics, cloud computing, global information systems, large scale knowledge bases, etc. Advancements are mainly driven in the field of computer science.

JIT - Just in Time - Just in time (JIT) is a production strategy that strives to improve a business return on investment by reducing in-process inventory and associated carrying costs. Just-in-time production method is also called the Toyota Production System. To meet JIT objectives, the process relies on signals or Kanban (看板 Kanban?) between different points in the process, which tell production when to make the next part. Kanban are usually 'tickets' but can be simple visual signals, such as the presence or absence of a part on a shelf. Implemented correctly, JIT focuses on continuous improvement and can improve a manufacturing organization's return on investment, quality, and efficiency. To achieve continuous improvement key areas of focus could be flow, employee involvement and quality.

Kbps – Kilobits per second – a measure of the transmission speed of a network or interface. Expressed as number times one thousand data bits transmitted per second.

KPI - Key Performance Indicators - A performance indicator or key performance indicator (KPI) is an industry jargon for a type of performance measurement. KPIs are commonly used by an organization to evaluate its success or the success of a particular activity in which it is engaged. Sometimes success is defined in terms of making progress toward strategic goals,[2] but often success is simply the repeated achievement of some level of operational goal (for example, zero defects, 10/10 customer satisfaction, etc.). Accordingly, choosing the right KPIs is reliant upon having a good understanding of what is important to the organization. 'What is important' often depends on the department measuring the performance - the KPIs useful to finance will be quite different than the KPIs assigned to sales, for example. Because of the need to develop a good understanding of what is important, performance indicator selection is often closely associated with the use of various techniques to assess the present state of the business, and its key activities. These assessments often lead to the identification of potential improvements; and as a consequence, performance indicators are routinely associated with 'performance improvement' initiatives. A very common method for choosing KPIs is to apply a management framework such as the balanced scorecard.

MAP - Manufacturing Automation Protocol - Manufacturing Automation Protocol was a computer network standard released in 1982 for interconnection of devices from multiple manufacturers. It was developed by General Motors to combat the proliferation of incompatible communications standards used by suppliers of automation products such as programmable controllers. By 1985 demonstrations of interoperability were carried out and 21 vendors offered MAP products. In 1986 the Boeing corporation merged its Technical Office Protocol with the MAP standard, and the combined standard was referred to as "MAP/TOP". The standard was revised several times between the first issue in 1982 and MAP 3.0 in 1987, with significant technical changes that made interoperation between different revisions of the standard difficult.

Mbps - A measure of data transmission. It indicates the number of megabits of data that can be transmitted over a network connections. Not to be confused with megabytes, which is a measure of memory and counts 8 bit words as a byte.

MBWA - Management By Walking Around - A term that emerged in the 1980s from companies like HP that emphasized getting out of the office to walk around and meet workers in their work locations to promote communications and understand issues.

MBVWA - Management By Virtually Walking Around - Doing MBWA by informal telecommunications.

M&A - Mergers and Acquisitions - Mergers and acquisitions (abbreviated M&A) refers to the aspect of corporate strategy, corporate finance and management dealing with the buying, selling, dividing and combining of different companies and similar entities that can help an enterprise grow rapidly in its sector or location of origin, or a new field or new location, without creating a subsidiary, other child entity or using a joint venture. The distinction between a "merger" and an "acquisition" has become increasingly blurred in various respects (particularly in terms of the ultimate economic outcome), although it has not completely disappeared in all situations.

MPLS - Multiprotocol Label Switching - Multiprotocol Label Switching is a mechanism in high-performance telecommunications networks that directs data from one network node to the next based on short path labels rather than long network addresses, avoiding complex lookups in a routing table. The labels identify virtual links (paths) between distant nodes rather than endpoints. MPLS can encapsulate packets of various network protocols. MPLS supports a range of access technologies, including T1/E1, ATM, Frame Relay, and DSL.

NDIS - Network Driver Interface Specification - The Network Driver Interface Specification is an application programming interface (API) for network interface cards (NICs). It was jointly developed by Microsoft and 3Com Corporation, and is mostly used in Microsoft Windows, but the open-source NDISwrapper and Project Evil driver wrapper projects allow many NDIS-compliant NICs to be used with Linux, FreeBSD and NetBSD. magnussoft ZETA, a derivative of BeOS, supports a number of NDIS drivers. The NDIS is a Logical Link Control (LLC) that forms the upper sublayer of the OSI data link layer (layer 2 of 7) and acts as an interface between layer 2 and 3 (the Network Layer). The lower sublayer is the Media Access Control (MAC) device driver. The NDIS is a library of functions often referred to as a "wrapper" that hides the underlying complexity of the NIC hardware and serves as a standard interface for level 3 network protocol drivers and the hardware level MAC drivers. Another common LLC is the Open Data-Link Interface (ODI).

NIH - Not Invented Here - Not invented here (NIH) is a term used to describe persistent social, corporate, or institutional culture that avoids using or buying already existing products, research, standards, or knowledge because of their external origins. It is normally used in a pejorative sense, and may be considered an anti-pattern. The reasons for not wanting to use the work of others are varied but can include fear through lack of understanding, an unwillingness to value the work of others, or forming part of a wider "turf war".

OCS - Office Communications Server - Microsoft Lync Server (previously Microsoft Office Communications Server) is an enterprise real-time communications server, providing the infrastructure for enterprise instant messaging, presence, file transfer, peer-to-peer and multiparty voice and video calling, ad hoc and structured conferences (audio, video and web) and, through a 3rd party gateway or SIP trunk, PSTN connectivity. These features are available within an organization, between organizations, and with external users on the public internet, or standard phones, on the PSTN as well as SIP trunking.

ODI - Open Data/Link Interface - The Open Data-Link Interface, developed by Apple and Novell, serves the same function as Microsoft and 3COM's Network Driver Interface Specification (NDIS). Originally, ODI was written for NetWare and Macintosh environments. Like NDIS, ODI provides rules that establish a vendor-neutral interface between the protocol stack and the adapter driver. It resides in Layer 2, the Data Link layer, of the OSI model. This interface also enables one or more network drivers to support one or more protocol stack.

OEM - Original Equipment Manufacturer - An original equipment manufacturer, or OEM, manufactures products or components that are purchased by a company and retailed under that purchasing company's brand name. OEM refers to the company that originally manufactured the product. When referring to automotive parts, OEM designates a replacement part made by the manufacturer of the original part. In this usage, OEM means "original equipment from manufacturer".

OS - Operating System - An operating system is a set of software that manages computer hardware resources and provides common services for computer programs. The operating system is a vital component of the system software in a computer system. Application programs require an operating system to function.

PBX - Private Branch Exchange - A business telephone system is any of a range of a multiline telephone systems typically used in business environments, encompassing systems ranging from small key systems to large scale private branch. A business telephone system differs from simply using a telephone with multiple lines in that the lines used are accessible from multiple telephones, or "stations" in the system, and that such a system often provides additional features related to call handling. Business telephone systems are often broadly classified into "key systems", "hybrid systems", and "private branch exchanges".

PC - Personal Computer - A personal computer is any general-purpose computer whose size, capabilities, and original sales price make it useful for individuals, and which is intended to be operated directly by an end-user with no intervening computer operator. In contrast with the batch processing or time-sharing models which allowed larger, more expensive minicomputer and mainframe systems to be used by many people, usually at the same time. Large data processing systems require a full-time staff to operate efficiently.

P&L - Profit and Loss - The income statement (also referred to as profit and loss statement (P&L), revenue statement, statement of financial performance, earnings statement, operating statement or statement of operations) is a company's financial statement that indicates how the revenue (money received from the sale of products and services before expenses are taken out, also known as the "top line") is transformed into the net income (the result after all revenues and expenses have been accounted for, also known as Net Profit or the "bottom line"). It displays the revenues recognized for a specific period, and the cost and expenses charged against these revenues, including write-offs (e.g., depreciation and amortization of various assets) and taxes. The purpose of the income statement is to show managers and investors whether the company made or lost money during the period being reported.

R&D - Research and Development - This refers to the Research and Development group of the company. This group does the work of delivering new products or services that can be sold. IN the P&L model this refers to the cost of the R&D function.

RFP - Request for Proposal - A request for proposal (RFP) is issued at an early stage in a procurement process, where an invitation is presented for suppliers, often through a bidding process, to submit a proposal on a specific commodity or service. The RFP process brings structure to the procurement decision and is meant to allow the risks and benefits to be identified clearly up front. The RFP may be proceeded by an RFI that does not include detailed requirements.

SG&A - Sales, General and Accounting - SG&A (alternately SGA or SAG) is an acronym used in accounting to refer to Selling, General and Administrative Expenses, which is a major non-production cost presented in an Income statement.

S&M - Sales and Marketing - Sales and Marketing refers to the portion of SG&A expense that is dedicated to the Sales and Marketing rather than General and Accounting.

SI - Systems Integrator - A systems integrator is a person or company that specializes in bringing together component subsystems into a whole and ensuring that those subsystems function together, a practice known as

System Integration. Systems integrators may work in many fields but the term is generally used in the information technology (IT) field, the defense industry, or in media.

SIP - Session Initiation Protocol - The Session Initiation Protocol (SIP) is an IETF-defined signaling protocol widely used in VoIP systems after 2010 for controlling communication sessions such as voice and video calls over Internet Protocol (IP). The protocol can be used for creating, modifying and terminating two-party (unicast) or multiparty (multicast) sessions. Sessions may consist of one or several media streams.

SKU - Stock-Keeping Unit - SKU refers to a Stock-keeping unit, a unique identifier for each distinct product and service that can be purchased in business. IN an organization, each individually purchasable item has a unique SKU.

SMB - Small/Medium Businesses - Small and medium enterprise or small and medium-sized enterprise (SMEs, small and medium-sized businesses, SMBs and variations thereof) are companies whose personnel numbers fall below certain limits. The abbreviation "SME" is used in the European Union and by international organizations such as the World Bank, the United Nations and the World Trade Organization (WTO). The term "small and medium businesses" (or "SMBs") is predominantly used in the USA. In most economies, smaller enterprises outnumber large companies by a wide margin. SMEs are said to be responsible for driving innovation and competition in many economic sectors. Generally SMBs are considered to have less than 250 employees, though some consider companies of under 1,000 employees to be medium.

SMLT - Split Multi-Link Trunking - Split Multi-Link Trunking is a Layer-2 link aggregation technology in computer networking designed by Nortel (now Avaya) as an enhancement to standard multi-link trunking (MLT) as defined in IEEE 802.3ad. SMLT was first developed by Nortel in 2001 as part of the v3.2 software release for the then Ethernet Routing Switch 8600, and is now positioned by Avaya under the marketing name of "Avaya VENA Switch Clustering".

SOA - Service-Oriented Architecture - In software engineering, a Service-Oriented Architecture is a set of principles and methodologies for designing and developing software in the form of interoperable services. These services are well-defined business functionalities that are built as software components (discrete pieces of code and/or data structures) that can be reused for different purposes. SOA design principles are used during the phases of systems development and integration.

SQL - Structured Query Language - SQL , sometimes referred to as Structured Query Language, is a programming language designed for managing data in relational database management systems (RDBMS). Originally based upon relational algebra and tuple relational calculus,[4] its scope includes data insert, query, update and delete, schema creation and modification, and data access control. It also defines the interface to databases using a SQL format for other applications.

SWOT - Strength, Weakness, Opportunity, Threat - SWOT analysis (alternately SLiabilityOT analysis) is a strategic planning method used to evaluate the Strengths, Weaknesses/Limitations, Opportunities, and Threats involved in a project or in a business venture. It involves specifying the objective of the business venture or project and identifying the internal and external factors that are favorable and unfavorable to achieve that objective. The technique is credited to Albert Humphrey, who led a convention at Stanford University in the 1960s and 1970s using data from Fortune 500 companies.

TBD - To Be Determined - A placeholder term used very broadly to indicate that although something is scheduled or anticipated to happen, a particular aspect of that thing remains to be arranged. Aslo refers to when the actual answer is not yet known as in, "the answer is TBD."

THX - THX is a trade name of a high-fidelity audio/visual reproduction standard for movie theaters, screening rooms, home theaters, computer speakers, gaming consoles, and car audio systems. The current THX was created in 2001 when it spun off from Lucasfilm Ltd. THX was developed by Tomlinson Holman at George Lucas's company, Lucasfilm, in 1983 to ensure that the soundtrack for the third Star Wars film, Return of the Jedi, would be accurately reproduced in the best venues. THX was named after Holman, with the "X" standing for "crossover" as well as a homage to Lucas's first film, THX 1138. The distinctive crescendo used in the THX trailers, created by Holman's coworker James A. Moorer, is known as the

Philip Edholm

"Deep Note".

TCO - Total Cost of Ownership - Total cost of ownership is a financial estimate whose purpose is to help consumers and enterprise managers determine direct and indirect costs of a product or system. It is a management accounting concept that can be used in full cost accounting or even ecological economics where it includes social costs.

UB - Ungermann Bass - Ungermann-Bass, also known as UB and UB Networks, was a computer networking company in the 1980s to 1990s. Located in Santa Clara, California, in Silicon Valley, UB was the first large networking company independent of any computer manufacturer. UB was founded by Ralph Ungermann and Charlie Bass. John Davidson, vice president of engineering, was one of the creators of NCP, the protocol suite of the ARPANET before TCP/IP.

UI - User Interface - The user interface, in the industrial design field of human–machine interaction, is the space where interaction between humans and machines occurs. The goal of interaction between a human and a machine at the user interface is effective operation and control of the machine, and feedback from the machine which aids the operator in making operational decisions. Examples of this broad concept of user interfaces include the interactive aspects of computer operating systems, hand tools, heavy machinery operator controls, and process controls. The design considerations applicable when creating user interfaces are related to or involve such disciplines as ergonomics and psychology.

UMTS - Universal Mobile Telecommunications System - Universal Mobile Telecommunications System is a third generation mobile cellular technology for networks based on the GSM standard. Developed by the 3GPP (3rd Generation Partnership Project), UMTS is a component of the International Telecommunications Union IMT-2000 standard set and compares with the CDMA2000 standard set for networks based on the competing cdma technology. UMTS employs Wideband Code Division Multiple Access (W-CDMA) radio access technology to offer greater spectral efficiency and bandwidth to mobile network operators. UMTS specifies a complete network system, covering the radio access network (UMTS Terrestrial Radio Access Network, or UTRAN), the core network (Mobile Application Part, or MAP) and the authentication of users via SIM cards (Subscriber Identity Module).

VAR - Value-Added Reseller - A value-added reseller (VAR) is a company that adds features or services to an existing product, then resells it (usually to end-users) as an integrated product or complete "turn-key" solution. This practice occurs commonly in the electronics industry, where, for example, a VAR might bundle a software application with supplied hardware. The added value can come from professional services such as integrating, customizing, consulting, training and implementation. The value can also be added by developing a specific application for the product designed for the customer's needs which is then resold as a new package. VARs incorporate platform software into their own software product packages

VoIP - Voice over Internet Protocol - Voice over IP (VoIP, or voice over Internet Protocol) commonly refers to the communication protocols, technologies, methodologies, and transmission techniques involved in the delivery of voice communications and multimedia sessions over Internet Protocol (IP) networks, such as the Internet. Other terms commonly associated with VoIP are IP telephony, Internet telephony, voice over broadband (VoBB), broadband telephony, and broadband phone.

VPA - Volume Purchase Agreement - A volume purchase agreement is a formal agreement between a seller and a buyer to a specific volume of purchases over a time period, typically one year. Based on a larger volume commitment by the buyer, the seller will discount or give better terms.

WiFi - Wireless Fidelity - Wi-Fi, sometimes spelled Wifi or WiFi, is a popular technology that allows an electronic device to exchange data wirelessly (using radio waves) over a computer network, including high-speed Internet connections. The Wi-Fi Alliance defines Wi-Fi as any "wireless local area network (WLAN) products that are based on the Institute of Electrical and Electronics Engineers' (IEEE) 802.11 standards". However, since most modern WLANs are based on these standards, the term "Wi-Fi" is used in general English as a synonym for "WLAN". The term Wi-Fi was a play on the term Hi-Fi (High Fidelity) from the home audio market.

3D - Three Dimension - Used as a reference to presenting information in three dimensions versus the two of a single flat screen display. A 3D television is a television set that projects a television program into a realistic three-dimensional field by employing techniques such as stereoscopic display, multi-view display, or 2D-plus-depth, and a 3D display.

3G - Third Generation Wireless - 3G or 3rd generation mobile telecommunications is a generation of standards for mobile phones and mobile telecommunication services fulfilling the International Mobile Telecommunications-2000 (IMT-2000) specifications by the International Telecommunication Union. Application services include wide-area wireless voice telephone, mobile Internet access, video calls and mobile TV, all in a mobile environment.

4K video - 4000 Pixel Video Displays - 4K is an emerging standard for resolution in digital cinematography and computer graphics. The name is derived from the horizontal resolution, which is approximately 4,000 pixels (this designation is different from those used in the digital television industry, which are represented by the vertical pixel count). There are several different resolutions that qualify as 4K.

5G - Fifth Generation Wireless - 5G (5th generation mobile networks or 5th generation wireless systems) is a name used in some research papers and projects to denote the next major phase of mobile telecommunications standards beyond the 4G/IMT-Advanced standards effective since 2011. At present, 5G is not a term officially used for any particular specification or in any official document yet made public by telecommunication companies or standardization bodies such as 3GPP, WiMAX Forum, or ITU-R. New standard releases beyond 4G are in progress by standardization bodies, but are at this time not considered as new mobile generations but under the 4G umbrella.

Bibliography

Booker, C. (2005). *The Seven Basic Plots: Why We Tell Stories.* Continuum International Publishing Group.

Brown, G. (2011). Taking Action to Sustain Customer Relationships. *Newsletter to the New York Society of Association Executives* .

Cherry, S. (2004, July). Edholm's Law of Bandwidth. *IEEE Spectrum* .

Christense, C. M. (2003). The Innovator's Dilemma: The Revolutionary Book That Will Change the Way You Do Business. Harper Paperbacks.

Corps, U. A. (1943, May 9). *Mobile Machine Shop US Army 1943.jpg.* Retrieved May 19, 2012, from Wikipedia: http://commons.wikimedia.org/wiki/File:Mobile_Machine_Shop_US_Army_1943.jpg

Herek, S. (Director). (1989). *Bill & Ted's Excellent Adventure* [Motion Picture].

Isaacson, W. (2011). *Steve Jobs.* New York: Simon & Schuster.

Jim Duffy. (2012, February 12). *Cisco Q4 Ethernet switch revenue up, HP's down* . Retrieved May 17, 2012, from Network World: http://www.networkworld.com/news/2012/022412-cisco-ethernet-switch-256544.html

Johnson, B. (2008, April 5). *Ben Blogged.* Retrieved May 19, 2012, from Free vector Coffee Cup: http://benblogged.com/?p=167

Leman, V. (2011, November 16). *My Dad's Old Drill.* Retrieved mAY 19, 2012, from Dust Furniture: http://www.dustfurniture.com/blogs/news/4602112-my-dads-old-drill

Marshon, S. (2010, May). *Help Identifying this Drill Press - Delta advertisement.* Retrieved May 19, 2012, from Practical Machinist:

Philip Edholm

http://www.practicalmachinist.com/vb/antique-machinery-history/help-identifying-drill-press-204313/

Marty Padgett. (2012, February 1). *January 2012 Car Sales Are Strong--Except At GM*. Retrieved May 17, 2012, from The Car Connection: http://www.thecarconnection.com/news/1072422_january-2012-car-sales-are-strong--except-at-gm

Moore, G. A. (1991). Crossing the Chasm: Marketing and Selling Disruptive Products to Mainstream Customers. Harper Business Essentials.

Ohmae, K. (1982). he Mind Of The Strategist: The Art of Japanese Business. New York: McGraw Hill.

O'Reilly, C. (1989, Summer). Corporations, Culture and Commitment: Motivation and Social Control in Organizations. *California Management Review*.

Pollack, S. (Director). (1995). *Sabrina* [Motion Picture].

Ross, G. (Director). (1998). *Pleasantville* [Motion Picture].

Savad, M. (n.d.). *Machine Shop Circa 1900's*. Retrieved May 19, 2012, from Suburban Scenes: http://www.zazzle.com/machinist_welcome_to_the_workshop_poster-228524108853820038

Unknown. (2012). *Computer Hardware*. Retrieved May 19, 2012, from Plyojump: http://plyojump.com/classes/hardware.php

US-DoL. (2011). Distribution of private sector employment by firm size class: 1993/Q1 through 2011/Q1, not seasonally adjusted. Retrieved May 17, 2012, from US Department of Labor: http://www.bls.gov/web/cewbd/table_f.txt

Waterman, T. P. (1982). In Search of Excellence; Lessons from America's Best-Run Companies.

Wikipedia. (2012, May 18). *Maslow's hierarchy of needs*. Retrieved May 19, 2012, from Wikipedia: http://en.wikipedia.org/wiki/Maslow%27s_hierarchy_of_needs

ABOUT THE AUTHOR

Phil Edholm is the President of PKE Consulting LLC. He consults to end users and vendors in the communications and networking markets. Mr. Edholm is recognized as both a technology visionary and a leader and innovator in business. He has over 30 years' experience in delivering results in the networking and communications industries.

Mr. Edholm has led teams ranging from a few people in Silicon Valley Start-Ups to hundreds in Fortune 500 companies. He is recognized as a visionary leader and is often asked to speak to companies and help their teams understand how to manage complex business situations. The concepts and companies he has founded or led have created over a billion dollars of market capitalization.

Mr. Edholm is recognized as an industry leader and visionary. In 2007, he was recognized by Frost and Sullivan with a Lifetime Achievement Award for Growth, Innovation and Leadership in Telecommunications for creating the VoIP industry. Mr. Edholm is a widely sought speaker and has been in the VoiceCon/Enterprise Connect Great Debate three times. He has been recognized by the IEEE as the originator of "Edholm's Law of Bandwidth" as published in July 2004 IEEE Spectrum magazine and as one of the "Top 100 Voices of IP Communications" by Internet Telephony magazine. Mr. Edholm has 16 patents and holds a BSME/EE from Kettering University.